COLLECTING GREEK COINS

COLLECTING GREEK COINS

JOHN ANTHONY

 LONGMAN London and New York

Longman Group Limited
Longman House, Burnt Mill, Harlow
Essex CM20 2JE, England
Associated companies throughout the world

Published in the United States of America
by Longman Inc., New York

© Longman Group Limited 1983

First published 1983

British Library Cataloguing in Publication Data

Anthony, John
   Collecting Greek coins.
   1. Coins, Greek   2. Numismatics – Collectors
and collecting
   I. Title
   737.4938   CJ335

   ISBN 0-582-50310-8

Library of Congress Cataloguing in Publication Data

Anthony, John, 1933–
   Collecting Greek coins.
   Bibliography: p.
   Includes index.
   1. Coins, Greek. 2. Coins, Greek-Collectors and collecting. I. Title.
CJ335.A57   1983   737.49495   82-9947
ISBN 0-582-50310-8 (pbk)   AACR2

Set in 10/12 pt VIP Times
Printed in Singapore by
Selector Printing Co Pte Ltd.

CONTENTS

Preface   vii
I   On Forming a Coin Collection   1
II   Greek Coin Production   4

COINAGE IN THE CITY-STATES
III   The Greek City-State   13
IV   The Archaic Period   16
V   Magna Graecia   23
VI   Sybaris   29
VII   Tarentum   33
VIII   Naples   39
IX   Sicily   43
X   Athens   55
XI   Aegina   63
XII   Corinth   69
XIII   Rhodes   79

THE COINAGE OF ALEXANDER AND HIS SUCCESSORS
XIV   Alexander the Great   89
XV   Macedon   96
XVI   The Seleukid Empire   103
XVII   Egypt under the Ptolemies   120

THE SMALLER HELLENISTIC KINGDOMS
XVIII   Epeiros under King Pyrrhus   137
XIX   Pergamum   143
XX   Bithynia   148
XXI   Pontos   151
XXII   Cappadocia   155
XXIII   Armenia   158

THE COINAGE OF THE NON-GREEK AREAS
XXIV   The Phoenicians   163
XXV   Carthage   169
XXVI   Jewish Coins   175
XXVII   The Etruscans and Bruttians   184
XXVIII   Thrace   191
XXIX   Celtic Coins   198

THE EAST UNDER HELLENISTIC INFLUENCE
XXX   Parthia   211
XXXI   The Sasanians and their Coins   220
XXXII   Bactria and India   228

THEMATIC COLLECTING
XXXIII   Greek Religion   239
XXXIV   Athena   241
XXXV   Dionysos and his Companions   245
XXXVI   Hercules   250
XXXVII   Some Monsters: Medusa, Marsyas, Pegasos
             and the Chimaera   255
XXXVIII   The Non-Greek Gods   259
XXXIX   River-gods and Water-nymphs   265
XXXX   The Greeks and the Sea   271
XXXXI   The Voyage of the Argo   275
XXXXII   The Odyssey   284

Further Reading   293
Index   295

PREFACE

This is a book on coin collecting that I hope is rather different from those already available. There are many books on Greek coins produced by researchers for a highly academic readership limited to a few hundred, even a few score of people. At the other end of the scale, there are general surveys of coin collecting which, in their attempts to interest as many readers as possible, cover a vast amount of ground somewhat superficially. *Collecting Greek Coins* aims to strike a balance between those extremes.

It is intended for collectors and prospective collectors who are beginners or have a little experience in this field and would like to learn more. Though they may have no knowledge of Greek and a very sketchy grasp of ancient history, they should be able to read this book without difficulty. It is not a catalogue – there are already available to collectors the two volumes of Seaby's *Greek Coins and their Values*, which are indispensable though, in spite of a useful introduction, the thousands of coins listed in them bewilder a great many people who scarcely know where to start. With them in mind, I have, for twelve years, written a monthly article on Greek and Roman coins – the 'Among the Ancients' series, published in *Coin Monthly*. It has been a pleasure to share my enthusiasm with its readers, many of whom write appreciatively and ask me to identify their own coins. Now, I hope, this book will help to make a fascinating and complex period of coin production much more widely appreciated. Greek coins are miniature works of art and, like all art, they are best understood through knowledge of the circumstances that gave rise to them. Hence, it has been necessary to say something about people, places, production techniques, political and social history, commerce and literature in order to develop a 'feel' for the subject.

The numbers in parentheses are references to the numbered illustrations which are spread throughout the chapters.

I. ON FORMING A COIN COLLECTION

This chapter is written with beginners in mind. Anyone who already has a collection will have his or her own answer to the question, 'Why collect coins?'

It may be difficult to put into words, but the usual reasons given run something like this – they are things of beauty; durable relics of past ages; links with important personalities or events; appeal to lovers of things miniature; offer scope for research; and form an excellent investment.

Usually, people acquire a few coins, perhaps by gift or accident, try to find out more about them and then get 'bitten'. It is not cupidity but imagination that motivates them. Collectors are able to see something fascinating in their subject, no matter what it may be and every collection involves questions of acquisition, storage and display. Let us now relate these to Greek coins.

SUPPLY

At first sight, it might appear that objects so old would be difficult to obtain. This is not so. Centuries of collecting have led to the accumulation of thousands of Greek coins, many locked up forever in museums, but even more in private hands or dealers' stocks. The supplies are augmented from time to time by 'finds' – individual coins picked up by peasants, groups of them from archaeological 'digs', eventually put on the market to raise funds, and jars-full turned up on building sites and often carried to western Europe through a chain of semi-secret transactions.

Reputable dealers are very necessary, especially to the beginner and, fortunately, there are a considerable number in Britain. Their firms vary in size and personal preferences will lead to choices from among the 'big names' or much smaller establishments, which usually offset a comparative lack of prestige by offering individual treatment. As is the case in every other collecting field, there are forgeries and imitations among Greek coins. Established dealers can be trusted, though every year my *Coin Monthly* correspondents reveal how unwise it is to buy from even the most apparently unsophisticated waiter or shepherd boy encountered on a Mediterranean holiday. Our own junk shops and market stalls may perhaps have a rare bargain on offer, though the days of splendid coins sold for a song have long passed. At that level, the general dealer is unlikely to know much about Greek coins, so his offerings are probably bad buys, even if he does not realise it himself. Finding a reliable source of supply is the first step for any collector.

SELECTION

It is standard advice, proved true by many years of experience, that it is wise to buy coins in the best possible condition. Aesthetic appeal and the general dislike of imperfection make almost all coin collectors feel that their money is well spent if it is laid out for well-preserved specimens. These preferences affect the laws of supply and demand, which lead to a situation in which the condition of coins has a close relationship with their prices. One must expect to pay far more for 'extremely fine' than 'fine' and, if that irks, consider what is likely to happen when the time comes to resell. The better the coin, the better the chance of selling for a good price and, in hard times, it is difficult to sell poorly-preserved coins at all.

Do not expect Greek coins to be in quite the same state as coins produced by present-day mints. The passage of time, burial in the ground, corrosion and cleaning have inevitable effects. Nevertheless, one takes account of the evidence of wear and tear as one would in the case of a modern coin. In addition, since Greek coins were produced by hand, there is always a possibility that they were struck off the centre of the metal blank, instead of being properly centred. Missing letters or parts of the design are defects given to many an ancient coin at the moment of its creation. Few people cared when it went into circulation but, if it survives, collectors certainly do. In general, avoid badly-struck specimens and examine good ones for mount-marks. A considerable number of gold and silver coins were used for jewellery, particularly in the nineteenth century, and the resulting scratches, file-marks or lumps of solder reduce prices dramatically. Other marks which the beginner might miss are called 'tooling'. These were applied with an engraving tool in order to enhance the appearance of the coin by cutting the design more deeply or even adding details not originally present. It may not have mattered much in the days when wealthy dilettanti on the Grand Tour filled their coin cabinets, but it does now that we are all much more condition-conscious. Any coin that has been roughly cleaned loses much of its market value. Reject specimens treated with a wire brush, just as you would those with lumps of corrosion on them. But, bear in mind that 'patina', the smooth coating that is evidence of great age, enhances a coin, particularly a bronze one.

Only experts can recognise a good forgery. Cruder attempts may give themselves away by being the wrong weight; too round; too perfect; showing tiny holes caused by air bubbles in casting; or by the line around the rim that indicates that the upper and lower faces of the coin have been stuck together (remember, it might have been filed off).

No one can possibly collect a specimen of every Greek coin. It is obvious that we must all specialise to some extent, according to our preferences and budgets. A beginner should start by buying a few coins that take his fancy and, after that, he will develop his own interests. There are enough possibilities outlined in this book to suit virtually everyone.

STORAGE AND DISPLAY

The traditional way to store a coin collection is in a cabinet made with wooden drawers pierced to hold the coins, resting on cloth. In this way, they can be easily seen and handled. Handling is probably good for ancient coins though not for modern ones which are harmed by every finger-print. Plastic albums and envelopes are sold for housing coins so that they are visible but not touchable and these have much to commend them, though paper envelopes might be better for ancient coins. They absorb moisture which may be present in minute quantities in coins long buried and cleaned in chemical solutions. If the moisture cannot escape through the plastic it may discolour the surface of the coin, particularly if it is bronze. Mounting coins in specially adapted picture frames is proving popular, though it attracts burglars as well as admiring friends. Having one's coins in a container that can be locked away or deposited in a bank is a regrettably necessary modern precaution.

II. GREEK COIN PRODUCTION

The intrinsic value of the metal used for an early coin was what made it a medium of exchange. Consequently, Greek coins were of gold, silver and their naturally-occurring alloy, electrum, until, comparatively late in the period, a token coinage made from bronze appeared. Silver is the predominant metal of the great majority of surviving coins and, therefore, what follows refers to them.

Carefully-weighed blanks of silver were cast or cut from a bar. They were trimmed to shape, heated, placed between two dies and 'struck'. Striking involved a heavy blow, presumably with a large hammer on the back of the upper die. This was mounted on the end of a metal bar resembling a cold chisel and the lower die was fixed firmly in place to act as an anvil. When the piece of silver was squeezed between the two dies, it became slightly distorted. The upper die was pushed into it and it curled away slightly from the lower one. Convention now leads us to refer to the convex side as the obverse and the concave one as the reverse of the coin. If the design on one side was more important than the other, it was usually incorporated into the obverse or anvil die, because it would last longer and more coins could be produced from it. We know this because, in cases where we have a great many similar coins available for study, it is possible to work out die sequences ie the combinations of obverse and reverse dies used in manufacture. There are always more reverses than obverses.

Another form of distortion was the spreading of the silver away from the circular form in which it was cut. This was virtually inevitable, though the degree of spreading varies from issue to issue. Blanks that were not struck fairly and squarely could be impressed off-centre, as already mentioned. Another common mishap occurred when the flan split, resulting in a 'striking crack' (460), or the die might do the same. If that happened, a raised line appears on the coin where the silver sank

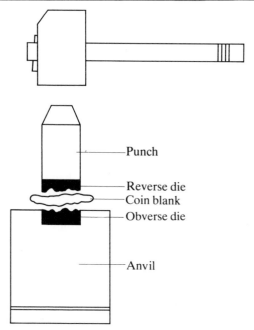

Punch

Reverse die
Coin blank
Obverse die

Anvil

Striking a coin

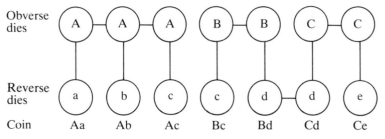

Die sequences

into the die crack (489). (Both kinds of crack are price-reducing blemishes at the present day.) Dies had a comparatively short life. They were all cut by hand from metal soft enough to allow this, but harder than the silver they impressed – bronze is believed to have been generally used. How the die-cutters managed to do such exquisite work without the aid of modern reducing machines, or even magnifying lenses, remains a mystery. Hundreds of dies were needed for a large issue, though the individual coins from it would not be identical. In fact, no two Greek coins are precisely similar – if the dies were the same, the metal behaved slightly differently.

WEIGHTS AND DENOMINATIONS

Since intrinsic value was of supreme importance, the weight of a coin decided its buying power. Before coins came into general use, lumps of metal passed from hand to hand and, as they lacked generally-agreed marks to indicate what they were worth, they had to be weighed each time a transaction took place. At least, that is what a prudent trader is likely to have insisted upon. He might also want to be quite sure that what he was accepting was solid silver and not base metal with a deceptive thin silver coating. The only way to find out was to cut into the metal and the results of this practice can be seen in the 'banker's marks' found on Greek coins (1,2,3). They vary from chisel cuts that almost slice a coin in half to small impressed patterns that may have been the personal stamps used by some important merchants to guarantee the reliability of coins that passed through their hands. Damage of this kind would make modern coins worthless to collectors, but it has comparatively little effect on the prices of Greek ones. Provided the cuts are not too savage, they may add extra interest to a specimen.

The sizes of coins in circulation and the relationships between them enable us to speak of denominations. However, the extensive region in which 'Greek' coins were used did not have a unified currency, a fact which is scarcely surprising in an age when communications were rather primitive, though it is equally true today. Commercial activity was localised and, as a result, the coinage provided had to suit the normal expectations and conventions of the people living in each trading area. Hence, several weight standards for coins became established. We recognise the distinctive standards used in Athens, Aegina, Phoenicia, Rhodes, Euboea, Phokia, Miletos, Corinth, Chios, Babylon and Persia, and can construct tables showing the weights of each denomination in them. To give them all here would lead to unnecessary and confusing detail, so only one has been set out. This is the Athenian weight standard, which is also the most elaborate. Denominations are multiples or fractions of the drachm or obol.

Dekadrachm	10 drachms	43 g
Tetradrachm	4 drachms	17.2 g
Didrachm	2 drachms	8.6 g
Drachm	6 obols	4.3 g
Hemidrachm	¹/₂ drachm	2.15 g
(or Triobol)	(or 3 obols)	2.15 g
Obol	¹/₆ drachm	0.72 g
Tritartemorion	³/₄ obol	0.54 g
Hemiobol	¹/₂ obol	0.36 g
Trihemitartemorion	¹/₄ obol	0.18 g
Hemitartemorion	¹/₈ obol	0.09 g

Surviving coins are unlikely to be of these precise weights because of minor errors in manufacture and the ravages of time. In the case of the very small coins, there is often doubt about their denomination and it is remarkable that they survive at all (5,6,7). In Athens, the commonest silver piece was the tetradrachm (4), as it was in many other areas. Elsewhere, the corresponding place in the currency system was occupied by coins of different weights so that, for convenience, we often refer to them as staters. This name was given by the Greeks to a wide range of coins and, in practice, it just means 'a piece of silver'.

It is unusual for Greek coins to bear the name of the denomination. Presumably, the designs and size were an adequate guide for the people who handled them. They also knew whose initials or badges were put on the coins as a guarantee by the officials in charge of the mints, though this information is no longer obtainable. Hundreds of monograms can be found on coins and only a very few mean anything to us. It is remotely possible that some of the series of letter groups are dates, though the only certain ones on Greek coins are on the issues of the Ptolemaic and Seleukid Kingdoms (192,217). Dating is often a matter of informed guesswork, taking account of historical events and the style adopted by the die-engravers. There is a conventional division of Greek coins into periods:

Archaic	from the invention of coinage to the defeat of the Persian invasion in 479 BC.
Classical	from the Persian Wars to the conquests of Alexander the Great, which began in 336 BC.
Hellenistic	from Alexander to Cleopatra, who died in 30 BC.
Imperial	the five centuries of Roman rule.

All the periods overlap, in the sense that marked changes did not occur throughout the Greek world in a single year.

Coins from the Imperial Period are not covered by this book. They are better treated as part of the Roman coinage.

THE SCOPE OF GREEK COINAGE

The term 'Greek' is very much one of convenience, used to cover coins which circulated in a vast area over a period of at least a thousand years. Greek-speaking people could be found in settlements stretching from the Atlantic coast of Spain to northern India and their neighbours included Celts, Jews, Phoenicians, Italian tribes and the nomads of Central Asia. They all used coins, as did the Romans, whom we treat separately because of the supremacy they eventually attained. It is impossible in a book of this size to cover the whole of this complex field, so the emphasis has been placed on collectable coins (ie those that appear for sale reasonably frequently and at prices that are not outside the reach of anyone except millionaires). Of necessity, the more obscure mint cities have been omitted, even though they may have produced some beautiful coins. Some compensation for this will be found, it is hoped, in the chapters on the coinages that have been selected.

A BRIEF COMMENT ON NAMES

It was, for many years, the practice to refer to Greek cities and rulers by the Romanised forms of their names. Recently, the original Greek forms have returned to use and these will be found in Seaby's catalogues, which most collectors rely on. Generally speaking, it is the Greek forms that are preferred here, though in cases where the names are very familiar in the Latin or Anglicised version, they have been retained (for example, Athens, Alexandria, Perseus and Hercules).

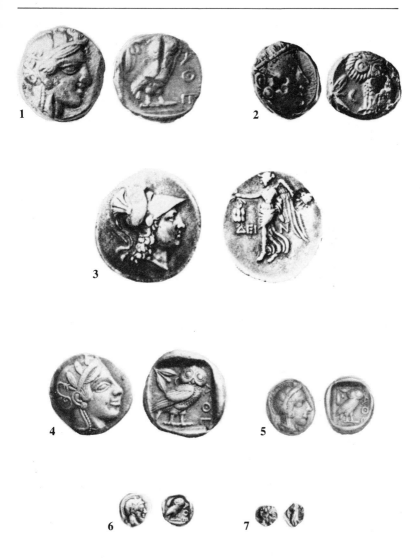

1 Athenian tetradrachm, 449–413 BC. Banker's cuts both sides. **2** Athenian tetradrachm, 393–300 BC. Banker's mark in the form of a cross, both sides. **3** Tetradrachm of Side, Pamphylia, *c*. 190 BC. Countermarked with a small head of Helios, possibly to make it acceptable in Rhodes. **4** Athenian tetradrachm, 455–449 BC. **5** Athenian drachm, *c*. 450 BC. **6** Athenian obol, *c*. 460–455 BC. **7** Athenian hemiobol, *c*. 450 BC.

COINAGE IN THE
CITY-STATES

III. THE GREEK CITY-STATE

A great many Greek coins were minted in city-states of a size that would make them utterly insignificant among modern countries. Nevertheless, each made a point of asserting its independence and, indeed, one way of doing so was to issue a distinctive coinage.

There is no good English equivalent for the word 'polis' used by the Greeks. It implied a walled town with sufficient territory to make it self-sufficient. The population might be a few hundred or many thousand and its territory could be a small valley, an island or something more extensive. An idea of the small size of political units can be gained from literary evidence. We learn, for example, that Athens was the largest polis and it was a matter for admiration that, to cross its territory (Attica), on foot took two whole days. In contrast, there are several instances of small city-states mustering their troops who numbered less than a hundred.

Every form of government could be found in one or other of the city-states. There were monarchy, democracy, aristocracy (rule by the best people), oligarchy and tyranny (dictatorship), and hybrid forms of these. The art of conducting public business satisfactorily is still called politics and every polis had its own laws, constitution and religious cult. Warfare and trade rivalry were common among the city-states. Over the centuries, supremacy passed from one to another of the larger ones and did not remain for long with any. Dominance tended to involve putting more coins into circulation and obliging weaker states to use them or, at least, to adopt the appropriate weight standard for their own currency, which may have shrunk to a token amount.

If the population of a polis outgrew the food resources, the problem was solved by encouraging a group of citizens to emigrate. Typically, those with little to lose, led by an adventurous or scapegrace young aristocrat, sailed away to found a colony. This was the name for a new settlement somewhere in the comparatively empty Mediterranean world. The inhabitants retained strong ties with their mother city over many generations, worshipping the same god and observing obligations to help in time of need, in the same way as they expected help themselves. Political links would be emphasised by the designs on the colony's coins, as well as through its foreign policy.

In spite of their diversity, the city-states were inhabited by people who had a strong sense of the fundamental unity of the Greek world. All Greeks had these aspects of life in common: their language; their religious beliefs and moral code; their sense that non-Greeks were inferior; and the right of participation in the Olympic Games. They could also unite against a common enemy, such as the Persians though, in normal times, dissension made them vulnerable to any of their number who had the strength to make a bid for dominance on land, at sea or in commerce.

Alexander the Great was able to overcome the poleis one by one and then seize control of the Persian Empire. He, and the kings who succeeded, him extinguished independence in most city-states in Greece and Asia Minor. A little later, the Romans and Carthaginians did much the same in the western Mediterranean. In the belief that freedom gave way to bureaucratic tyranny, earlier generations of historians maintained that the greatness of the Greeks ended with Alexander, what followed being an unedifying period not worth their close attention. Modern research tends to emphasise that the Hellenistic Period is more interesting than used to be claimed. The standard of living rose considerably, people's lives were more settled, and these centuries produced much of the philosophy and science that we admire. It is far too easy to rely on the literature produced in Athens which, though the most highly developed, was only one of many city-states. If we had comparable records of what went on in the others, before and after Alexander's conquests, we should probably make drastic alterations in traditional assumptions. Unfortunately, the histories of most city-states are badly-documented or told only by their enemies. We cannot claim to know much about what went on there, though archaeology may have a big contribution to make. It must be obvious from this that there will always be many unanswered questions about Greek coins. Nevertheless, collectors often say that their enigmatic qualities add to the fascination of the subject.

The history of coinage in a selection of city-states is reviewed in subsequent chapters though, first, it is necessary to say something about the Archaic Period.

IV. THE ARCHAIC PERIOD

The earliest period of coin production has left us a distinctive group of coins which have their own aesthetic appeal and also the attractions of being 'the oldest' and 'the first' – characteristics that appeal to collectors in many fields.

Any assessment of archaic coins starts with the historical questions, 'how' and 'when' did the use of money begin? Though our answers lack precision, there is general agreement about what probably happened. From Egyptian and Hebrew records, it seems clear that precious metal was valued by weight and that units for measuring it evolved. The most familiar name among them is the talent, which doubtless varied from one area to another, according to local custom. Convenience required that gold and silver should be cast into handy pieces, corresponding in size to the weights in use. The next step was to stamp them with marks guaranteeing their weight and purity, thus avoiding the need to check both every time they changed hands. Finally, when a ruler or magistrate accepted responsibility for doing this, coinage had appeared.

The date when coins were first minted is still subject to debate. Nineteenth-century numismatists thought it was about 700 BC, whereas twentieth-century research has brought it down to 600 or even later. There is, however, little doubt that the sixth century BC was the period when the city-states of Greece and Asia Minor were learning to use money.

It is very probable that the credit for minting the first coins should go to Lydia, a small kingdom in western Asia Minor. Our major evidence for this came in the form of very early coin deposits placed in the foundations of the Temple of Diana at Ephesos, which was excavated in 1904–5. The silver pieces found there included very primitive lumps with only striations or the marks of nail punches on them and, also, some others with recognisable designs on one side.

Such designs are believed to have been the personal badges, perhaps the same ones as were on their signets, used by leading merchants. One is actually inscribed 'I am the badge of Phanes', though no one now knows who he was. Like numerous other archaic coins, this piece is the only one of its kind yet discovered and there are no written records to throw light on the matter. Further archaeological work may eventually provide more information though, at present, we have to admit that we do not know whether the devices on the first coins belonged to merchants, mint officials or kings.

Such prototype coins are very rare and, if ever sold, very expensive. The earliest specimens available to collectors are the 'lion heads' of Lydia. There are dumpy little pieces of electrum (white gold) dating from any time between the extremes 650–550 BC. Their weights range from 14g, which we assume to be the stater, down to 0.15g which is a ninety-sixth part of the stater (8,9,10). The lion's head on them has a prominent wart on its nose and is believed to be the heraldic sign used by the kings of Lydia. They had made a big advance in coin production by providing standardised denominations with designs on them that guaranteed their acceptability over a considerable area. However, there were two disadvantages to this currency. One was the fact that the smaller denominations were too tiny for convenient daily use. The other involved the metal. Electrum is a naturally-occurring alloy of gold and silver, which can contain the two metals in varying proportions. People knew this, even though specific gravity could not yet be measured. Two or three hundred years were to pass before Archimedes took his celebrated bath (if he ever did).

According to the Greek historian Herodotos, King Kroisos (Croesus) of Lydia (560–546 BC) was the first to mint coins in gold and silver. He had invented bimetallism, the principle of having a fixed relationship between the values of the two metals used for currency. In this case, ten silver pieces were worth one gold stater. Croesus minted large quantities of coins, which had designs that were continued for a generation after his death (11,12,13,14). The heads of a lion and a bull face each other on one side, and the other side was blank, except for the indentation left by the punch that forced the silver into the die. Such an unprecedented volume of currency may well have given rise to the legend that Croesus was the richest man in the world.

City-states in Asia Minor soon followed Lydia's example and

equipped themselves with coins suited to local conditions (15–20). They used whatever weight standard and denominations commerce required. As coinage spread into Europe and across the Mediterranean, these weight standards served much the same purpose as currency areas in the modern world. Through mapping the places that used each one, we can estimate the political and economic influence of Persia, Athens, Corinth, Phoenicia and the other important states. Bronze was a later addition to the currencies in circulation. Its use as a token coinage (ie one not dependent on intrinsic value) was begun in fifth-century Sicily and bronze remained the metal for small change throughout the Greek period.

The designs on archaic coins are varied. Animals, plants, deities and various symbolic objects were chosen for reasons we can only surmise (21–27). Since large numbers of hardstones cut with designs for seals date from this period, it seems a reasonable hypothesis that the early coin dies were made by the seal cutters. They probably used designs they were familiar with, though most city-states soon adopted heraldic devices, the 'parasemon' by which each coin could be identified. The great majority of archaic coins have designs on one side only. The other is dented by the punch and is described as 'incuse'. It seems to have taken many years for people to realise that both sides of a coin could carry designs. This development first occurred in Athens, where the portrait of the patron goddess was backed by her owl (28). Even so, early reverse designs sunk into the depressions, by die makers that had been a feature of coins for so many years (29–31), are distinctive, though more easily recognised by looking at the coins than described in words. They are stiff, deeply cut and show a peculiar perspective. One instance of the latter is that human figures are shown with both shoulders visible while the stomach is in profile (42,79). Another involves Athena's eye, which faces the viewer, although her face is in profile (32). On later Athenian coins, the eye was rendered looking forward, as we would expect (33). There is an unmistakable solidity and a feeling of age about archaic coins that attracts collectors. Some would say that this is a speciality for the elite and what they could acquire is best demonstrated by a representative selection of silver pieces from the period.

After 486 BC, the Lydian Kingdom was part of the Persian Empire, throughout which circulated the coins called sigloi and darics. The difference is that they are silver and gold respectively, though the design is the same (110–113). A bearded archer, carrying a bow in one hand and a spear or sword in the other, is seen in a crouching position. According to the conventions of archaic art, this was the way to show the action of running. It used to be thought that here was the image of the 'Great King' himself and variations on the basic theme were labelled with the Persian emperors' names. Now, scholarly caution restricts us to calling him an archer.

Among the coin-issuing cities of Asia Minor that adopted distinctive badges, was Teos, which used a griffin (25); Mallos, whose religion involved a mysterious winged figure and a conical stone (479); Lycia where a bull and lion's scalp were chosen (34) and Kelendris that preferred a horseman and goat (35). The list could be made several times as long – the point is that, though such designs made for easily identifiable coins, we cannot usually explain why they were adopted in the first place.

Some of the Aegean islands were under the control of states in Asia Minor. For example, Samos used a lion's head similar to Lydia's and, in addition, there was a lion's scalp and bull's head. When a small hoard of these staters was found a few years ago, the experts estimated that this increased the number in existence to forty. Crete used coins from Aegina at first and then produced its own. Those featuring the labyrinth (474), and the Minotaur (473) as a monster-headed human, are particularly interesting. Aegina was the first city-state in Europe to produce coins. Its 'turtles' are described in a subsequent chapter, as are the 'owls' of Athens. Some of the most outlandish issues come from Thrace in northern Greece which, also, is treated in more detail later in this book. One could go on and on listing archaic coins that should appeal to modern collectors. Since this is not intended to be a catalogue, a limit is quickly reached and, although it has been painted with very broad strokes, the Archaic Period must be left for detailed investigation by readers to whom it particularly appeals. It is to be hoped that, though restricted in number, the illustrations will lead to greater appreciation of the period, for a picture is often worth a great many words.

The next few chapters review the history and coinage of some of the city-states. They could be taken in any order, so it is convenient to observe the convention employed in most reference books by starting with the westernmost and working eastwards.

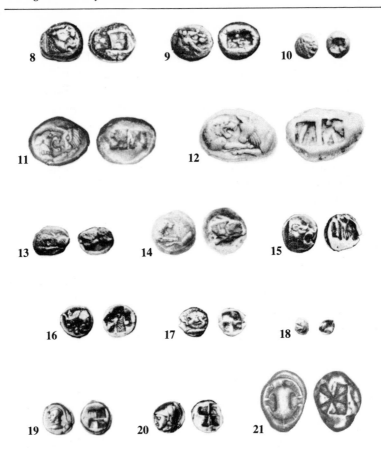

Kingdom of Lydia, 650–561 BC. Electrum lion-head coinage
8 ¹/₃ stater. **9** ¹/₆ stater. **10** ¹/₁₂ stater.

Electrum coinage of King Kroisos, 560–546 BC.
11 Stater. **12** Stater. Reverse depression clearly divided.
13 ¹/₃ stater. **14** Stater. Rounder: somewhat later? **15** Mytilene, Lesbos. Electrum ¹/₆ stater, 480–450 BC? Lion's head; calf's head intaglio. **16** Similar coin. Bull's head: intaglio reverse. **17** Kyzikos. Electrum ¹/₁₂ stater, sixth century BC. Gorgon's head. **18** Uncertain mint in Ionia. ¹/₆ stater, sixth century BC Griffin's head. **19** Kyzikos. ¹/₁₂ stater, fifth century BC. Head of Athena. **20** Phokaia. ¹/₆ stater, fifth century BC. Head of Athena. **21** Boeotia. Stater, sixth century BC. Shield.

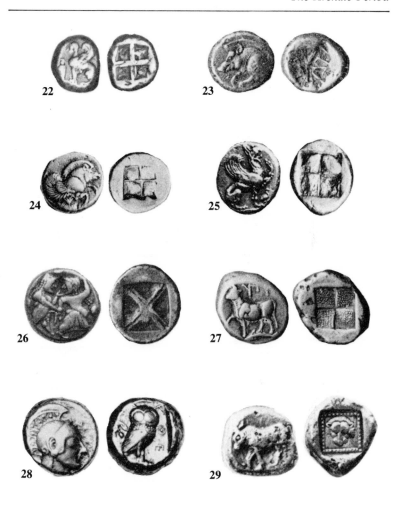

22 Chios. Didrachm, *c*. 500–480 BC.   **23** Lycia. Stater, 520–480 BC.
Forepart of winged boar.   **24** Klazomenai. Stater, similar.   **25** Teos. Stater,
late sixth century BC. Griffin.   **26** Lete. Stater, 530–480 BC. Satyr and
nymph.   **27** Byzantium. Stater, fourth century BC. Cow.   **28** Athens.
Tetradrachm, early fifth century BC.   **29** Lycia. Stater, fifth century BC.
Lion's head and bull.

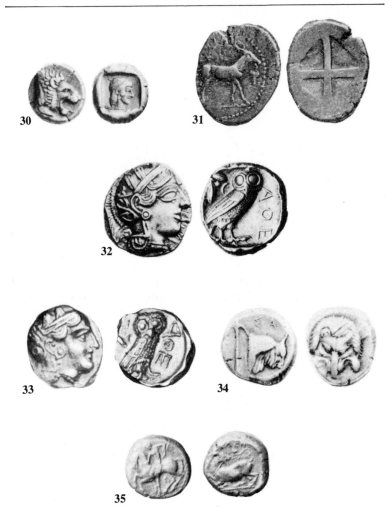

30 Knidos. Drachm, 480–450 BC. Lion's head and Aphrodite.   **31** Mende.
Tetradrachm, 480–465 BC. Ass with bunch of grapes in mouth; cross.
32 Athenian tetradrachm, 455–449 BC. Eye facing viewer.   **33** Later
tetradrachm, fourth century BC. Eye in profile.   **34** Lycia. Stater, fifth
century BC. Lion's scalp and bull's head.   **35** Kelendris. Stater, *c*. 450 BC.
Horseman and goat.

V. MAGNA GRAECIA

By the sixth century BC, the Greek cities established in southern Italy were flourishing to such an extent that the area was known as Magna Graecia – Greater Greece – for it promised to outshine the mother country. On the Bay of Taranto, between the 'heel' and 'tow' of Italy, were Tarentum itself, Metapontum, Sybaris, its dependency Sirinian Pyxos, Kroton, Kaulonia and Rhegion, while on the west coast, at Italy's 'ankle', was Poseidonia and, across the straits in Sicily opposite Rhegion, was the harbour of Zankle. We know little of the history of most of these cities and can only guess at what they were like in their prime, taking as a guide the magnificient temple of Poseidon at Poseidonia (known to the Romans as Paestum and to the Italians as Pesto).

There is plenty of scope for learned speculation in these cities' coins. Each produced tetradrachms struck on broad, thin flans and weighing 8.9 g, a standard found only in the earliest coins of Corinth. Though this is unexpected, the most remarkable thing about these coins is their design and method of production. The obverses have raised designs with cable borders and, at first sight, appear normal, but the reverses do not have a raised design at all and, instead, there is one similar to the obverse design sunk into them. To emphasise the point, the reverse design is *intaglio* as opposed to being simply the back of *repoussé* work, such as the raised designs on Victorian silver jugs or tankards. This is confirmed by close study which reveals details that vary between the two sides of the coins. The production of such coins presents problems – if they were struck in the usual way, the thin flans would probably split and, certainly, the designs would be spoilt if obverse and reverse were not exactly aligned – and they seldom were on coins of the period. Very few of the surviving coins from the cities in question are faulty and most are technically of a high standard. Experts have suggested

ETRURIA

● Rome

● Neapolis

● Poseidonia
● Velia

Metapontum
● Tarentum

Thourioi ● Sybaris

BRUTTIUM

● Kroton

● Segesta
● Selinos   ● Himera   Zankle-●
Messana

● Akragas

Leontini
●

● Syracuse

Italy and Sicily

that the dies must have been hinged and, possibly, produced by the 'lost wax' method used in casting sculpture. We should probably talk of pressure-moulding instead of striking. The silver came from other people's coins, which were hammered flat and, in the process, the metal spread – hence, the broad, thin flans. By indenting the thin flans with the reverse design and the border, coins of remarkable strength as well as beauty were produced.

Each city adopted its badge for the coins and added its name in abbreviated form. The three tetradrachms that modern collectors can hope to obtain are those of Metapontum (ear of barley) (36,37), Sybaris (a bull looking back) (38,39) and Kroton (a sacrificial tripod) (40,41). Coins of the other cities are rarities. Pyxos adopted a bull, similar to its mother city's; Kaulonia featured Apollo (42,43); Tarentum its two patrons, Apollo and Phalanthos (44); Rhegion employed a man-headed bull; Poseidonia portrayed the god after whom it was named, brandishing his trident (45) and Zankle showed a dolphin in its sickle-shaped harbour (46). The use of such coinage indicates that the cities had much in common. We know that they all sent representatives to the principal religious festival of Magna Graecia, held in honour of the goddess Hera Lakinia, whose cliff-top temple is still visible. Trade between them is also certain and there may have been a formal alliance. Another remarkable feature of their currency is that it would be of little use outside the area, because of its contrast with the contemporary coinage of the eastern Mediterranean, so different in weight and style.

Some scholars have sought to explain the issue of such unusual coins by attributing them to a remarkable individual. The obvious candidate for the honour is Pythagoras, the philosopher and mathematician. We know that about 535 BC he left his native island of Samos and settled in Kroton. At the time, this city was renowned for its physicians and the success of its athletes at the Olympic Games – since medicine was a matter of diet and exercise, there was little difference between the doctor and the athletics coach. Indeed, both might consider themselves philosophers and, since philosophers prescribed a carefully regulated way of life, Pythagoras no doubt expected to feel at home at Kroton. He was at the height of his fame and made a great impression. Aristotle records that the citizens identified him with Apollo and other traditions tell of the honours showered upon him, including his being immediately made a member of the senate and offered its chairmanship. Such statements must be treated with caution, for much that is recorded of Pythagoras (even his invention of the famous theorem) is clearly legendary. It seems unlikely, therefore, that he would have aspired to political power or that a stranger, however eminent, should have been offered it. On the other hand, there is a reliable record that a Pythagorean brotherhood was established. Resembling a secret society, it had several hundred members and branches in the other cities, eventually becoming so powerful that the apprehensions of the other citizens were aroused. The temple in which the brotherhood met at Kroton was burnt in a riot. Many members were killed and among them may have been Pythagoras himself. Similar disturbances were experienced in the other cities and the brotherhood was destroyed.

Were the Pythagoreans ever influential enough to dominate political and commercial life in Magna Graecia? Were its coins the products of their eccentric philosophical principles and did Pythagoras himself design them? Charles Seltman, the great authority on Greek coinage, believed so. He pointed out that Pythagoras was the son of a gem engraver and practised his father's art in Samos. Here the 'lost-wax' technique had been introduced about 550 BC, so Pythagoras would have known about it before coming to Kroton. He was also a man of artistic sensibility and, as a mathematician, had an adequate grasp of financial principles. Although without the sophistication of the modern economist, Pythagoras was quite capable of appreciating that the commercial interest of Magna Graecia could best be served by a coinage that would remain in the area, because its unacceptability further afield would ensure that there was no outflow of bullion. One can even suggest that an early coin of the island of Kalymna, near Samos, gave Pythagoras the model for 'his' coinage.

All this leads to a most attractive theory but, in the absence of hard facts, it remains in the realm of speculation. The coinage under discussion is usually dated between 550 and 480 BC and, on this reckoning, it first appeared before the arrival of Pythagoras. However, such dates are tentative and can easily be revised. The coinage certainly had a relatively short life and did not long outlast the philosopher. Relations between the cities deteriorated. In 510 BC (shortly after Pythagoras' death), Kroton destroyed Sybaris. Luxury and prosperity soon departed from all the cities for, probably as a result of their quarrels, they lost control of the inland areas to the

Italian tribes. Cut off from each other, most declined to the status of fishing ports and only Tarentum remained a commercial centre. Eventually, they all fell to Rome and their coinage ceased. In any case, their later coins were more conventional, not at all similar to the 'Pythagorean' issues, which are almost all we have to remind us of the remote but fascinating 'golden age' of Magna Graecia.

The intaglio-design coinage of the sixth century BC
36 Metapontum. Stater. Ear of barley.   **37** $^1/_6$ stater. Bull-head incuse.
38 Sybaris. Stater. Bull.   **39** $^1/_3$ stater.   **40** Kroton. Stater. Tripod-altar.
41 Kroton. Thicker fabric. Eagle incuse.

42 Kaulonia. Stater. Apollo. **43** Kaulonia. Stater. Smaller and thicker. **44** Tarentum. Stater. Phalanthos on a dolphin. **45** Poseidonia. ¹/₂ stater. Poseidon. **46** Zankle. Stater, slightly later period. Dolphin within sickle-shaped harbour; scallop shell in centre of incuse pattern.

VI. SYBARIS

The name Sybaris was synonymous with wealth and luxury. Several classical writers have left us descriptions of this remarkable city, situated on its plain at the back of the 'instep' on the 'foot' of Italy. Though many of its coins had been found, its exact site was unknown to us until the 1970s, when it was discovered deeply buried and very difficult to excavate properly by the archaelogical expedition financed by Pennsylvania University Museum. The deep deposits that cover Sybaris were probably carried there by earthquakes and soil erosion, though the Greeks and Romans had a different explanation.

The ancient writers leave us in no doubt that the Sybarites' luxurious way of life was their downfall. They dwell on their gluttony, extravagance, love of ease and failure to develop the qualities needed by fighting men. Perhaps it was a case of sour grapes on the part of the writers. After all, Sybaris was in the running for the title of richest city in the Greek world. Her fertile plain provided plenty of food. The choice of a bull for the coins indicates the importance of cattle-breeding at a period when few people ate beef. It was too scarce and expensive. Apart from agriculture, the other source of Sybaris' prosperity was her trade. Her position on the foot of Italy made her a centre for what is now called the export-import trade. In order to avoid the difficult passage round the Italian toe, where natural hazards were accompanied by notorious pirates, merchants unloaded their goods for transhipment overland and then made contact with ships sailing north, where they traded with the Etruscans. All this happened when Rome was an obscure little town that no one expected to make much impact on international relations. Several cities of Magna Graecia were considered much more important. Two flourishing colonies of Sybaris that were established on the opposite coast were Laus and Poseidonia, perhaps better known as Paestum. The latter's splendid temple to the sea god is frequently illustrated in architectural books as the finest example of such a building outside Greece itself. Both cities had their own coins, as did two others with whom they usually maintained friendship. These were Kroton and Metapontum, both on the south coast. All these cities were founded by the Achaeans, who came from the region south of the Gulf of Corinth and, following the usual custom in Greece in remote times, left to settle elsewhere due to population pressure at home. After two or three centuries, the Achaean colonies developed into important cities with their own distinctive characters. Enough has already been said about Sybaris to emphasise the contrast between it and Kroton. That city was renowned for the prowess of its athletes and the learning of its intellectuals. Its citizens took care to cultivate the military virtues. No one raised his status by living a life of ease. One really could not attempt to do so under the eye of philosophers such as Pythagoras. However, in spite of their different life-styles, Sybaris and Kroton got on together well enough until a crisis arose in 510 BC. A sustained demonstration by the poorer inhabitants of Sybaris led to a tribunal which exiled the most arrogant and ostentatious of the rich (they would have returned before long, no doubt). The exiles sought political asylum in Kroton and posed a problem by doing so. Although, man-for-man, the Krotoniates were more than a match for the Sybarites, there were far fewer of them. Besides, the Sybarites could use their wealth to hire any number of mercenaries. Consequently, the Krotoniates were anxious to avoid war. They sent a delegation of thirty prominent citizens to Sybaris in the hope that a conference would settle the situation and good relations would be restored. Unfortunately, the revolutionaries were still in control of Sybaris and they had the delegates murdered.

No one could overlook such a treacherous act and the Krotoniate army marched on Sybaris. Outside the walls, it was opposed by a confident army, strong in cavalry. According to legend, the Sybarite cavalry proved worse than useless. The horses had been carefully taught dressage and could dance to music. When the men of Kroton played a dirty trick on them and got their pipers to play the Sybarite tunes, the horses did what they were trained to do and danced into the infantry, causing general chaos. The Krotoniate troops seized their chance and inflicted a heavy defeat. The city withstood their seige for a further seventy days and then succumbed. Motives of revenge led to general butchery and destruction. Then, they diverted a river over its site.

Some refugees sought protection in the colonies of Laus and Poseidonia, though the most influential found their way to Athens. They kept their nationalism alive and, two generations later, their descendants returned to refound their city. It seems that they were unable to make use of exactly the same site, perhaps because of the changed course of the river. Another reason was the hostility of neighbouring cities, who had no wish to see their old commercial rival re-established. Everyone knew that the latest arrivals were really building New Sybaris, but they found it wise to change the name. Their city became Thourioi (Thurium in Latin) and, in due course, it issued some splendid coins (47–51). Dating from about 420 BC, they have seldom been surpassed as numismatic art. On the obverse is a head of Athena, in acknowledgement of the help received from her city, Athens. She is provided with a distinctive helmet on which the sea-monster Scylla and a griffin are carefully depicted. Presumably, these creatures implied some reference to trade or seafaring. No doubt attaches to the design on the reverse. The charging bull is a reminder of the earliest coins and a statement that the Sybarites were making a come-back. We know a great deal about Thourioi, even the names of its principal streets, from descriptions given us by the ancient writers. It was an early example of sensible town planning, grew as its trade brought prosperity, sided with Athens in her struggle against Sparta, suffered occupation by Hannibal and established a lasting alliance with Rome. It would be satisfying to excavate such a site but, like its predecessor, Thourioi has disappeared.

47 ¹/₆ stater, 443–425 BC. With the name 'Sybaris', later changed to
Thourioi. **48** Stater, 435–400 BC. Laurel wreath around Athena's
helmet. **49** Di-stater, 350–281 BC. Scylla on Athena's helmet. **50** Stater,
similar. These two coins are of the very best style. **51** Stater with a
hippocamp on Athena's helmet. On figures 48–51, there is a tunny fish
beneath the bull on the reverse.

VII. TARENTUM

About a hundred miles east of Sybaris, where the 'heel' of Italy meets the arch of the 'foot', Greek ships found an excellent natural harbour. It was defensible, strategically situated and abounding with edible shellfish. Here, for five centuries, flourished the richest Greek colony in Italy. Its name, Tarentum, has scarcely changed in becoming the modern Taranto. This was the town of Taras, son of Poseidon, lord of the sea, better known to us by his Latin name, Neptune. Taras was carried there on the back of a dolphin and, when a port grew up, it honoured him as its patron god.

The first inhabitants were, according to tradition, driven out by a group of Spartans who arrived in 708 BC under the leadership of Phalanthos, a shadowy, possibly mythological, hero. He and his followers had been expelled for breaking the rigid code of behaviour observed among their race. The 'crime' in question was refusal to accept status as second-class citizens, which was imposed on them because of the circumstances in which they had been born. Their mothers were the young wives of soldiers, who had been obliged to spend twenty years away from home fighting the Messenians, the inhabitants of the western Peloponnesus. During their husbands' absence, the women shared their beds with helots, members of the serf class who did manual work for the Spartans. When these couples had children, they could not be granted full citizenship, though they were not treated as helots either. Known as Partheniae, they were numerous enough to pose a problem in Sparta and, when they reached adulthood, the Oracle of Delphi was consulted. Her advice was for them to emigrate, so they set sail and reached the site of Tarentum, drove out the handful of people already living there and settled down to create a prosperous city. They found that the crops did well, vines and olives flourished and livestock thrived. Furthermore, the murex, a kind of mussel, provided much-prized purple dye that became an important article of trade with the ships that frequently called on their voyages westward from Greece. After several generations, Tarentum had become the most prosperous city in Magna Graecia and its inhabitants had adopted some un-Spartan habits, becoming rather like the Sybarites. They had difficulty fending off the tribes who lived in the hilly inland areas, though there was plenty of money to pay mercenaries to do their fighting for them.

Tarentine coins were minted in very large quantities. The great majority were didrachms which feature, on one side, Taras riding his dolphin and on the other a horse with its jockey or a cavalryman. A surprising number of variations were made on the basic themes, giving a long series – 'the Horsemen of Tarentum' – which some collectors specialise in. Taras holds a number of different symbolic objects – wine cup, amphora, trident, helmet, spear, shield, oar and so on. The jockey is shown in many poses associated with racing – galloping, walking, prancing, dismounting and even removing a stone from his horse's hoof. Frequently he is crowning his winning mount and, in one variation, someone else is doing this for him: presumably this gesture was the equivalent of our custom which allows the owner to 'lead in' the successful horse. Racing seems to have been a Tarentine passion. The jockeys were boys, who doubtless outgrew the occupation and, eventually, became fighting men, unless they succumbed to the temptations of life in this fortunate city. Very probably, the silver pieces that feature mounted warriors were intended to impress the mercenaries whose pay they formed.

So serious was the threat posed by the local tribes, referred to as the Lucanians that, in 338 BC, the Tarentines had to appeal to their mother-city for aid. The Spartan leader, Archidamos, led an expedition which relieved the pressure on them, though he was killed in the fighting. A few years later, they called in another distinguished general, Alexander, King of Epeiros (63), the area of the Balkans closest to the heel of Italy. He, too, was temporarily successful and, later, met his death in battle. Even more formidable rivals were advancing from the north. The Romans, with whom the Tarentines had had a treaty of friendship since 450 BC, were gradually extending their control over the rest of Italy. It must have been obvious that Tarentum's days of commercial supremacy were numbered, though the resentment of the common people could scarcely justify the behaviour that turned Rome into an enemy. A visit by ships of the Roman fleet sparked off a riot. Taken unawares, the crews of five vessels were overwhelmed, the admiral was killed and any surviving sailors were sold into slavery. Next, the Tarentines went to Thourioi, which had accepted a Roman garrison, and forced it to surrender. In spite of this provocation, the Romans behaved with great moderation, hoping to restore good relations at a time when their principal enemy appeared to be the distinguished military leader, King Pyrrhus of Epeiros. He was quite likely to follow the example set by his predecessor and came to the aid of the Tarentines. After a long debate in their assembly, they decided to continue their opposition to Rome and sent Pyrrhus an invitation. He arrived in 280 BC with an army said to have been composed of 20,000 infantrymen, 2,000 archers, 500 slingers, 3,000 cavalry and 20 elephants, all of whom had to be paid for in Tarentine silver, or even gold, for here was an emergency which required the unusual step of minting the very valuable gold staters. The design chosen – Zeus and his eagle – was an implied compliment to Pyrrhus, whose kingdom contained one of the best-known sacred groves dedicated to the Father of the Gods. Nevertheless, the Tarentines were unhappy at the way their money seemed unable to buy instant victory and, therefore, Pyrrhus had to treat them as if they had surrendered to him, billeting troops in private houses and enforcing martial law. Having secured his base, he proceeded with campaigns that put heart into the inhabitants of cities that resisted the Roman advance, though each of his battles was won at such cost that 'a Pyrrhic victory' became proverbial. After several years of fighting that took him to Sicily, back to Italy and, eventually, to his homeland, Pyrrhus met his death in a street brawl, leaving his Italian allies leaderless against Rome. The Tarentines were fortunate to be able to become nominal allies of Rome, though they were no longer permitted to maintain an army. They were, however, allowed to retain the privilege of minting coinage and adopted, either through necessity or convenience, a lighter standard, which made their didrachms equal in value to those being produced by the Romans. Coin designs followed the established pattern and a great variety of officials' names and mint-marks were used to identify each issue. Unfortunately, none has an obvious meaning, such as was implied by the little elephant placed below the dolphin on silver struck in Pyrrhus' time, though all contribute to the fascination of this long series. It continued until

228 BC, when the mint was closed by the Romans, though there was to be one last flurry of activity. In 212, during Hannibal's campaign in Italy, the southern Italian cities made a final bid to regain their independence and allied with him against Rome. Tarentum was occupied by the Carthaginians, for whom gold and silver were struck. Five years later, the Romans retook the city and had their revenge. 30,000 Tarentines are supposed to have been sold as slaves and 3,000 talents sent from the treasury to Rome. These must have been terrible days, when many a hoard of savings was buried by their anxious owners. Some of the people who were unable to return for them left substantial numbers of 'horsemen' to be discovered in subsequent centuries and, thereby, unwittingly ensured that Tarentine coins are now fairly common.

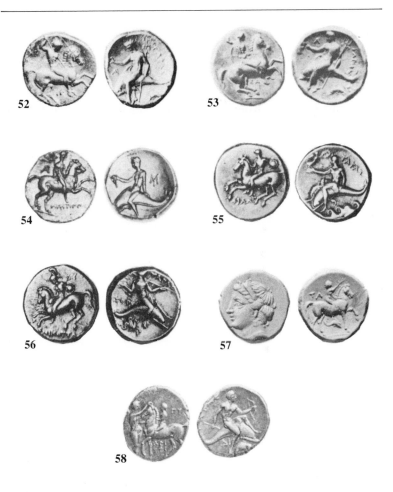

The 'Horsemen' of Tarentum. A selection of didrachms.
52 344–334 BC. Naked horseman brandishing a spear; Taras holds a trident.   **53** The horseman holds two spears; Taras carries a trident and holds out a wine-cup.   **54** The horseman holds a sceptre and Taras a wine-cup.
55 302–281 BC. The naked horseman carries a shield and Taras holds a miniature Nike, who crowns him: waves beneath him.   **56** The horseman is helmeted: Taras holds a staff; hippocamp beneath him.   **57** A coin which may result from an alliance between Naples and Tarentum. Female head: boy rider crowning his horse; dolphin beneath.   **58** 281–272 BC. The horse is ridden by a boy and crowned by a man; Taras holds a bow and arrow.

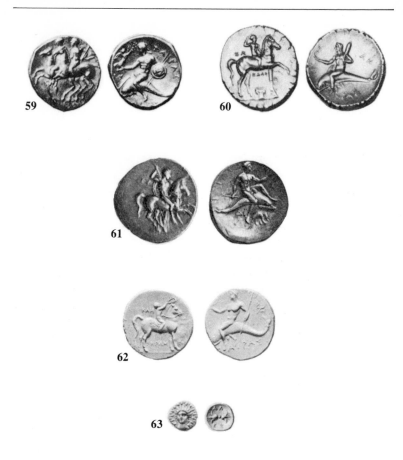

59 The Dioskouroi ride their horses. Taras has Nike, spears and a shield with a hippocamp on it.   **60** Boy rider crowning himself; Taras holds a distaff.
61 Coin with King Pyrrhus' elephant as a mint-mark.   **62** This coin is believed to date from the occupation of Tarentum by Hannibal.   **63** A gold stater struck by King Alexander of Epeiros when aiding Tarentum, 334–330 BC. Head of Helios and a thunderbolt.

VIII. NAPLES

A northern ally of the Tarentines made peace with the Romans in 327 BC and honourably stood by the agreement, much to her advantage. This city is known to the English-speaking world as Naples, a close approximation of the Greek Neapolis. The name had not always been used. According to the earliest historical traditions, some Cumaeans from the island of Ischia founded the first settlement in about 650 BC, at a spot where the tomb of Parthenope was thought to be, and named it after her. Three centuries later, it fell to one of the Italian tribes, the Samnites, who were ostracised by the original inhabitants. They were refused space to settle within the city walls, so a new Samnite suburb grew up and a new wall was built to enclose it. Thus, there were two adjacent towns – the Old Town, Palaeopolis and the New Town, Neapolis. In the course of time, the latter grew so large that it swallowed up its ancestor.

But to return to Parthenope – she is probably the lady who appears on the extensive silver coinage issued by Naples in the fourth and third centuries BC. Different artists portrayed her variously. For instance, on one of these coins, she has a kind of pony tail and on the other she is wearing a diadem – a headband that signified royalty or divinity (64–67). Parthenope was one of the Sirens, those terrible sea-nymphs whose captivating songs lured sailors to death on their island, the beautiful meadows of which were scattered with human bones. Early artists depicted them as birds with female heads but, later, they were seen as mermaids and, as such, passed through medieval sea-lore, surviving in travellers' tales until quite modern times. The best-known escape from the Sirens was contrived by Odysseus on his homeward voyage from Troy. He stopped up his crew's ears with wax so that they were unable to hear the singing and had himself tied to the mast in such a way that, however much he struggled, he was unable to follow the example of those who had previously sailed that way – leaping overboard, swimming to the island and languishing to death there. Some time afterwards, another band of heroes, the Argonauts, made a similar journey. They had the advantage of help from Orpheus, the most gifted musician of all, whose melodies made the very trees uproot themselves to follow him. When they listened to Orpheus, the Argonauts were safe from the Sirens, who were deeply dismayed at seeing their powers counteracted. Legend has it that one of them, Parthenope, of course, threw herself into the sea. Her body was cast up on what we now call the Bay of Naples and buried at the spot where the town was later founded.

As a sea-nymph, Parthenope was a daughter of the strange creature on the reverse of these coins. The man-headed bull is Acheloos, the god of rivers. The offspring of the primeval Greek gods – Oceanus, the Sea, and Tethys, daughter of Heaven and Earth – Acheloos gave his name to the longest river in Greece and several others in various places. Hesiod, the early Greek poet, describes him as having 3,000 sons, the rivers known to him, and countless daughters, the Naiads, nymphs of fresh-water springs. In time, he came to represent all running water and was worshipped by communities which were closely linked to rivers. As a rule, they refrained from burning the rams, horses or bulls brought for sacrifice, but threw them into the river instead. This practice alluded to the legends associated with Acheloos. He was born in human form and, as a young man, became the rival of Hercules for the hand of Deianira. This tragic lady eventually saw her mother, Althea, commit suicide after bringing about the death of Meleager, her heroic son and Deianira's brother. Deianira herself was a good wife to Hercules until she unwittingly brought him a robe that proved to be impregnated with poison and caused his death. On seeing the result of her action, she too committed suicide. After Hercules had defeated him to win Deianira's hand, Acheloos turned himself into a bull and, subsequently, tried to gain his revenge. Once again, Hercules out-wrestled him and was able to break off one of his horns.

This horn was eventually returned to him in exchange for another, which he had kept closely guarded. It had originally belonged to Amalthea, a nymph who took the form of a goat to nurse the infant Zeus in Crete. When he grew up, Zeus broke it off and conferred upon it magic properties. It instantly filled with whatever the possessor might wish and became known as the Horn of Plenty. Ovid, the Latin poet, tells us a slightly different tale in which the Naiads made Acheloos' horn the Cornucopia. Whichever tradition you may prefer, there is no doubt that, in Mediterranean countries, rivers brought fertility and prosperity. Poor Acheloos was so humiliated by his second defeat that he leapt into the river and drowned himself.

Worship of the god who dies and rises again to give life to the soil is a characteristic of a great many fertility rites. However, we are uncertain which river or spring was worshipped by the inhabitants of Neapolis and, moreover, these coins present another problem. The flying Victory (Nike) crowning Acheloos must commemorate some triumph of the Neapolitans, but we have no record of the particular battle alluded to. Very probably, they had been fighting on the same side as the Romans for, at an early stage in her expansion, Rome found a firm ally in Naples, who stood by her against the Samnites and, later, against Hannibal. After 290 BC, Naples was under Roman domination, but her citizens were rewarded for their traditional loyalty with full voting rights and exemption from military service. Her coinage was replaced in about 220 BC by Rome's. In the case of other cities, a similar development almost always indicated defeat and decline. However, Naples retained her Greek constitution, Greek language and Greek way of life. These attractive features encouraged many wealthy leisured Romans to settle there to enjoy the dolce vita amid some of the world's most beautiful scenery. As their numbers grew, they built the resort towns of Herculaneum and Pompeii – but this was a mistake!

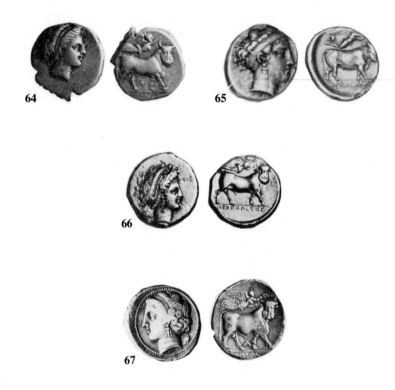

Didrachms. The siren, Parthenope and the man-headed bull, Acheloos, crowned by Nike.
64 450–340 BC. Parthenope with waved hair. **65** Parthenope with a prominent headband. **66** 340–241 BC. Parthenope's coiffure is more elaborate. **67** She has curls at the back of the head.

IX. SICILY

This island produced coins which have long been favourites among collectors and are now very expensive indeed. Even so, the once-neglected minor silver pieces and bronzes can still be had at reasonable prices, which allow us to acquire specimens of numismatic art from what is arguably the finest period.

Sicily was colonised by expeditions that set out from various cities in Greece during the seventh century BC. They met little opposition from the people living there already, whom they called Sikels. On the other hand, the western tip of the island was controlled by the Carthaginians, whose capital city was on the site of modern Tunis. As its power grew, it challenged first the Greeks and, later, the Romans, for supremacy in the Mediterranean. Consequently, the history of the Greek cities in Sicily is a story of constant vigilance and intermittent warfare, throughout which it was possible to build up considerable prosperity. Most cities grew in population and provided themselves with handsome public buildings, among which are the best-preserved examples of Greek temples. Even so, their architectural achievements were competent rather than outstanding, as was most of their art. They certainly had the usual embellishments of Greek life – statuary, painted vases and so on – but the local product was not very distinguished and those wealthy people who expected the best of everything knew that they had to import either the goods or the craftsmen who made them.

The exception to this state of affairs was the coinage, which must have received far more attention than elsewhere. A tradition of artistic care and innovation was established and the result was a series of coins, the beauty and craftsmanship of which have never been surpassed. Dies were cut with great precision. It still arouses the admiration of modern craftsmen, particularly when we remember that the Greeks had to work without the help of magnifying lenses.

The eye can, of course, be trained to close work, though natural aptitude is important. I much prefer to think of the splendid work on coins as the result of long training and experience rather than coming from the hands of men who were so short-sighted that, in normal life, they were as blind as the proverbial bats. However, this theory has been seriously put forward by scholars who cannot imagine how dies of the quality involved could have been made without optical aids. Perhaps they did, in fact, have some form of magnifying glass even though there is no record of the fact but, whatever the case, everyone accepts that their coins are outstanding examples of classical art.

Like many other Greek cities, those in Sicily first produced coins with a design on only one side and the incuse mark of the punch on the other. The archaic period was not prolific. Its chief interest lies in the use of the 'mill-sail' and 'swastika' reverses and the prototypes of later designs. Akragas used its eagle and crab (68); Gela had its river-god (71); Himera had chosen a cock as its badge (72); Zankle-Messana featured its sickle-shaped harbour (as already mentioned in the chapter on Magna Graecia) (46); Selinos had its wild parsley and Syracuse was already using a female head and a chariot on its silver (74). After a generation or two, this chariot was adopted by other cities in acknowledgement of the superior position of Syracuse which, for a time, dominated the whole island. It produced a long series of splendid coins, which must have eclipsed other currencies but, before turning our attention to it, a few words must be said about the smaller cities. They all tended to push the date of their foundation as far back as possible though, nowadays, we doubt claims to very early origins.

Even so, one of the oldest was Gela on the south coast. Numismatically, it is appreciated for its representation of the river god. He takes the form of a man-headed bull, often called Acheloos, the name of the largest river in Greece and, supposedly, the father of all other rivers. Presumably, the inhabitants of the town had their own river in mind or, even, fresh water in general – a vital commodity not too plentiful in Sicily.

In the sixth century BC, a group of Gelans moved up the coast and founded Akragas. Their power grew steadily and, in 485, their ruler, whom we know as Gelon (the man from Gela), was able to make himself master of Syracuse. Though he eventually became very popular, he needed help at first and, therefore, transferred half the inhabitants of Gela to his new realm. After that, Gela gradually fell into decay and, by the time of Augustus, it was an uninhabited site.

Its 'colony', Akragas, is rather confusingly referred to in catalogues by two names: Akragas, which is Greek, and Agrigentum, which is Latin. The coin badges it used were the eagle and the crab, symbols of Zeus and Poseidon, gods of the sky and sea. The usual explanation is based on the tradition that, since the city was sited on a steep hill, people approaching it remarked that it was midway between the sky and the sea. On typical early didrachms, the eagle shows the formality of the style then in vogue (68). Later versions (69), and even bronze pieces (70), were designed with greater ingenuity. The eagle sometimes stretches its wings, or is seen eating its prey or accompanied by its mate. The later version is on a handsome silver piece believed to commemorate the victory of one of its citizens in the chariot race at the Olympic Games and is now one of the treasures of the British Museum.

Another Olympic celebration explains the unusual choice of design for the coins of Messana (75–77). The mule team entered by the wealthy Anaxilas won the race held in 480, so it was placed on silver pieces, which would remind everyone who handled them of this achievement. Another fast runner, the hare, is on the reverse, though it is doubtful whether there is a connection. This animal is more probably the companion of the god Pan, whose following was strong in the area. Sometimes, a miniature portrait of him is provided as well.

Pan could be found in the countryside and, particularly, in the wild places, where the music of his pipes might scare people so that they fled in panic – to use the word derived from his activities. We may think it fanciful to believe in such a creature though, when they worshipped Pan, the Greeks were usually using him as a focus for their hopes of receiving the fruits of nature. In a similar way, they personified their river gods, as already mentioned in the case of Gela.

It was not essential to follow the convention of using the man-headed bull. In Selinos, the river was shown as a young man sacrificing (78,79). Beside him are the cock and the bull that he might have killed in the ceremony and, also, the selinon leaf to tell everyone whose coin it was. The small city of Segesta, which was not a Greek foundation, was usually on bad terms with Selinos, though it also followed its example of putting its water supply on its coins (80). The stream was a tributary of the river Krimissos, the god of which changed himself into a dog in order to take advantage of a Trojan maiden. Their son was supposed to have founded the city. In general, it was a point of pride to claim descent from the Trojans, whose heroic conduct was celebrated in the Iliad.

After the fall of the city, many of its inhabitants fled to the west and one of them, Aeneas, was credited with fathering the Romans. Even in those remote days, credulity must have been strained when the old stories were retold, especially if someone counted the number of ladies who allowed disguised gods to make love to them. On the other hand, the listeners may have been more appreciative than we assume, realising that the myths were symbolic accounts of historical situations.

In very early times, lions were to be found in most Mediterranean countries. 'Lion Town' (Leontini) was the name given to one of the Sicilian cities and predictably, a lion was used on its coins. At first, it was accompanied by a naked horseman and, later, by Apollo (81). Its very fertile land yielded an abundance of corn and, therefore, corn grains were placed around the lion's head. Though important economically, this city played only a minor role in politics, because it was situated too near Syracuse, which easily dominated it.

Even more blatantly, Syracuse defeated Katane, the other city which used Apollo for its coins, and deported its citizens. This was in 476, when they were replaced by Syracusan and fresh Greek immigrants. The name of the city was changed to Aetna, on the lower slopes of which it was situated though, eventually, the original inhabitants were able to change it back again. While under Syracusan domination, the chariot appeared on its coins as an indication of the fact (82,83).

The chariot had always been the badge of Syracuse and was a theme which gave its die engravers plenty of scope for experiment. It evolved from the stiff, archaic style, through the convention of depicting four horses by giving two of them the shadowy outline of the other pair, to a point when all the horses are individually sculpted as spirited animals requiring all the skill of the charioteer to control them.

Power and prosperity in Syracuse were the result of the activities of Gelon, who devoted all his energies to developing the city. Though renowned for his moderation and leniency, he was a forceful general who was able to inflict a crushing defeat on the Carthaginians at the Battle of Himera in 480. According to tradition, his wife persuaded him to treat the prisoners humanely and, in due course, an ambassador from Carthage expressed thanks by presenting her with a gold crown.

The proceeds from its sale were used to produce commemorative coins, some of which were the large 10 drachma pieces named after her. She was called Demarete, so the coin is the demaretion.

The specimen in the British Museum is often singled out as the most handsome of all Greek coins and it has attracted the attention of generations of scholars. At one time, it was believed that the portrait was one of the queen herself though, nowadays, opinion has shifted and favours the view that it is only a particularly well executed version of Arethusa, the nymph who appears again and again on Syracusan silver. She was supposed to be the deity who lived in the fresh-water spring that bubbled up on the island of Syracuse and, thus, provided that extremely defensible position with the most vital requirement if it was to withstand a siege. Since little was known about rock strata, there seemed to be no explanation of how the spring was to be found on an island, except that it must, somehow, pass under the sea and come to the surface again. The way the myths put it was to describe how Arethusa escaped from Poseidon and, on coins, she was shown surrounded by dolphins. They served another purpose as Syracuse grew into a major city because they could represent sea power.

The demaretion is a large version of the tetradrachm, which was standard currency in Syracuse. Unlike other cities, such as Athens, which stuck to designs that changed very little over the years, the Syracusans preferred to experiment with the way they depicted the chariot, Victory flying above it and, most obviously, Arethusa's portraits. They can be arranged in sequence according to style, though there seems no obvious reason why the nymph should change her hair-style so often, apart from the probability that ladies' fashions in Syracuse have been perpetuated on the coins. Some of them have been chosen to give an indication of the evolution in design, and it would have been possible to have provided two or three times as many from the hundreds of dies used.

First, is a small semi-archaic head with long hair held in place with a headband (84). On the next coin, the head is larger and the hair ornamented with a string of beads (85). This is much the same kind of portrait as found on the demaretion, except that, on the victory coin, the beads are replaced by a laurel wreath. The third coin shows a big change in style. The semi-archaic rigidity has given place to a realistic portrait and the horses have also been transformed. Arethusa's hair is worn in a roll, bound by a cord, and she seems pretty rather than regal

(86). A few years later, she was wearing a net (sacchos) to keep her hair in place and, on the reverse of the tetradrachm (87), Victory is crowning the charioteer instead of the horses. On the next coin, they have clearly come into their own as two splendid animals and Arethusa has put up her hair into a top-knot (88).

The artist's signature beneath her head on the sixth tetradrachm brings us to another important aspect of Syracusan coinage. For a craftsman to sign his work, he must have had permission from the authorities and granting it would have been an unusual decision in the Greek world. Generally speaking, craftsmen were not highly esteemed and many of the famous works of art that have survived are by unknown hands. Attitudes must have been rather different in Syracuse where, as has already been suggested, great attention was paid to coin designs. Accomplished engravers were probably celebrities and, if this was so, the next logical step would be to allow them to sign their work.

Unfortunately, we know nothing about them, apart from their names, and assume, on the basis of the styles, that Eumenes and Soison began work about 425 and, after about ten years, they were joined by four other artists – Euainetos, Phrygillos, Eukleidas and Kimon (89,90). Some tetradrachms carry the name of Eukleidas, who has given us a lovely portrait with elaborately curled hair. The people he is thought to have trained were responsible for other coins which show Arethusa's hair blown by the wind or, perhaps, floating in the water, which was her element.

Kimon and Euainetos, who were probably professional rivals, were entrusted with the production of another issue of dekadrachms somewhat like the demaretion (91,92). The occasion for this issue, which indicates a military victory by placing enemy armour beneath the chariot wheels, is not in serious dispute. In 413, the Syracusans almost annihilated a powerful Athenian expedition sent to attack them. This was another round in the thirty-year struggle between Athens and Sparta which we call the Peloponnesian War. Their allies got dragged into it and, in the case of Sicily, the only long-term benefits went to the Carthaginians, who were able to stage an invasion in 409. Their forces seized Selinos, Himera, Akragas, Gela and smaller cities the coins of which have not been mentioned here. The captured citizens were enslaved and, in one case, the city was completely destroyed. This was Himera, later rebuilt on the opposite bank of the river and called Thermae – hot springs – a welcome by-product of

Aetna's volcanic activity.

Syracuse held out under the able leadership of Dionysos, whose reign, of twenty-five years, was dominated by the struggle with Carthage. He needed plenty of money to pay his troops and, therefore, the mint was very busy. As well as producing the usual tetradrachms, it continued to strike dekadrachms and even issued gold coins. As has already been said, gold was seldom used for Greek coins and, when it does appear, an emergency is indicated. Even though Dionysos needed supplies quickly, the die cutters lived up to the city's traditions and produced well-designed pieces. Though they are small, the workmanship is excellent.

Our examples are 20-litrae and 100-litrae coins, weighing only 1.15 g and 5.79 g (5 litrae equalled 4 drachms) (93,94). The portraits are well carved, even the minute head of Arethusa in the centre of the incuse pattern on the smaller coin. Hercules, who appears on both, may be taken to be the champion whose example the Syracusans were following and the lion he is overcoming may well be intended to represent the Carthaginians. They came from Africa and that is where the lions were most commonly found, even though the original animal strangled by Hercules lived in Greece.

With these gold coins, our survey of fifth-century Sicily comes to an end. Of course, issues of coinage continued and several very interesting types appeared in succeeding centuries. However, the artistic inspiration declined and, with a few exceptions, students of the subject agree that the 'golden age' was over. Coins from this period often come up for sale, though they are bought by investor-collectors who want to put their money into 'nothing but the very best'.

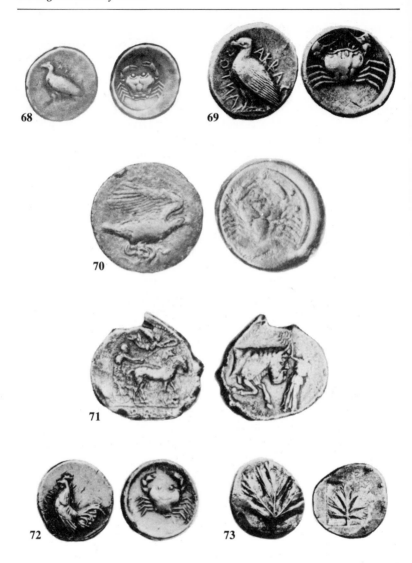

68 Akragas. Didrachm, 510–472 BC. Eagle and crab.   **69** Tetradrachm, 472–420. Similar.   **70** Bronze hemilitron, 425–406 BC. Eagle with a snake in its talons; crab and pellets.   **71** Gela. Tetradrachm, 440–430 BC. Chariot and man-headed bull crowned by a nymph.   **72** Himera. Didrachm, 482–472 BC. Cock and crab.   **73** Selinos. Didrachm, 490–466 BC. Wild parsley leaf.

74 Syracuse. Tetradrachm, 510–490 BC. Chariot; swastika incuse with archaic female head. **75** Messana. Tetradrachm, 480–461 BC. Chariot and hare. **76** Tetradrachm, 450–425 BC. Female charioteer (the city-goddess); hare with a fly used as a mint-mark. **77** Tetradrachm, 425–396 BC. Charioteer crowned by Nike; hare and corn stalk. **78** Selinos. Tetradrachm, 466–415 BC. Chariot driven by Apollo and Artemis; river-god sacrificing a cock on an altar; statue of a bull on a pedestal.

79 Tetradrachm, similar types. River-god holds a patera over a fire.
80 Segesta. Didrachm, 480–461 BC. Head of the nymph, Segesta, and a dog.
81 Leontini. Tetradrachm, 466–425 BC. Heads of Apollo and a lion, surrounded by corn grains. 82 Katane. Tetradrachm, 450–420 BC. Head of Apollo and chariot. 83 A similar coin.

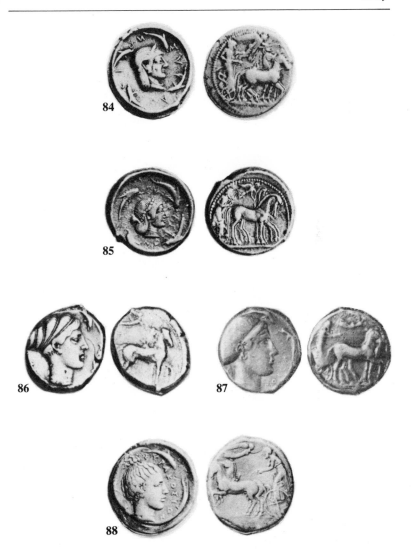

Syracuse: Tetradrachms. Arethusa and a chariot; Nike crowns the horses.
84 485–478 BC. Small head, long hair and headband.   **85** *c*. 479 BC. Hair
ornamented with a string of beads.   **86** 474–450 BC. Hair bound with a
cord.   **87** 450–439 BC. Hair worn in a net.   **88** 413–405 BC. Hair in
top-knot.

89 425–413 BC. Signed by Eumenes.   **90** 405–380 BC. Signed by Eukleidas.
91 Dekadrachm, 405–380 BC. Signed by Kimon.   **92** Dekadrachm, 405–380
BC. Signed by Euainetos.   **93** 20 litrae piece, 405–380 BC. Head of Hercules
and a small head of Arethusa in an incuse square.   **94** Gold 100 litrae piece.
Arethusa; Hercules wrestling with a lion.

X. ATHENS

This most famous Greek city enjoyed three advantages – its territory was extensive in comparison to other poleis; its position made possible the creation of a maritime commercial empire; and its silver mines were the most productive in the known world. Prosperity encouraged the intellectual pursuits of a leisured class of citizens, accustomed to relying on slaves to do most of the manual work. Almost every historian of Greece stresses the contributions made by Athens in laying the foundations of western drama, philosophy, mathematics, art, architecture and history. The surviving records are far more complete for Athens than for any other city-state, so much so, that we are always in danger of seeing ancient Greece through Athenian eyes. All the same, it is very useful for the numismatist to have detailed accounts of events that had a bearing on the design and production of coins.

Nevertheless, the earliest Athenian issues are the source of controversy. Sometimes called 'Wappenmünzen' or 'heraldic coins', because a nineteenth-century German scholar advanced the now-discredited view they were produced by the leading families, they carry a variety of designs – wheel, amphora, gorgon's head, triskeles and so on (95). It is not easy to explain all these choices and a few experts doubt whether they are, indeed, Athenian, though the fact that they are found in Attica makes it probable. All of them are rare and the average collector is unlikely to acquire one. He will be thinking of buying a representative specimen or two from the long series of silver pieces that feature Athena and her owl.

About 510 BC, Athens began to provide herself with a distinctive coinage. On the obverse was the head of the patron goddess and, on the reverse, was her owl, which flew about the world each evening and returned with news of what had happened the previous day. There was

Greece, the Aegean Islands and Asia Minor

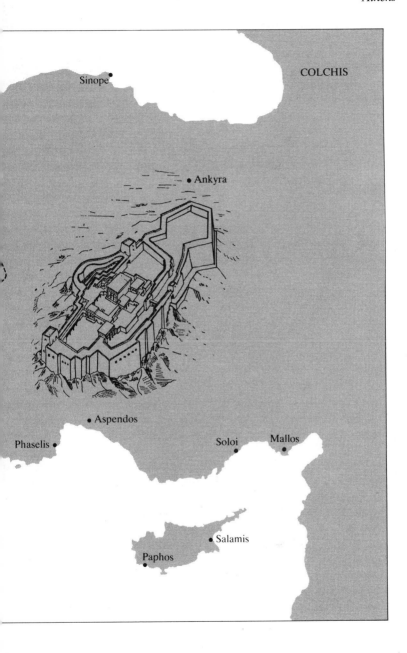

COLCHIS

Sinope

Ankyra

Aspendos

Phaselis

Soloi

Mallos

Salamis

Paphos

no more efficient way of keeping informed and, as goddess of wisdom, Athena needed to know everything worth knowing. She was also the personification of defensive warfare and, consequently, wore a helmet. Full-length impressions of her on other cities' coins usually show her with a spear and shield as well. Her temple was on the Acropolis and she was thought of as presiding over the affairs of her city in both war and peace. Thanks were regularly paid to her for prosperity and the coins show the source of much of Athenian trade, a sprig of olive. This reminded everyone who handled them that great quantities of oil came from Athens and so did the pottery vessels to keep it in. As we would expect, the earliest versions of Athena and her owl are in the archaic style (28,96,97). A few are very well executed, though the majority are dumpy pieces of little artistic merit, clearly mass-produced from the silver pouring out of the Laurian mines. Great quantities reached the state treasury and were wisely used to pay for the construction of a fleet.

It saved Athens from the Persians, whose huge armies twice invaded Greece. The first was halted in 490 BC at Marathon and the second was forced to retreat ten years later when the Athenians won mastery at sea through the battle of Salamis, and the Persians found their supplies cut off. Herodotos, the Athenian historian, gives a detailed account of the forces involved, the scene when the Persian Emperor reviewed his troops, debates among the commanders and what happened at the principal engagements. Unfortunately, he does not tell us when a change in the basic coin design occurred. Athena was given a crown of olive leaves to wear on her helmet (98,99). This symbol of victory could have been first used after either Marathon or Salamis, we shall never know which. It is sufficient to appreciate it as a facet of the 'golden age' of Athens when, for about fifty years, she was supreme among the Greek cities. At that time, the damage done by the Persians was made good and the major public buildings rebuilt to the highest standards. The Parthenon and other famous architectural gems were paid for from the treasury, the arts flourished and intellectual life was at its peak. Immense quantities of silver were minted to pay for the various projects that had been undertaken. Thucydides tells us that, at the time when the Peloponnesian War began in 431 BC, Athens was receiving 600 talents of silver per year in tribute from her allies and a reserve of ten times that amount (175 tons), all in coin, was kept in the Parthenon. Athenian coinage dominated commerce in the Aegean and was carried far and wide. Hoards have been discovered in Afghanistan and even more distant ones may come to light.

The dockyards and defensive walls linking Athens with its port, the Peiraeus, proved to be invaluable when her supremacy was challenged by several resentful states, led by Sparta. As long as the Athenians had a secure base and a strong fleet, little could be done to defeat them decisively, though Attica was devastated. The reserve of money in the Parthenon was gradually used up, even though supplies of silver still came from the mines. After eighteen years' fighting, the Spartans cut the road to Laurium and deprived the Athenians of these vital supplies. Next year, in 413, the naval expedition sent to Sicily to capture Syracuse was heavily defeated and most of Athens' remaining allies abandoned her. Matters grew more desperate and crisis point was reached in 407–406, when the silver ran out. Copper plated with silver had to be used as a token coinage and, as was normal in emergencies, an issue of gold was made. The statue of Nike on the Acropolis and other offerings or temple furnishings were melted down and turned into coins. They paid for yet another fleet but it, too, was defeated and, in 404, Athens surrendered.

The Spartan occupation was not as onerous as had been feared and did not last long. More sadly, democracy was a war casualty and was replaced by oligarchy or tyranny. After a decade, recovery had reached a point when minting could begin again. The coins retained their traditional designs, thus posing dating problems. A rule-of-thumb guide for identifying fourth- and third-century silver is Athena's eye (100). It is in profile, with the eyeball facing forwards, as we would probably sketch it in a present-day portrait. The archaic style gave her an eye that seems to be seen from the front, even though her head is in profile. An additional guide is the general style, which is softer and, sometimes, rather careless, though there are plenty of examples of carelessness among the thousands of dies used in the fifth century, too. The custom of producing every denomination from the tetradrachm to the minute eighth of an obol in silver gradually gave way to a more convenient bronze coinage for small denominations.

Alexander the Great seems to have allowed Athens to continue producing her traditional coins, though other mints in his empire had to turn out his standard Hercules-Zeus silver pieces. After his death, the issues went on, though the volume was much reduced and they petered out around 200 BC. However, during the next century, Athens produced another major coin series, the 'new style' tetradrachms (101,102). They are much broader, thinner and more elaborate. Athena's portrait is based on Pheidias' statue in the Parthenon, where she wore a triple-crested helmet, which had decorations that included Pegasos and other, normal, horses. The owl on the reverse stands upon an amphora, accompanied by magistrates' initials and symbols, while the whole design is enclosed within a wreath. 109 separate issues have been identified through these mint officials' names, though it is uncertain when the series began. To call them 'magistrates' or 'mint officials' is to make the conventional assumptions. Possibly, the people named were being honoured, in some way, for they might have put up the resources for minting in a particular year. The rich were expected to use their money for public service in Athens and were duly honoured if they paid for a building or a warship: why not for an issue of coins? If this was the case, a few people must have been exceptionally wealthy because, in some years, the volume of coins required large numbers of dies. Forty-seven obverse ones is the most yet discovered for a single year. In contrast, the last quarter of the period saw only a few dies used annually. For some years, only one is known, though there is always the chance that others will be discovered. The outstanding exception among these names is Mithradates, King of Pontos, whose war against Rome made him a welcome ally for the Athenians. The tetradrachms associated with his expedition to Greece can be precisely dated to 87–86 BC.

Round about 50 BC, the Athenian silver coinage came to an end, partly because the mines were exhausted and, more probably, because the ever-increasing influence of Rome made it obsolete. Like many other cities, Athens was permitted to mint a bronze coinage for local circulation, though this was only a diplomatic gesture made by the Romans to soothe the feelings of once proudly-independent poleis. She had the additional privilege of putting on the obverses a portrait of Athena, instead of the reigning emperor, but memories of true greatness must have been very dim by that time, because the quality of life in Athens changed very much for the worse when the Peloponnesian War began and it never truly recovered. With a little imagination, we can sense this as we handle her coins.

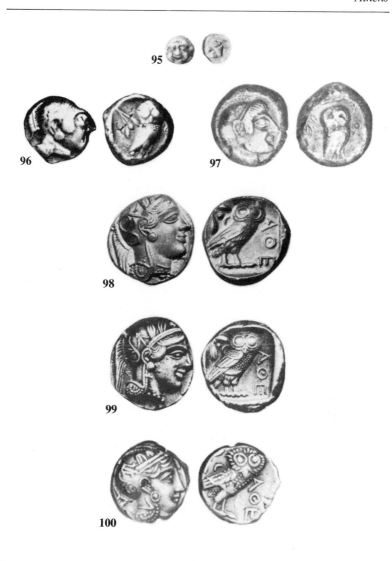

95 'Wappenmunzen'. Obol, *c*. 530 BC. Gorgon's head.

Tetradrachms, Athena and her owl.
96 *c*. 480 BC. Archaic style.   **97** *c*. 470 BC. Similar.   **98** 455–49 BC. Crown of olive leaves.   **99** 449–413 BC. Crown of olive leaves.   **100** 393–300 BC. Eye in profile.

101 'New style' coinage. Elephant mint-mark.   **102** Similar coin.
Tripod-altar mint-mark.

XI. AEGINA

A very popular series of ancient coins are the turtles and tortoises of Aegina (sometimes spelt Aigina). These engaging designs are all basically the same, starting with the smooth-shelled turtle in the sixth century and ending with a life-like tortoise late in the fifth. The reverses – incuse patterns – are also very similar (103–108).

This state was the first in Europe to issue coinage and had its own weight standard. The credit is traditionally given to King Poseidon, though the dates of his reign are uncertain. The mid-sixth century BC is a widely supported estimate of when the earliest Aeginetan coins appeared. Individual specimens are dated according to their style. At first, the turtle had a smooth shell with a row of dots down the middle of its back. Later, it acquired an additional row across the top of the shell, where we might say its 'shoulders' would be found. In the middle of the fifth century BC, the turtle was replaced by a land-tortoise, with the segments of its carapace realistically rendered. The incuse pattern used for the reverse changed from a crude outline to one that was carefully divided into five segments and these, eventually, were made to contain the abbreviated name of the island and a small dolphin which may be a mint-mark or a symbolic assertion of sea-power. Aeginetan coins have been found in many islands of the Aegean and far beyond: their spread indicates the extensive influence of the island that was the first naval power in Greece. Aegina is a small island visible from the Acropolis of Athens and was, at one time, a serious commercial rival.

When commerce and command of the sea are at stake, neighbouring cities or states usually find it difficult to live amicably together. No one really knows when Aegina and Athens began their feud. Herodotos, who may have shown Athenian prejudice in this instance, tells us that it was all the fault of the Aeginetans. There was a ridiculous quarrel over some cult statues made from the wood of Athenian olive trees and, originally, given to another city, which was expected to acknowledge Athenian supremacy while holding its religious rites. Fortuitously, the Aeginetans acquired them and refused to perform the appropriate ceremonies or to return them to Athens. Her people also maintained that, on the first occasion that the two states went to war, there was a gratuitous attack by Aegina. It was supposed to have come about because of an appeal by the Thebans, who were getting the worst of a conflict with Athens.

A martial people, represented on a stater by their characteristic shield and by one of the vessels that held the wine for which they were also renowned (109), the baffled Thebans did the conventional thing and consulted the Delphic oracle. In her answer, she told them to ask assistance from their next of kin. At first, this was difficult to interpret, because the cities with which Thebes had close ties were already her allies. Then, someone thought of mythology. The foundress of the city (Thebe) had been the sister of the nymph Aegina, after whom the island had been named. So, the Thebans sent an embassy and the Aeginetans agreed to help. Their fleet caused Athens considerable embarrassment, but the outcome of this first round in the struggle is unknown. The period is rather remote – *c*. 525 BC or, as the Greek historians called it, the 68th Olympiad. They reckoned time in four-year intervals between the Olympic Games. The first Olympiad, 'When Coroebos won the foot race', was about 776 BC, and the last (283rd) was held in AD 394, after which Christian influence had them suppressed.

The war was still on when a much more dramatic conflict began. Darius, the great King of Persia, began his invasion of Europe. He and his successors put themselves on barbaric gold darics (110–113). On the obverse of one, the emperor appears complete with impressive beard, royal robes and powerful bow (surely not the mere 'archer' sometimes suggested?). The reverse is a simple incuse. No other message was needed. Many thousands of gold and silver pieces like this bought mercenaries for Persia and bribed potential enemies.

Before the arrival of his armies, Darius' heralds went ahead and demanded the traditional symbols of submission from the smaller cities – a helmet full of earth and a jar of water. Several cities agreed and Aegina was one of them. She had probably learnt the danger of opposing Darius from the fate of the settlements which were her trading centres in Asia Minor and neighbouring islands. Athens, of course, refused to submit and, to the Spartans, such action was inconceivable. The two states formed the nucleus of an alliance to oppose the Persians and were soon joined by many others – even Aegina. She changed her mind after the Athenians, with Spartan help, appealed to her to unite with them for 'the good of Hellas'. This is the first recorded instance of strong feelings of solidarity among the fiercely independent Greek cities and helps to explain their success in the campaign which turned back the Persians at Marathon.

Very soon after the Persian threat had been averted, Athens and Aegina were again at war. Hostages were taken on both sides and much diplomatic fencing followed. One result was an abortive revolution in Aegina which was sadly mistimed. The expected Athenian support arrived a day late, because ships had to be borrowed from Corinth. Meanwhile, the Aeginetan ruling class had recovered its poise and executed 700 rebels. One perished in a most sacrilegious manner, with the result that Demeter, the Aeginetan patron deity, was alienated (or so many believed). This fugitive ran to her temple and sought sanctuary by clinging to the door handle. His panic gave him strength so that no one could pull him away. He could not be killed in that position, so the rough and ready solution was to cut off his hands and drag him away for execution. The hands remained on the door-handle for a considerable time.

When the Athenian fleet finally arrived, Aegina appealed for help and mercenaries responded, principally from Argos. The war dragged on till 481 BC and, as usual, ended indecisively. However, the Athenians had learnt a lesson and resolved to build a large fleet of their own. Eventually, it was to destroy Aegina and threaten Corinth.

Hostilities between Athens and Aegina were suspended again when the Persian threat reappeared. Xerxes was crossing into Greece with a far larger army than his predecessor, in fact, the largest force known to have been assembled up to that time. Recognising the seriousness of the situation, the southern Greek states held a conference at the Isthmus of Corinth. There they pledged their solidarity, grudgingly admitting Aegina to their ranks, though remembering her earlier willingness to submit to the Persians.

The Greeks held up the Persian advance at Thermopylae, a battle famous for the gallant last stand by the Spartans, but a defeat for the Greeks, who were forced to retreat. The inhabitants of Athens took an agonising decision and abandoned the city. The refugees were shipped to the islands of Salamis and Aegina (of all places!) from whence they could watch the flames billowing up from their city, which the Persians were treating in the normal way. When the Persian fleet tried to reach the refugees, it was lured into a narrow stretch of water around Salamis and deprived of the power to manoeuvre. The Greek ships were able to set on fire or capture their trapped adversaries and soon the Persian fleet was reduced to a shadow of its former self. Deprived of sea-borne supplies, the Persian army was forced to retreat. It was some time before the Persians were finally driven from Greece and, until that happened, Aegina served as an important naval base.

But the feud went on. In 459 BC, Athens again attacked her enemy and inflicted a crippling blow. Seventy Aeginetan ships were captured, leaving the island defenceless against invaders. The Athenian army besieged the citadel and, after a five-year struggle, Aegina surrendered. Her fortifications were dismantled, her remaining warships handed over and her independence brought to an end. Many of the surviving Aeginetans chose to leave or were expelled and they took refuge in Thyrea, the inhospitable frontier strip between Laconia and Argolis.

Athens was now mistress of the Peloponnesian coast and the Aegean Sea. She quickly became by far the largest of the Greek states and threatened to dominate the others. Eventually, Athenian pretensions provoked the neighbouring states to form an alliance under Spartan leadership and the Peloponnesian War began (431 BC). In its eighth year, an Athenian force sailed to Thyrea and slaughtered the Aeginetans there. The massacre was relatively easy, because there had not been sufficient time or resources for them to build effective defences. Nevertheless, a few survivors were collected by the Spartan king, Lysander, and they were enabled to return to their island after the Spartan victory in the war.

The Spartans acknowledged their obligations to all their allies and, in the case of Aegina, the Athenian settlers were driven out and their holdings were returned to the islanders (or their descendants). However, it proved impossible to resurrect a viable state without sufficient inhabitants or resources. The best that the Aeginetans could manage was to become privateers who plundered Athenian shipping – a situation that could not last for long. Soon after the Spartan army withdrew, the Athenians were able to suppress the privateers and that is the last we hear of Aegina as an independent state.

Her last 'tortoises' appeared in about 404 BC, at the end of the Peloponnesian War and, after that, Athenian coinage was used there.

One final point – searching for contemporary Spartan coins will be fruitless. At the time when the other Greek states were issuing beautiful gold and silver pieces, the ultra-conservative Spartans stuck to iron bars!

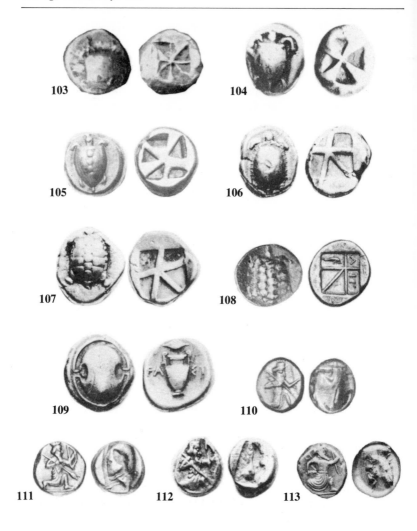

103 Stater, sixth century BC. Smooth-shelled turtle. **104** Similar. Deeper, cleaner-cut incuse pattern. **105** Similar. Row of dots on turtle. **106** After 450 BC. Tortoise. **107** Similar. Segments clear. **108** 404–340 BC. Letters and dolphin in incuse. **109** Thebes. Stater, 395–387 BC. Shield and amphora.

Persian Empire: Fifth–fourth century BC. The king-archer.
110 Gold daric. **111** Similar. **112** Silver siglos. **113** Similar.

XII. CORINTH

One of the most prolific mints in the Greek world was situated in Corinth. This city stands at the head of the gulf after which it is named and at the foot of a steep hill, 2,000 feet high. The slopes were utilised as strategic defensive positions and the narrow isthmus at the head of the gulf was made navigable for the small ships of the time by means of rollers, over which they were pulled. This way, ships reached the Aegean from the Adriatic without having to make the voyage round the Peloponnesus, that famous peninsula where so much Greek history took place. On the hill, the Acrocorinthus, were two fountains. Legend had it that one (the Hippocrene, or horse fountain) was created when Pegasos struck the rock with his hoof and the other (the Peirene) was where he drank. The origin of the story possibly came from the fact that the Hippocrene was shaped like a hoof-print, but every Corinthian was convinced that, on this hill, the winged horse was captured by Bellerophon. After many unsuccessful attempts, he succeeded with the help of Athena, who kept Pegasos sleeping beside her altar while Bellerophon placed on his head a golden bridle, specially provided by the goddess. Hence, we find Athena and Pegasos on Corinthian coins though, in later centuries, it was Aphrodite who was the principal goddess in the city. She has her place on the smaller silver pieces but, in comparison, it is insignificant (114,115). Another reason why Athena has such prominence is that she could be associated with the sea.

The sea linked Corinth with the wider world to the west of Greece and she dominated trade in that direction. It made her prosperous, as the imports were funnelled up the Corinthian Gulf and distributed among the other Greek cities. An abundant supply of silver was essential for all this commercial activity and this is the reason why there are so many surviving coins. The Corinthian 'colts', named after Pegasos by the Greeks and called staters by us, were divided into three

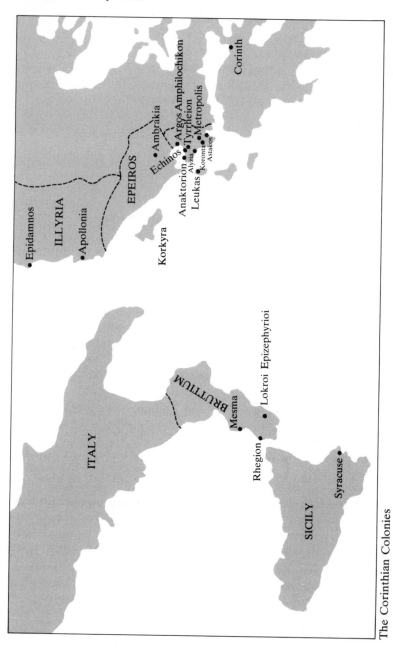

The Corinthian Colonies

drachms – a system that seems to have originated in Asia Minor. Athens used a different weight standard, with the result that one of her 'owls' was worth two 'colts'.

The Corinthian weight standard came into use in many westerly cities, especially those of southern Italy. Here, and in several other areas, the Corinthians founded colonies, ie citizens emigrated and built new towns, which maintained close links with their mother-city. Their coins were very similar to those used in Corinth. In fact, many of them were struck at the Corinthian mint. Apart from carrying a political message of solidarity with the other settlements, the colts were of great advantage to the colonies, because they were such a readily-acceptable medium of exchange. Subtle differences, well understood by the Greeks, but not so obvious to the modern collector, distinguished the coins of each city and this chapter is intended to serve as a guide to identification. If any reader decides to specialise in the series, he will have enough to occupy him for the rest of his life!

First, a few words about the coinage of Corinth. It began about 550 BC when, like other cities at that time, Corinth produced coins with a design on only one side and a punch-mark on the other (116). The design was Pegasos and the punch-mark was, oddly enough, similar to a twentieth-century European symbol – either a 'union Jack' or a swastika. By the end of the sixth century, the technique of putting a design on each side of the coin had led to the appearance of Athena on the reverses. Dies cut in the archaic style show her in an incuse depression and provide Pegasos with a curled wing (117,118). As time went by and styles developed, the incuse disappeared and the horse and goddess became more life-like (119–121).

Great care was devoted to the details of the designs and the thousands of devices that served as mint-marks. Very probably, the moneyers were changed each year and, therefore, the newly appointed officials had to use symbols to indicate that they were responsible for the products of the mint. Animals, birds, musical instruments, parts of ships, flowers, pieces of armour, fabulous beasts and even gods and goddesses were used. Unfortunately, we cannot link these beautifully-produced 'signatures' with historical figures, because we have no detailed history of the internal politics of Corinth. The most important symbol, as far as ordinary collectors are concerned, is the letter Qoppa placed beneath Pegasos. In its early form, it resembles a lollipop and, later, it was tilted so that it is recognisable as a 'Q', the initial of Corinth, though this particular letter disappeared eventually from the Greek alphabet.

The colonies were given other letters. One group of cities was in the area called Akarnania, which is between the head of the Gulf of Corinth and the small inlet to the north, known as the Gulf of Akarnania. Some of them were very small – villages by our standards – and others, important trading centres. In spite of the fact that their sites have been identified, not much is known about their history, though a few historical notes are included in this list of colonies that have left us their colts. We start at the entrance to the Corinthian Gulf and move northwards.

Astakos. Mentioned by Thucydides as being captured by the Athenians at the beginning of the Peloponnesian War and recaptured a few months later by a powerful expedition from Corinth. AΣ beneath Athena.

Koronta. An inland village. K behind Athena.

Metropolis. A neighbouring settlement that certainly did not grow large enough to justify its name in the modern sense. MH monogram beneath Pegasos. AΣ monogram behind Athena. Sometimes countermarked with a star or AM monogram.

Alyzia. Noted only for the temple of Hercules there. A beneath Pegasos. The other side of the coins has AΛ) IAIΩN in front of Athena's face.

Tyrrheion. A fairly large town in the third and second centuries BC. The Greek letter equivalent to our 'Th' on both sides of the coins (122).

Anaktorion. At the entrance to the Ambrakian Gulf, it issued coins in considerable quantities. It was founded with the help of the people of Korkyra (see below) and, like its neighbours, faced the hostility of the local people for many years. In the seventh year of the Peloponnesian War (425), it was captured by the Athenians. Illustrated is an early drachm as an example of a coin bearing the head of Aphrodite whose worship was so important in Corinth and, also, a stater, to show the identifying monogram AN below Pegasos with the full name ANAKTOPIΩN in front of Athena (123).

Echinos. A village on the southern shore of the gulf. Its coins are identified by an E behind Athena.

Argos Amphilochikon. The town called Argos, founded by Amphilochos, the Argive or native of the original Argos, capital of Argolis, the eastern corner of the Peloponnesus. A below Pegasos. APΓEA above Athena's head (124).

Leukas. The chief town on the island of the same name, which is south of the gulf. Its inhabitants were said to have cut through the narrow peninsula joining their territory to the mainland so that they could improve their security by creating an island. The town issued coins over a long period: the standard types have an Λ on both sides and the name ΛΕΥΚΑΔΙΩΝ or an abbreviation of it (125).

Akarnanian Confederacy. The Leukas mint produced some coins intended for either the smaller Corinthian colonies in the area or for all the native inhabitants. These have the name AKAPNANΩN.

Korkyra. North of Akarnania was the region called Epeiros, which was dominated by another island state, Korkyra. Founded by the Corinthians, it was never on very good terms with the mother city. According to Thucydides, triremes (galleys with three sets of oars) were invented in Corinth and used against Korkyra in the first sea battle ever recorded, in 664 BC. Though it cooperated with Corinth from time to time, Korkyra had a distinctive coinage for most of its existence. The main design was a cow and calf with an apparently abstract pattern on the reverse. Doubtless, it was symbolic, though the meaning has now been lost. In the second half of the fourth century, Corinthian-type staters were in use in Korkyra. They have KOP, sometimes as a countermark, on them.

This city helped the Corinthians in the foundation of several colonies. The two where the Korkyrans were dominant were Apollonia and Epidamnos in Illyria – the coast opposite the heel of Italy.

Apollonia. Situated on the fertile coastal plain, it flourished. Little is recorded about it, except that its oligarchic government became more democratic, yet it ferociously excluded any foreign traders. At first, it used cow and calf coins based on the Korkyran model though, like its mother-city, it changed to Corinthian staters. These have AΠOΛ on them.

Epidamnos. Known to the Romans as Dyrrhachium, it had a history somewhat similar to Apollonia's. In the period immediately before the Peloponnesian War, there was a revolutionary situation in the city. The people drove out the ruling families, who did their utmost to get back into power. Meanwhile, the neighbouring tribes, the Illyrians, were taking advantage of the city's weakness and making life difficult for the inhabitants. Korkyra would not come to their aid because the families who had been driven out originally came from there and still retained their ancestral tombs. So, the desperate Epidamnites appealed to Corinth and help was sent, mainly to spite Korkyra. The result was a full-scale naval war between the old rivals, into which was drawn Athens as an ally of Korkyra. Corinthian staters replaced the cow and calf coinage about 350 BC and these carry the name ΔYPPAXINΩN – the Dyrrhachii – used to refer to the local people (126).

Ambrakia. On the northern side of the Ambrakian Gulf, in Epeirus, this was one of the most important Corinthian settlements. Founded about 600 BC, it eventually became the capital of the area in the reign of King Pyrrhus (295–272). The Corinthian-type staters were in use here by 480 BC and continued until it became the capital of the Epeirote Republic in 238. There are over a hundred varieties of staters. Nearly all have the initial A and some have the name in full, AMBPAKIΩTAN (127).

Lokroi Epizephyrioi. This was an even older colony, in Bruttium, the 'foot' of Italy, its name indicating that it was situated at Cape Zephyrium. Tradition maintained that this colony was founded in 683 BC by people from Lokris. Though there were two towns of this name, the mother-city has been forgotten. Aristotle says that the founders were runaway slaves, so it is not surprising that they did not keep up the links with their homeland. Their behaviour was supposed to have justified the imposition of a very strict law code, which was more severe than usual in Greek cities. Possibly, these laws prohibited the issue of coins during the period when Lokris was an independent state. Whether it had a treaty with Corinth, or not, is an open question for there is no record of the Corinthians establishing influence there. Whatever the case, Lokris issued Corinthian-type staters in the fourth century, possibly simply to facilitate trade. They are distinguishable by the name ΛOKPΩN (128). Rhegion, on the Sicilian Straits, was another town that used similar coins for reasons not fully understood. Its monogram was PH. Mesma, a Lokrian colony on the northern coast of the Italian 'foot', did the same and used ME.

These cities may well have been under the influence of Syracuse rather than Corinth. This city, one of the most important of the Greek world, had been founded by a Corinthian expedition to Sicily. Its prosperity was undermined by civil war and the threat from the Carthaginians, who were extending their empire beyond north Africa. In 344, the situation had grown so desperate that the Syracusans sent an embassy to ask for help from their mother-city. Though success seemed doubtful, an expedition was got together under the leadership of a somewhat obscure young man called Timoleon and good fortune smiled on it. The emigrants were able to re-establish Syracuse's position and prestige and, as part of the process, provided it with a new coinage – Corinthian-type staters, of course. ΣΥΡΑΚΟΣΙΩΝ appears in front of Athena (129). Such coins were an appropriate acknowledgement of the help received and, as has been mentioned earlier, were probably an asset in an area where Corinthian coins were the commonest in circulation. Similar advantages would have been derived by the Italian cities, Lokris, Mesma and Rhegion already listed, and by the other Sicilian cities associated closely with Syracuse.

Leontini. The Lion City, which used a lion's head on its early, attractive coins, became dependent on Syracuse about 422. A quarrel between the landed aristocracy and the landless common people led to a situation in which the Syracusans were able to take control of Leontini, demolish its fortifications and annexe its territory. It soon recovered and became an important centre in the prolonged struggles between the Sicilian cities and the Carthaginians. When Timoleon's expedition landed, Leontini was allied to the Carthaginians though, after they were defeated, its people surrendered their leaders to Timoleon and changed sides. The numismatic evidence is in the form of Corinthian staters with the name ΛΕΟΝΤΙΝΩΝ on them.

That concludes the brief survey of Corinthian colonies and it is appropriate to end with a few words about the later history of Corinth. All of Greece lost its independence when Philip II of Macedon was elected king. This ceremony was staged at Corinth in 337 and soon had to be repeated for Alexander, after his father was assassinated. The choice of Corinth for the necessary congresses indicates its high status and comparative neutrality. When Alexander was there, he encountered the philosopher, Diogenes, famous for his contemptuous attitude to material possessions. He did not actually live in a tub, though he was in the habit of sleeping in the streets on porches of houses and, sometimes, in a huge jar intended for offerings at a temple. When Alexander offered him any favour he cared to name, Diogenes asked him to step aside because he was keeping the sunshine off him. The new king was impressed and went away muttering: 'If I were not Alexander, I would like to be Diogenes' – which of the two men had a greater opinion of himself, I wonder.

Alexander did not stop Corinth issuing its staters, even though many mints in his empire were obliged to produce the well-known Hercules-Zeus silver pieces, which he used to finance his campaigns. The Corinthian staters continued to appear until the early third century. Corinth, like many cities, could not survive as an independent state with its own coinage, in the years when the post-Alexandrian kingdoms struggled for supremacy. For a time, it benefited from membership of an alliance of cities called the Achaean League, though they were unable to resist the expanding power of Rome. In 146, Corinth was destroyed and abandoned. A century later, with deliberate timing, Julius Caesar refounded it and made it a settlement for veteran soldiers. There were to be no more staters, though a series of bronzes are mementoes of the recovery made by the city under Roman rule.

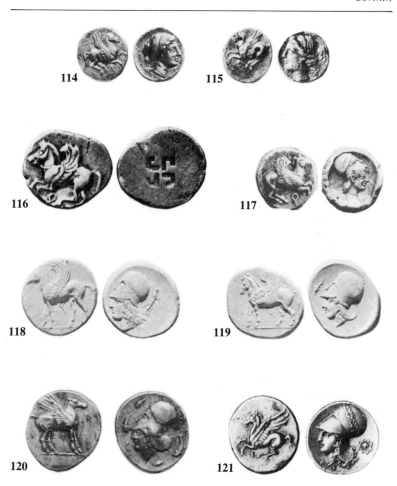

114 Drachm, 350–306 BC. Aphrodite and Pegasos. **115** Similar coin, 306–300 BC. **116** Stater, 525–500 BC. Pegasos and incuse swastika. **117** Stater, 500–482 BC. Pegasos with curled wing; Athena's head in incuse depression. **118** A similar coin. Stater, 400–350 BC. Pegasos with curled wing, walking. Athena no longer in a depression; mint-mark, statue of Zeus. **119** A similar coin. Dolphin mint-mark. **120** Pegasos standing with straight wing; dolphins around Athena's head. **121** Stater, 350–306 BC. Pegasos flying; olive-wreath around Athena's helmet.

Corinthian colonies: Fourth century BC staters.
122 Tyrrheion. Letter θ both sides.   **123** Anaktorion. AN below Pegasos;
mint-mark, altar within wreath.   **124** Argos Amphilochikon. AP below
Pegasos.   **125** Leukas. Λ below Pegasos; mintmark, caduceus.
126 Dyrrhachium. ΔYP around Athena.   **127** Ambrakia. A below Pegasos;
mint-mark, spear.   **128** Lokroi Epizephyrioi. Name in front of Athena;
thunderbolt below Pegasos.   **129** Syracuse. Name in front of
Athena.   **130** Epidamnos-Dyrrhachium. Stater, 400–350 BC. Cow and calf,
floral pattern.

XIII. RHODES

Rhodes is the most eastern of the Aegean Islands and is comparatively large, measuring at its extremities approximately 72 km (45 miles) by 40 kms (25 miles). For a long period, it was one of the most prosperous Greek settlements and produced a plentiful coinage, which gives modern collectors an opportunity to specialise in a series that offers variation on a constant theme.

The first coins minted there date from the sixth century BC, a time when the island was divided between three city states – Lindos, Ialysos and Kamiros. According to tradition, they had all been founded at the same time by the members of an expedition from Argos, led by a commander called Althaemenes. In the search for somewhere to establish themselves, his followers went first to Crete where some of them stayed. The rest moved on to Rhodes. They were able to seize the island from the handful of people already living there and then proceeded to divide the territory amicably between themselves. It is a simple story from fairly remote times, but it does provide a good example of how Greek civilisation spread. The traditions of common origins preserved by the people of Rhodes explain, at least in part, why they got on so well together and with their island neighbours, too. It was their policy to maintain friendly relations with everyone, even to the extent of not providing their cities with walls. Their naval supremacy was sufficient to keep them safe from enemies.

Each of the three cities provided itself with coins bearing its badge. Lindos used a lion's head (131), Ialysos chose the forepart of a winged boar and Kamiros preferred a fig-leaf (132). Like most coins of the archaic period, these silver pieces are chunky, simply-designed and obviously made for use rather than propaganda. Although they were minted in the same island, they used different weight standards, presumably because their primary purpose was to facilitate overseas trade. Each of the three cities traded independently. Kamiros, which was on the west coast, used the Aeginetic standard, ie its coins were of the same weight as those of Crete, the Peloponnesian peninsula and, especially, the island of Aegina which was at the time the principal commercial rival of Athens. Ialysos and Lindos were on the north and west coasts, respectively, and they used the Phoenician standard, a fact that indicates trade with the mainland.

Life in Rhodes seems to have gone on fairly peacefully during the first half of the fifth century BC. We know little about it, except that, as Athens developed into a great commercial power, Rhodes was drawn more and more into an alliance with her. The Rhodians imitated some of the Athenian constitutional devices, such as the jury system. We still admire the concern to see justice done that led to the formation of large groups of jurors called dykasteries, which were too big to be bribed. Friendship and trade with Athens naturally led Rhodes to support her when the war against Sparta broke out in 431 BC. Comparatively little happened to the island until one day in 412 BC, when the Spartan fleet of ninety-four large galleys appeared. The islanders had little choice but to allow them to establish a base there and had to pay a levy of 32 talents to cover their expenses. If the thousands of silver coins collected on this occasion were carried away and eventually melted down, we have an explanation of why early Rhodian coins are very scarce.

The dissatisfied Rhodians had to remain nominal allies of Sparta until the opportunity arose to break away. Meanwhile, the three cities decided to pool resources and build a new well-fortified capital for the island. It was designed, as far as possible, to resemble Athens and, when they provided it with coins, they were minted according to the Athenian weight standard. New designs were required, so Helios, the Sun-god, to whom the whole island was sacred, was placed on the obverses. The reverse design was a rose, a pun on the name of the island. (Rhodos is the Greek for rose.) The engravers produced deeply-cut dies with a vigorous rendering of Helios, seen full-face with luxuriant hair, blown back by the wind as his chariot carried him across the sky (133–135).

An Athenian naval victory in 394 BC enabled Rhodes and several other cities to break away from Sparta. The coins they produced for the occasion are known as the issues of the Maritime League, an alliance about which we have very scanty records. The numismatic evidence is almost all that remains to indicate the League's importance. Each city put its badge on the reverse of coins that had a common obverse design – the infant Hercules strangling two snakes (439, 440). All these coins are scarce. Those from Rhodes can be recognised by the rose.

For two generations or so, Rhodes was able to re-establish its commercial supremacy and its coins became quite plentiful. There is a long series that the experts attempt to place in chronological order, according to style and mint-marks. In the last third of the century, the magistrates responsible for the mint put their full names on the coins. It is unfortunate that we have no detailed record of Rhodian political history.

The island submitted to Alexander the Great without a struggle and the coinage seems to have gone on without a break. Alexander died in 323 BC, leaving a huge empire over which his generals quarrelled. The details of this epic struggle do not concern us here, except as far as Rhodes was involved. Predictably, the Rhodians took the first opportunity of driving out the Macedonian garrison left by Alexander and then reasserted their independence. After a few years, they were dragged into the wars by Demetrios, the extraordinary general whose career, while struggling to carve out an empire in Asia Minor, is one of the epics of Greek history. He attempted to conquer Rhodes which, fortunately, had support from Ptolemy, king of Egypt, Lysimachos, king of Thrace and Kassander of Macedon. The city of Rhodes was subjected to a siege in which everyone concerned behaved with great credit. Demetrios built huge mobile siege towers, the like of which had not previously been seen. Ever after he was called Poliorketes, the Besieger of Cities, though the Rhodians did not give in easily. Eventually, they agreed to join Demetrios, but only on condition that they were not expected to fight against their old ally Ptolemy. Demetrios chivalrously acknowledged the citizens' fortitude which had given them a moral victory. He presented his siege towers to them and left.

The money raised from the sale of these towers, which were made of valuable timber and other materials suitable for shipbuilding, was put into a memorial. As much bronze as possible was collected and a leading sculptor, Chares of Lindos, was commissioned to produce a statue. The result was the Colossus of Rhodes, one of the wonders of the ancient world. It was a huge statue of Helios, exactly how big we do not know. One historian tells us it was 85 m (280 ft) tall, but we should allow for the customary exaggeration found in ancient accounts. The technological problems of creating anything bigger than 30 m (100 ft) were immense and the reconstructions showing it bestriding the entrance to the harbour, while ships sail between its legs, are fanciful. Nevertheless, it must have been spectacular.

Consistent with the Greek custom of understatement that more than a century before had led the Athenians to provide Athena with laurel leaves on coins issued after their victory at Marathon, the Rhodians designed a new issue that showed Helios wearing a crown of rays (136,137). This design is probably based on the Colossus. At any rate, everyone who saw it would recognise a victor's crown. Everyone, that is, who knew about the siege. Centuries later, medieval monasteries sometimes treasured these coins because it was then believed that the head was, in fact, Jesus wearing the crown of thorns and that these were the coins referred to in the Bible, which tells us how Judas betrayed his master for thirty pieces of silver.

Peaceful trading and good relations with everyone continued in the third century. The coins went on with interesting minor variations of mint-marks. An exception is the imitations of Rhodian coins struck by the Macedonian king Philip V about 200 BC. He needed to pay his mercenaries and was, at the time, occupying territory in which such coins were the normal currency. Catalogued as issues of 'Rhodian Peraia', which only means 'territory near Rhodes', their style is distinctive. Helios has tighter curls and the rose bud flares more sharply. The name HEPMIAΣ appears above it (138). Neither Philip nor the other warring kings made much impact on Rhodes and we hear little of it from contemporary historians. They do, however, tell us about the great Helios Festival held every year. There were chariot races, gymnastic events and music contests. The climax came when four consecrated horses were sacrificed by hurling them into the sea. The thinking behind this act of apparent cruelty was that Helios rose and set, seeming to come out of the sea and returning to it. He needed to change the horses that pulled his chariot and, therefore, the people of his sacred island provided him with a new set.

Rhodes became enmeshed in the growing power of Rome when she joined an alliance against the Macedonians. Her fleet proved useful in this enterprise and, also, against Antiochos of Syria. The Romans rewarded her by granting her territory in Karia on the mainland of Asia Minor. Characteristically, the Rhodians employed mercenaries to defend it and concentrated on their usual commercial activities. In 168 BC, the Romans went to war against King Perseus of Macedon and, this time, the Rhodians objected because their trade was suffering. The furious Romans seized the mainland possessions and imposed a ban on two vital Rhodian trade commodities. Salt could no longer be taken to Macedon in return for shipbuilding timber. Furthermore, the Romans did their best to encourage the development of Delos as a rival commercial centre to Rhodes.

These events had an impact on the coinage. It was no longer appropriate for Rhodes to produce large silver pieces. Instead, a new issue of drachms was minted. They show Helios in profile and the rose appears in an incuse square (139). By reverting to the obsolete incuse design, the Rhodians were probably telling everyone that their coins and their credit were as good as they had been centuries ago.

However, things were not going well for Rhodes. Apart from a boost in 84 BC, when Sulla restored some of her mainland possessions as a reward for help against Mithriadates, her fortunes gradually declined. She wavered between Pompey and Caesar in the Civil War and, consequently, was rewarded by neither. Caesar had first visited Rhodes as a young man when, like many of his kind, he had spent some time there learning philosophy and rhetoric, as a preparation for a political career in a Rome where clever speeches counted for a great deal. After his death, Cassius destroyed most of the Rhodian fleet, putting the last touch to a period of decline which had lasted for a hundred years.

In the long run, it would have been impossible to maintain independence in the face of Roman expansion, though the Romans must not be blamed for all Rhodes' misfortunes. The island suffered from earthquakes. One brought down the Colossus in 222 BC and, since there was no one with the skill to repair it, the remains were sold for scrap.

Some time in the first century BC, Rhodes ceased to mint silver coins (140). The last currency produced there consisted of large bronzes, some of which carry the word 'didrachm' though they were really token money (141). One design features, rather ironically, Nike, goddess of Victory (142). The latter may be derived from a statue erected to commemorate victories against Antiochos. It fell into the sea, probably in an earthquake, and has been re-erected in Paris where it is one of the most cherished possessions of the Louvre. Rhodian independence was officially ended by Claudius and the island sank into obscurity, suffering even worse earthquakes in AD 155, when the city was destroyed. During the Middle Ages, it was provided once again with a mint by the Knights of St John, who made it their base.

131 Lindos. Stater, *c*. 520 BC. Lion's head.   **132** Kamiros. Stater, *c*. 500 BC. Fig leaf.

The Helios–head and rose coinage.
133 Tetradrachm, *c*. 360 BC. High relief.   **134** Didrachm, 387–304 BC. Wind-blown hair.   **135** Didrachm. Hair loose.   **136** Tetradrachm, 304–167 BC. Radiate head.

137 Didrachm. Similar.   138 Rhodian Peraia. Drachm, second
century BC.   139 Drachm, 167–88 BC. Head in profile; rose in incuse
depression.   140 Trihemidrachm, 88–43 BC. Full-blown rose. The last silver
coins?   141 Bronze coinage, first century BC–first century AD. Helios and
Victory.   142 Helios has become Dionysos, shown on both obverse and
reverse.

THE COINAGE OF ALEXANDER
AND HIS SUCCESSORS

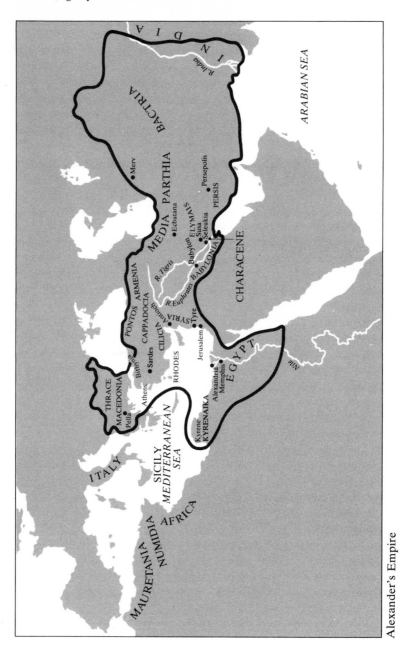

Alexander's Empire

XIV. ALEXANDER THE GREAT

Alexander, known as 'the Great', made an impact on contemporaries, and on subsequent generations, that is truly astonishing. Even modern historians trying to understand him, and to strip away the accumulated traditions to reveal the true Alexander beneath, are deeply impressed, despite their academic detachment.

Macedon, his inherited kingdom, was a mountainous area of northern Greece, inhabited by a tough race of shepherds and peasants, often at war among themselves and, to the sophisticated Athenians, scarcely civilised. They were tolerated as members of the Greek community because they spoke a dialect that was just comprehensible and participated in the Olympic Games. The kingdom was founded about 480 BC by Alexander I (143–147) and made little impact on international relations for more than a century, until Philip II came to power in 359. This ambitious king developed the gold and silver mines as rapidly as he could, with the result that production reached an unheard-of scale. He deliberately minted so many gold pieces that they were sufficient to become the standard denomination for what was then considered to be the world. His staters have a head of Apollo on the obverse, backed by a chariot (148), an allusion to the victory won by Philip's team at the Olympics. There were so many of them that the ratio of gold to silver in Greece fell from twelve to one to ten to one.

Well aware how conservative people are about money, Philip maintained the tradition of equating a stater with twelve silver drachms by the expedient of altering the weights of Macedonian coins. His gold staters weighed approximately 135 g and his 4 drachma pieces, 56.25 g. This was the normal standard in use in Athens, the coinage of which had dominated the Greek world and was about to be eclipsed. Philip's silver pieces bore a forceful head of Zeus backed by a horseman (149–151).

In one version, we can see that the rider is a boy, presumably the jockey who rode Philip's horse to win at the Olympics. The other reverse design shows a mounted warrior who could be Philip himself.

Although numerous, the silver pieces did not have as much impact as the gold which was carried many miles away, even reaching Britain, where it was copied and turned into the stylised Celtic designs on early staters (316–322). For twenty years or so after Philip's assassination in 336, the mints continued to turn out his staters, so that they formed a semi-permanent element in the circulated coinage.

By the time of his death, Philip had defeated or won over the major Greek cities and made himself the most powerful and the wealthiest ruler of his time, bar one, Darius, Emperor of Persia.

Darius ruled Asia Minor, the Holy Land, Mesopotamia, Persia and the sparsely-populated lands stretching towards India. This vast empire was by far the largest political unit yet known and it posed a continual threat to Greece. Nevertheless, Philip had plans to free the Greek cities in Asia Minor from Persian rule and had organised the Hellenic League to unite his allies in the project when he was assassinated. Alexander was then twenty, a fair-headed, handsome young man, an accomplished athlete, and very ambitious. Educated by the best available tutors, among whom was Aristotle, the young prince absorbed the learning and philosophy of the day and modelled himself on Homer's heroes. The Iliad became his constant reading and, on campaign, he kept it under his pillow at night along with his dagger.

Alexander may have seen himself as rather more than human. Coming from a family that claimed descent from Hercules and Perseus, he undertook the conquest of the world and, whatever else about him may be legendary, he certainly possessed extraordinary powers of leadership. His foresight and talent for public relations can be seen in his first coins which were issued after he had dealt severely with his father's allies who contemplated desertion. The Hellenic League was reformed and, as its general, Alexander authorised the production of an appropriate coinage to pay the expenses of the coming Persian campaign. His gold staters bore the head of Athena (152), a compliment to Athens, his unenthusiastic ally, and the reverses show Nike, the goddess of Victory, holding the conqueror's olive wreath and a naval standard – symbols of triumphs yet to come. The silver coinage of tetradrachms, drachms and smaller pieces featured Hercules, the greatest of the mythical heroes, wearing the skin of the Nemean lion, which he strangled with his bare hands. His features are remarkable in that, although Hercules was usually depicted as a bearded mature man, on Alexander's coins he is young and beardless and is, in fact, Alexander himself. This is the first time that any ruler had put his portrait on coins but, in view of his ambitions and the traditional origins of the Macedonian royal house, Alexander probably saw nothing inappropriate in this action. The reverses of these coins show Zeus Olympios, greatest of the gods who dwelt in the palace on the sacred mountain, seated on his throne, holding an eagle in his outstretched right hand and a sceptre in his left (153).

This personification of power and authority appealed not only to Greeks, but to Alexander's future oriental subjects, who could recognise in the image their own great gods and could identify themselves with the concept of a universal empire that was involved. Their loyalty, or at least their awe, was further stimulated when they saw the name of Alexander behind Nike and Zeus, and it is these coins that give the first indication that Alexander may have considered himself superhuman. His greatest failing was pride in his achievements and, at the end of his life, he expected his subjects to pay him divine honours though, in fairness to him, it should be said that the Persian emperors whom he displaced had also been accustomed to behave as if they were gods.

The campaign against Darius went well. After crossing into Asia Minor and, characteristically, finding time to visit the site of Troy, Alexander marched from victory to victory, usually in spite of superior odds. Darius was driven further and further into Asia as his armies met defeat and his cities surrendered to Alexander. Eventually, he was murdered by his last companions as he fled to take refuge in the mountains of the Caucasus. Egypt, also, surrendered to Alexander after only token resistance. While inspecting the new conquest, Alexander insisted on marching his men far out into the desert to the oasis, now called Siwa, where the temple of Zeus Ammon was situated. He went to consult the oracle there, as Hercules and Perseus were reputed to have done and, when he emerged from the sacred shrine, he had obviously undergone a most moving experience. No one knows what happened or what he was told but, after this incident, he may well have believed himself to be the incarnation of the god.

Elsewhere in the Persian Empire, he found great wealth as well as prestige. Susa, the Persian capital, contained thousands of talents of precious metal, including 40,000 talents in coined money (ie the Persian 'archers', small gold and silver coins showing the emperor with his bow on the obverse and an incuse depression on the reverse). A quantity was immediately dispatched to the mints and such wealth, representing many millions of pounds at present-day values, proved ample for the expenses of the new empire and pay for Alexander's armies. Although extremely generous in distributing rewards, he was never content with his conquests and continued to march eastwards after overcoming Persia. When his troops reached the Indus, eight years after they had left Macedon, they refused to go further. They had marched beyond the limits of the known world and were anxious to return home with their loot. Perhaps, Alexander really did burst into tears because there were no more worlds to conquer for, at this point, he was obliged to transform himself from the conquering hero into the administrator of enormous territories.

We are principally interested in his coinage policies. Twenty mints were established and they poured out silver coins. The most prolific was Amphipolis in Macedon, which produced tetradrachms in such quantity that 700 obverse dies and 1,300 reverses have been identified. Coins of Amphipolis must be identified by style and the new collector will more easily recognise the tetradrachms from mints that used distinguishing initials – Damascus (ΔA) (156), Sidon (Σ) and Babylon (M = Metropolis, the mother-city of the East). If one wishes to specialise, there is no limit to the scope offered by Alexander's coinage, for there is such fascinating variety of detail in designs that are basically uniform. One can collect specimens from each mint – some are by no means rare. Then, there are the symbols used by the magistrates responsible for the mints – small animals, birds, implements, monograms and so on (154,155,157–159). Alternatively, there is the comparatively neglected copper coinage featuring Hercules and, on the reverse, his club and bow-case or, sometimes, an eagle instead (160). Many Alexandrine coin hoards have been discovered, most, presumably, being the accumulated wealth of his soldiers, who hid them for safety and were unable to return to collect them. Alexander himself never returned to Macedon, dying of fever in Babylon where he was scarcely thirty-five.

He left no competent heir. His half-brother was an epileptic and his only son was born posthumously. Given the name Philip III, the latter became the nominal ruler of the Empire. Coins were struck with his name in place of his father's but he was, of course, too young to rule and Alexander's generals were his protectors. For a time, they maintained a plan to keep the Empire in trust for him, but they soon quarrelled and established kingdoms of their own.

143 Stater, 510–480 BC. Akanthos, an independent Macedonian city. Lion attacking a bull. **144** Tetrobol, King Alexander I, 495–454 BC. Horse and helmet. **145** Tetrobol, Perdikkas, 454–413 BC. Horseman and lion. **146** Tetradrachm, Archeleaus, 413–399 BC. Horseman and goat. **147** Another of his tetradrachms. Young male head and horse in square.

Coinage of Philip II, 359–336 BC.
148 Gold stater. Apollo and chariot. **149** Tetradrachm. Zeus and mounted warrior. **150** Tetradrachm. Boy jockey instead of warrior. **151** Similar. Boy holds a palm branch.

Coinage of Alexander the Great, 336–323 BC.
152 Gold stater. Athena and Nike. **153** Tetradrachm. Alexander as Hercules; seated Zeus; Amphipolis mint. **154** Pella mint.

155 Alexandra mint.　**156** Damascus mint.　**157** Posthumous issue. Broad flan.　**158** Drachm. Similar types.　**159** Drachm. Eagle reverse. **160** Bronze coin. Club and bow-case on the reverse.

XV. MACEDON

When Alexander set out to conquer the world, he left Macedon in the hands of an elderly general called Antipater. Though loyal to his young master, his position was almost that of a king and, a few years after his death in 319 BC, his son, Kassander assumed the title. 'Kassander' is another form of 'Alexander', which we use to distinguish him from his much more famous predecessor. He had no need to alter the coins because they already carried his name. To make the throne secure for his own dynasty, he murdered the young son of Alexander the Great and was succeeded by his own son, Philip.

There was another son, however, who was dissatisfied with his inheritance and turned for help to the most dashing commander of the age. This was Demetrios Poliorketes, the Besieger of Cities, whom we have briefly encountered at Rhodes. Son of Antigonos, the One-Eyed, he had begun his military career at twenty, when he was acting as his father's military commander in Syria and Phoenicia. The next ten years or so had been spent winning various territories from Kassander. A spectacular victory over the Egyptian fleet in 306 gave him control of Cyprus, which proved to be a vital naval base. The siege of Rhodes, which sided with the Egyptians, ended indecisively and Demetrios' fortunes sank to their lowest when he was forced to flee from the battlefield of Ipsus in 301, leaving his father dead and Seleukos and Ptolemy victorious. He still had Cyprus and a few Greek cities. After a time, he was able to attack Athens and was conducting the siege when Kassander of Macedon died. Demetrios was far too busy to march northwards then, but, eventually, Athens capitulated and Demetrios was in a position to respond to the invitation to come to Macedon. Demetrios seized his chance, came to Macedon and persuaded the nobility to accept him as king. He had a slim claim to the throne, since he had married Kassander's sister though, by then, they were divorced.

More convincing was his record, which must have made him seem like a new Alexander the Great. Once established on the Macedonian throne, he used his kingdom as a base from which to recover his father's dominions in Syria and, therefore, his best-known coins commemorate his successes. They show Poseidon, god of the sea, who gave victory to Demetrios in the battle with the Egyptian fleet (161,162). For the obverses, Demetrios used his own portrait or a design based on the statue set up to commemorate the event. Victory stands blowing her trumpet on the prow of a galley. The statue in the Louvre called 'The Winged Victory of Samothrace' is believed to be the same one, or possibly a copy. The event thus commemorated had occurred before Demetrios became king of Macedon, a dramatic increase in his power that had the effect of uniting his enemies against him. Ptolemy sent another fleet, while Pyrrhus of Epeiros and Lysimachos of Thrace invaded Macedon from east and west. They chose a time when Demetrios was campaigning on the Asiatic mainland and they undermined his position so badly that he was captured and ended his days in honourable detention.

For the next decade (286–277), Macedon experienced a chaotic succession of political changes. Pyrrhus, Lysimachos, Ptolemy, Seleukos and other contestants for power held sway there. No coins can be attributed for certain to this period, though it has been suggested that the standard Alexander types were still minted. In 279, the migrating Celts, known to the Romans as Gauls, invaded Macedon, searching for loot and, possibly, a place to settle. The lead in driving them away was taken by Demetrios' son Antigonos Gonatas, who had been holding out in the area around Corinth. As a result, he was accepted as king and soon proved himself to be a capable diplomat as well as a general. He made peace treaties with his neighbours and did his best to allow his kingdom time to recover from the damage caused in the unsettled period. His most common coins have an obverse design showing a Macedonian shield with a head of the god Pan in the centre (163). It was he who sent the Gauls into a panic and permitted the Macedonians to win the battle. Somewhat less common, though more spectacular, are the tetradrachms commemorating Antigonos' victory over yet another Egyptian fleet (164). He had taken a vow that he would dedicate his flagship to Apollo if he was granted a victory and, consequently, Apollo is shown seated on it, making an appropriate reverse design for a portrait of Poseidon. Side by side with these splendid coins, the Alexander types continued to appear. As well as gold and silver, bronzes became very numerous. These have a head of Hercules, his club and bow-case. They were the small change of the area and can still be bought cheaply, providing opportunities for the less affluent collector to include an Alexander piece in among his treasures. After a reign of forty-one years, Demetrios died, leaving the usual disputed succession.

After another disturbed period, the seventeen-year-old Philip V came to the throne. He, too, was to reign for forty years, though it can scarcely be called a glorious period. For three years, he struggled with the Aetolians and, after making peace, he considered what policy to follow in his relations with Rome and Carthage, who were locked together in the epic struggle called the Punic Wars. He sympathised with Carthage though did little to help her. The Romans deliberately stirred up enough trouble to keep him occupied, by encouraging the Aetolians, in alliance with other Greek states, to renew the war against Macedon. Though Philip was successful against them, so was Rome in her conflict with Carthage. Consequently, the Roman armies were able to turn against Macedon and Philip was defeated. He became a client king afraid to reassert his independence, though he was preparing to do so when he died. Some fine silver pieces have preserved his portrait for us (165,166). Other, less orthodox, issues, struck in the name of the Macedonian people, date from the latter part of his reign. One has on it a Macedonian shield and helmet (167). Another coin features a sea-nymph backed by the prow of a galley (498). It resembles contemporary coins of Histiaia on the Island of Euboea (497), though the precise reason why is unknown.

Philip regarded the mythical hero Perseus who, among other adventures, had killed the snake-haired Gorgon, as his personal protector. His wife claimed descent from Perseus and their son was named after him. Philip substituted his own portrait, wearing Perseus' winged cap, for the head of Pan on the tetradrachms and the practice was continued by Philip VI, a later claimant to the throne, who can be distinguished by the absence of a beard. The new king, Perseus, who began his reign in 179, continued the preparations for the inevitable war against Rome. Building up money reserves to pay the troops and buy allies was essential. Thanks to this policy, we have a series of tetradrachms with portraits of the king, some of which are signed by Zoilos, the mint-master (168). The eagle on the reverse occupies most of the space inside the oak-wreath on the earlier, heavy pieces, whereas, on the lighter coins he minted later, it has shrunk – possibly, to indicate the change. Though handsome, charming and diplomatic, Perseus was not the man for the task imposed on him. He was too mean with his money to win support in his time of need and too hesitant to succeed in battle against the Romans. It was not a time to reduce his soldiers' wages and, instead of refusing to pay the Gauls fighting on his side, he should have doubled their hand-outs. The treasury was full and there was no excuse for behaving in such an uninspiring way. His tactics were also faulty since, instead of taking the initiative, he stayed on the defensive, waiting for the inevitable Roman attacks. After three years of fighting, he was defeated at the battle of Pydna, captured and taken to Rome, where he died two years later.

Perseus was the last of the Macedonian kings. The Romans split up the area into four provinces, mainly to prevent further trouble. 'Divide and rule' was a traditional policy for them. They adapted coins by removing Philip's head from the Macedonian shield and substituting the head of Artemis (Diana), providing a non-controversial design (169). However, the Macedonians do not seem to have been content with the situation and gave considerable support to a young man calling himself Philip VI and claiming to be the illegitimate son of the fifth Philip. He was able to put his own portrait in the centre of the shield on the tetradrachms, though his two-year period of independence was apparently not long enough for many to be minted. When the Romans brought up reinforcements, he was driven over the border into Thrace, one of the chieftains of which handed him over to his enemies.

Macedon was made secure and was firmly held by the Roman governors. About fifty years after the crushing of Philip VI, the unusual step was taken of providing the province with an abundant silver coinage. In general, the provinces were encouraged to adopt Roman coinage and had their own suppressed on the ground that it encouraged aspirations towards independence. Suddenly, for reasons now unknown, the policy was reversed in Macedon. Aesillas, the Quaestor, ie the official responsible for taxation and monetary affairs, authorised tetradrachms that bear his name and symbols of office – the money-chest and quaestor's chair. The other side of the coin carries a portrait of Alexander, presumably a gesture to local feeling, but it is a very weak and degenerate rendering of the great man's features (170).

It cannot, surely, have been intended to demonstrate that Macedon was only a shadow of her former self and must be the result of a general decline in artistic standards. In many people's opinion, these coins are a sad ending to the series of splendid silver pieces that commemorate one of the most important kingdoms of the ancient world.

161 Tetradrachm, Demetrios Poliorketes, 294–288 BC. Poseidon and Victory on the prow of a galley.   **162** Tetradrachm. His portrait and Poseidon. **163** Tetradrachm, Antigonos Gonatas, 277–239 BC. Head of Pan in the centre of a shield; Athena.

164 Tetradrachm. Head of Poseidon; Apollo seated on the prow of a galley. (Possibly minted by Antigonos Doson, 229–221 BC.)   **165** Tetradrachm, Philip V, 221–179 BC. Philip as the hero Perseus; club in wreath.
166 Drachm. His portrait and club.   **167** Drachm. Philip V and Perseus; Macedonian helmet and club.   **168** Tetradrachm, King Perseus, 179–168 BC. His portrait and an eagle within a wreath.

169 Tetradrachm, 158–150 BC. Head of Artemis; club within wreath.
170 Tetradrachm issued by the Roman Quaestor, Aesillas, after 146 BC.
Head of Alexander the Great; club between money-chest and Quaestor's
chair.

XVI. THE SELEUKID EMPIRE

Seleukos (this is the modern spelling based on the original Greek, instead of Seleucus, the Latin form of the name) stood aside when the Alexandrian Empire was first divided at the Council of State arranged by some of Alexander's principal commanders to decide who was to govern its huge provinces. He was content to be cavalry commander for Perdiccas, the middle-aged Macedonian aristocrat to whom the dying Alexander had given his signet ring and, in this capacity, he accompanied him to Egypt, where Ptolemy had set himself up as an independent king. This was contrary to Perdiccas' wishes as self-designated regent of the whole empire, but he got himself into an impossible situation. His imposing army had to cross the Nile and attempted to do so by making use of a shallow place where there was an island in the middle of the river. Men and animals could wade out to it and there was plenty of room for regrouping and organising the whole of the proceedings. The feet of thousands of soldiers, horses, mules and so on, disturbed the sand, which was washed away. The ford got deeper and deeper, until men were swept away and drowned. Those already on the island could not get back and those left on the bank could not go forward. In the confusion, three senior officers slipped into Perdiccas' tent and killed him. One of these was Seleukos, who subsequently laid claim to the province of Babylon and was able to take it from the control of Perdiccas' appointee.

Seleukos proved a just and efficient administrator, though this did not save him from Antigonos, who took Perdiccas' place as overlord of the empire. When Antigonos, backed by a large army, paid a state visit, he was received in Babylon with every courtesy diplomacy required but, when he demanded that Seleukos give an account of his financial policies since he was appointed, it was clearly time to leave. Seleukos slipped away to Egypt, where Ptolemy remembered that he had helped remove the threat posed by Perdiccas and, consequently, gave him a post in keeping with his status and experience. For three years, he commanded the Egyptian fleet, a stage in his career that probably explains the choice of an anchor as his personal badge, used first as a countermark and, later, as part of the reverse design of his coins (171,173,478). On land, he helped defeat Antigonos' son Demetrios Poliorketes, whose army was a dangerous threat to Egypt. As a reward, Seleukos asked for troops to help him regain Babylon. It reads like a fairy story, though the record of events may be essentially true. A thousand troops were all that could be spared, yet Seleukos set out and, on the way, he gained recruits in large numbers. The people of Babylon were glad to have their respected former ruler once again in office, so they welcomed him with open arms. This triumphal return led to the establishment of 312 BC as the beginning of the Seleukid Era, which is used to date coins, giving us one of the few dated series among all the Greek issues.

Seleukos still had to fight for his kingdom. Antigonos sent two armies against him. The first was ambushed, its officers killed or forced to flee, and the rank and file, who were mercenaries like almost all the men involved in the conflicts described here, readily changed sides. With greatly augmented forces, Seleukos moved east, securing his control of the sparsely-populated territories that stretched away towards India. While he was away, Demetrios led a force against Babylon, where the garrison realised they could not withstand a siege in which they were heavily outnumbered, so they melted away into the desert, leaving the city to be pillaged. Like Napoleon, who knew this story when he marched to Moscow, Demetrios had to withdraw with little to show for his efforts and, soon afterwards, Seleukos returned. He was presented with an opportunity to build a new capital city and he chose a site further down the Tigris, away from the malarial swamps. Following Alexander's example, he named it after himself and, in time, Seleukia-on-the-Tigris became the largest city in the East. It ruins are situated about 40 km (25 miles) south of Baghdad and, in other parts of his kingdom, archaeological sites have been identified as the thirty or more cities Seleukos established to be bases for the Macedonian garrisons whom he posted at strategic places to hold his territories for him in case of rebellion. Seleukos overreached himself when he led an expedition to India to reclaim Alexander's conquests. There, he met the powerful Chandragupta, with whom he was obliged to make a treaty of friendship. The 500 war elephants received in the exchange of gifts proved very useful later and were featured on coins. Whether there were really as many as 500, and how they were fed, have to be left as open questions. What is certain is that some of the elephants proved decisive at the battle of Ipsus in 301 BC, when Seleukos, in alliance with Lysimachos, king of Thrace, defeated and killed Antigonos.

In the share-out of Antigonos' territory, Seleukos received Syria and, thus, had access to the Mediterranean. He built a new western capital on the river Orontes and called it Antioch, after his father. (Antiochos later became a traditional royal name among the Seleukids.) Since the new city was about 24 km (15 miles) upstream, it needed a port and was provided with one. This was another Seleukia, usually referred to as Seleukia-in-Pieria. Yet another building project in the area was the temple of Apollo on a sacred site four miles from Antioch. Honouring the local gods was a convenient device used by numerous rulers to inspire loyalty, though the Seleukids went further, naming Apollo as their patron deity and placing him on many of their coins. For Seleukos, the process of consolidating and extending his power was an unending task. Seeing that the defeated Demetrios was still a dangerous man to have in his rear, Seleukos arranged a peace treaty with him. As part of the agreement, Demetrios' young daughter Stratonike became Seleukos' second wife (his first had been a Babylonian princess). The alliance between the men worked well, but the principal effect of the marriage was to make Seleukos' son and heir very jealous. The solution was to pass on the young queen to the next generation and she, eventually, bore two sons and a daughter for Antiochos.

The last step in regaining Alexander's possessions involved a campaign against Lysimachos, whose judgement, impaired by age, led him to put his eldest son to death and impose heavy taxes on the cities he controlled in Asia Minor. Some of them appealed to Seleukos for help and, eventually, he was able to defeat and kill Lysimachos. This victory gave him control of Macedon, his homeland but, while sightseeing there, he was assassinated. Seleukos was seventy-seven and had ruled for thirty-two years. During this time, he had provided himself with an extensive coinage that could well make a specialised collection in its own right. To begin with, he retained Alexander's gold and silver pieces, which must have become familiar to everyone in his territories. When he felt sufficiently firmly established – we do not know the exact year – Seleukos substituted his own name for Alexander's (172). Then came silver pieces that had on the obverses a head of Zeus, similar to the design used for Macedonian coinage authorised by Alexander's father, Philip II (151). The reverses were very distinctive because they showed Athena in a chariot drawn by elephants (173). Above them was Seleukos' anchor badge. It appeared, again, on the reverse of drachms that featured a horned horse's head, another device with which the dynasty became associated (174). Both can be found on the bronzes as well (175), along with many other designs emanating from several of the cities Seleukos founded. The only portrait of him is, perhaps, the magnificent helmeted head on tetradrachms that also show Victory crowning a trophy of arms, though some eminent numismatists hold the view that it is, in fact, Alexander (176).

So much space has been devoted to Seleukos because his work was very important in establishing the Empire. His successors will have to be dealt with more briefly, partly because detailed treatment would make this survey unduly long and partly because the historical records are often scanty, merely chronicling battles and deaths, without permitting many of the Seleukids to 'come alive'. Here and there, anecdote and scandal enliven the narrative and serve to whet our appetites for more knowledge about the family whose portraits make such attractive coins, several of which are illustrated to give an impression of the range available.

Seleukos' assassin, one of the Ptolemy family, established himself briefly in Macedon and looked a capable ruler, but he perished in a hasty defensive action against an invasion by the Celts, who lived in the Danube Basin and, periodically, tried to seize Greek territory. Seleukos' son, Antiochos, was in Babylonia at the time his father died and, as soon as possible, he marched westwards to deal with the threats to his authority. He was implored to hurry to their rescue by the cities on the Aegean coast who were at the mercy of the Celts and, when he had driven them away, he was called 'Saviour', Soter in Greek (177–179). He used this title frequently, thereby setting a precedent for his successors. Some of them put the officially-approved flattering descriptions of themselves onto the reverses of their coins. Others have gone down in history with rather different adjectives attached to their names and this convention certainly helps us distinguish between one Antiochos or Seleukos and another. There were fourteen of the former and six of the latter. Antiochos Soter was succeeded by a son who called himself Theos – God, no less! (180,181) Both of them appear to have been preoccupied with seemingly interminable campaigns to retain their possessions or, sometimes, to capture a city or two from neighbouring kings. Their mercenary armies required payment constantly and, therefore, large issues of silver were made. These provide us with realistic portraits of the two kings, which change as they aged.

Antiochos Theos married a cousin called Laodike and had two sons by her. Then he divorced her in order to wed an Egyptian princess, as was customary when treaties were made. There was a son born to this marriage but, nevertheless, Antiochos left his Egyptian wife and returned to Laodike. Predictably, civil war began as soon as he died; the Egyptians intervened; none of the principal characters trusted each other; the baby heir was killed; and the two adult sons of Antiochos I divided the empire between them. They soon quarrelled and met ignominious deaths. We call them Seleukos Kallinikos, the 'Gloriously Victorious' and Antiochos Hierax, the Hawk (182,183). Their successors were the sons of Seleukos. The elder took the family name but did little to enhance its prestige. This Seleukos is remembered as Keraunos (184), the Thunderbolt, not because he hit his enemies hard, but because he was driven to violent rages that disgusted his commanders. The young man ineffectively tackled the problem of regaining territory in Asia Minor from the increasingly powerful kingdom of Pergamum and, when it became obvious that he was unlikely to be victorious, his officers did away with him and, after some disputes, they agreed to serve under their dead king's younger brother, who had at first been ruler of only the eastern provinces.

This Antiochos was to reign for thirty-six years and earn the epithet 'the Great'. The first few years of his reign were spent in finding his feet, gradually undermining the influence of his dominating chief minister and subduing revolts in the east. From 220 BC onwards, we have Polybius' History which gives many details about Antiochos, though its major theme is the expansion of the Roman Empire and the struggle with Carthage. He tells us how Antiochos antagonised many of his subjects while he was at his summer palace at Ecbatana in the land of the Medes, whose principal goddess was Anat, the warlike virgin whose task it was to see that her fellow deities were kept alive by being fed regular sacrifices. Her temple was a treasure house, with ample reserves to finance the religious observances if voluntary efforts failed. They were, also, just the thing Antiochos needed, so he confiscated the gold to pay his troops. Twenty years later, the goddess had her revenge. Meanwhile, the mercenary armies were on a campaign that lasted almost five years. Parthia, Bactria and the Indian borderlands were recaptured, giving Antiochos justification for calling himself 'the Great King', as the Persian Emperors had done. He also imitated his ancestor and issued some coins with Indian elephants on them (185), though most of his silver pieces were of the usual design – a portrait with Apollo on the reverse (186). By the time that he had subdued Asia Minor, apart from Pergamum, captured southern Syria from Egypt, successfully besieged the Phoenician cities, Tyre and Sidon, and then crossed with his army into northern Greece, Antiochos was undoubtedly the most powerful ruler alive. However, he made a serious mistake in backing Hannibal against Rome, crossing again into Greece with an army too small to take on the Romans effectively, then losing command of the sea to a Roman fleet, ably assisted by the Rhodian warships. A massive Roman force, led by the redoubtable Scipio, crossed into Asia Minor, inflicted a crushing defeat on him and forced him to pay a huge indemnity, to hand over hostages and even to pay a substantial sum to Rome's ally, Pergamum. Antiochos was shattered: his dreams of being a second Alexander were in ruins and, with the few soldiers who remained loyal, he retreated eastwards. Temple robbing was the only way to get hold of enough money to pay them and, when he tried it at Anat's temple in the important Persian city of Elymais, an infuriated crowd of citizens killed him.

Antiochos' elder son, Seleukos Philopater (187) – Lover of his Father – reigned for about eight years, steadily restoring the royal power, though doubtless hindered considerably by the annual payments of the indemnity to Rome. His younger brother was one of the hostages held in Rome and had just been exchanged for Seleukos' eldest son, when he learnt that a palace conspiracy had led to Seleukos' murder. Both Rome and Pergamum felt it was to their advantage to have Antiochos on the Seleukid throne, so he was helped to establish himself. Historians have been unkind to him, stressing his vanity and inordinate generosity to his mistress. The Bible roundly condemns him for defiling the Temple in Jerusalem and setting up 'the Abomination of Desolation', an altar to the Greek gods. Moreover, he chose as an official title a name that was certain to affront the Jews – Theos Epiphanes, 'God Manifest'. For a time, the gods seemed to be on his side and he was able to gain control of Egypt, though the Ptolemies remained as nominal rulers. Antiochos has left us some large bronze coins intended for use in Egypt and very clearly marked with his name to distinguish them from the earlier issues in the long series which they resemble (188). The Ptolemy family appealed to Rome for help and got it, for it was obvious to the Senate that to allow Syria to come under the rule of a single king would be very dangerous. A Roman ambassador reached Antiochos, when he was encamped near Alexandria, and handed him the Senate's order to evacuate Egypt. Playing for time, Antiochos answered that he would think it over but, according to one of the most dramatic anecdotes of the period, the ambassador took his walking stick and drew a circle in the sand around Antiochos' feet, saying that he required an answer before His Divine Majesty stepped out of it. Antiochos knew when he was beaten. Nevertheless, he celebrated a triumph when he got back to Syria and, later, successfully continued the seemingly endless task of keeping the remoter provinces under control. One disappointment was his failure to loot Anat's temple at Elymais where the inhabitants, warned by his father's behaviour, closed the gates of their well-fortified city. Another setback was the defeat of forces sent by his subordinates to crush the Jewish Revolt that his sacrilegious policies had sparked off. According to the First Book of Maccabees, he died in delirium brought on by frustration and remorse. Clearly, anyone who is thinking of collecting coins associated with the Bible will want one with his portrait on it (189).

Demetrios (190), Seleukos' eldest son, had grown to manhood in honourable captivity as a hostage in Rome, where, incidentally, he spent much of his time with Polybius, who later wrote the history of this period. On learning of his father's death, Demetrios managed to escape by sea and reached Syria where he was welcomed as the 'Saviour' who rescued his people from oppressive governors, exploiting the situation to their advantage. Though he took the title 'Soter', Demetrios was not a popular king because he was too mean. There were no lavish entertainments or distributions of largesse nor did he appear much in public, preferring to remain in his palace, keeping company with poets and philosophers or indulging the Seleukid weakness for alcohol. There was general support for a pretender known as Alexander Balas (191,192), a young man backed by Pergamum and Egypt, who managed to defeat and kill Demetrios. He was permitted to marry an Egyptian princess called Cleopatra Thea, a remarkable lady, one of the most interesting Seleukid rulers. She bore him a son and then returned to Egypt because her husband preferred the company of his mistresses. His imprudent life of luxury and neglect of politics weakened Alexander's position, with the result that there was little support for him when the son of Demetrios Soter, also called Demetrios, made a bid for the throne. With Egyptian help, he secured it, arranged Alexander's murder and married his widow, Cleopatra. Though he called himself Nikator, the Victorious One (193), Demetrios was not very fortunate in the civil war that dragged on between his supporters and recalcitrant warlords, one of whom fought in the name of the infant son of Alexander, striking coins that show the child with a rayed crown, like a god (194). After he had disposed of the infant, he put his own head on the coins (195), calling himself Tryphon, 'the Magnificent'. Meanwhile, Demetrios had blundered into the hands of the Parthians, who kept him prisoner for ten years.

Almost every Seleukid seems to have had a younger brother ready to step into his shoes and Demetrios was no exception. The brother this time was yet another Antiochos, known to us as Sidetes because he spent his youth at a port called Side (196). He was a personable, capable young man and Cleopatra Thea decided to marry him, even though he was ten years younger than her and Demetrios was still alive. There must have been scant hope of ever seeing him again. Cleopatra bore her new husband five children while he successfully dealt with Tryphon and restored order to his dominions. Unfortunately, he miscalculated the strength of the Parthians and was killed.

While Antiochos' last campaign was taking place, the Parthian king had sent Demetrios by a roundabout route to Syria with instructions to claim his rights as the true king and stir up trouble, thus undermining his brother's efforts. Demetrios unexpectedly found himself back in his kingdom with no serious rival. He took back Cleopatra, though she probably did not recognise him at first. The coin portraits show how he had adopted Parthian fashions and grown a long beard like all the other men at the court where he had been detained (197). His ambitions remained the same and he began a campaign against Egypt, only to be humiliated when a much stronger army took the field against him and a pretender threatened his position, in much the same way as he had been sent to harass his brother. Cleopatra had had enough of him, too. She gave orders that the city gates of Ptolemais should be closed against him when he tried to take refuge there and as, in desperation, he boarded a ship at Tyre, the crew murdered him. She paid well. The pretender, Alexander Zebina, the Bought One (possibly an indication that he had once been sold as a slave) was backed by the king of Egypt and managed to hold on to parts of Syria for about four years, issuing a considerable number of different coins (198).

Cleopatra Thea, who by now had become the widow of three Seleukids and was the mother of eight children, began to act as queen in her own right. Some rare tetradrachms feature her alone, but public opinion obliged her to take a son into partnership. Both their portraits were put on the coins and Cleopatra's was the more prominent (199). The son was Antiochos Grypos, the Hook-nosed – his coins make this peculiarity very clear (200,201). He was no statesman and left the conduct of affairs to his mother for a few years until he grew suspicious of her. If we are to believe the chronicles, they were not on the best of terms when, one day, as Antiochos returned from hunting, his mother met him with a cup of wine – just the thing for a hot, sweaty horseman. However, Antiochos was not a fool and instead of drinking the wine himself, he insisted that Cleopatra did so. It was poisoned, of course.

Antiochos reigned twenty-five years and spent much of the time fighting his half-brother, Antiochos Kyzikenos (202), the man from Kyzikos. Most historians seem to lose patience at this stage in the Seleukid civil wars. There is little of lasting interest in the struggles of the later princes to gain power. Grypos had five sons and Kyzikenos had one. Each had an opportunity to issue coins (203–205) but, in the long run, all their struggles succeeded in doing was to impoverish the country and turn the people against the Seleukids. An invitation was sent to King Tigranes of Armenia (252) to take over and restore good government. Remarkably, he was able to do this and ruled for fourteen years. His successful reign was ended by the Romans, who decided to take Syria into their empire. For about five years, they maintained a puppet king called Antiochos Asiatikos and, when he was murdered by an Arab chief, Pompey made the decision to treat Syria as a province, with a governor appointed by the Senate. The Seleukid dynasty and this finest series of ancient coin portraits had come to an end.

Seleukos I, Nikator, 312–280 BC.
171 Alexandrine tetradrachm, countermarked with Seleukos'
anchor. **172** Alexandrine tetradrachm with Seleukos' name.
173 Tetradrachm. Head of Zeus; Athena driving a chariot drawn by
elephants; anchor above it. **174** Drachm. Horned horse and anchor.
175 Bronze coin of similar design.

176 Tetradrachm. Helmeted portrait, either Alexander or Seleukos; Nike crowning a trophy of arms.

Antiochos I, Soter, 280–261 BC.
177 Drachm. His portrait and horned horse.   **178** Tetradrachm. Youthful portrait with Apollo.   **179** Tetradrachm. Older portrait.

Antiochos II, Theos, 261–246 BC.
180 Gold stater. His portrait with Apollo.   **181** Tetradrachm. Similar designs.

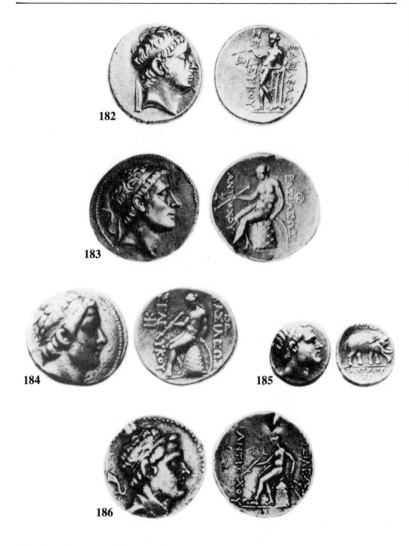

182 Tetradrachm, Seleukos II, Kallinikos, 246–226 BC. His portrait and Apollo. **183** Tetradrachm, Antiochos Hierax, 246–227 BC. His portrait and Apollo. **184** Similar coin, Seleukos III, Keraunos, 226–223 BC.

Antiochos III, the Great, 223–187 BC.
185 Drachm. His portrait with an Indian elephant. **186** Tetradrachm. His portrait and Apollo, test cut.

187 Tetradrachm, Seleukos IV, Philopater, 187–175 BC. His portrait and Apollo.   **188** Large bronze coin, similar to Egyptian issues, Antiochos IV, Epiphanes, 175–164 BC. Zeus and his eagle.   **189** Portrait tetradrachm. Zeus holding Nike.   **190** Portrait tetradrachm, Demetrios I, Soter, 162–150 BC. Tyche enthroned.

191 Portrait teradrachm, Alexander I, Balas, 150–145 BC. Zeus holding Nike. Seleukid Era data, 163 = 150/49 BC.   **192** Portrait drachm with Apollo.   **193** Tetradrachm, Demetrios II, Nikator, first reign, 145–140 BC. His portrait and Apollo.   **194** Portrait tetradrachm, Antiochos VI, Dionysos, 145–142 BC. He wears a rayed crown; the Dioskouroi are on the reverse.   **195** Portrait tetradrachm, Tryphon, 142–138 BC. Horned helmet.

196 Portrait, tetradrachm, Antiochos VII, Euergetes (Sidetes), 138–129 BC. With Athena. **197** Tetradrachm, Demetrios II, Nikator, second reign, 129–125 BC. Bearded portrait and Zeus. **198** Portrait tetradrachm, Alexander II, Zebina, 128–123 BC. With Zeus. **199** Tetradrachm, Cleopatra Thea and Antiochos VIII, 125–121 BC. Their portraits and Zeus.

200 Portrait tetradrachm, Antiochos VIII, Grypos, 121–96 BC. With Zeus. **201** Portrait tetradrachm. Reverse: the pyre of Sandan, the lion, at Babylon. **202** Portrait tetradrachm, Antiochos IX, Kyzikenos, 113–95 BC. With Athena. **203** Portrait tetradrachm, Seleukos VI, Epiphanes Nikator (eldest son of Antiochos VIII), 95–94 BC.

204 Portrait tetradrachm, Philip Philadelphos (another son of Antiochos VIII), 93–83 BC. With Zeus. **205** Portrait tetradrachm, Antiochos X, Eusebes Philopater (son of Antiochos IX), 94–83 BC. With Zeus.

XVII. EGYPT UNDER THE PTOLEMIES

One of the most popular commanders, who had set out as a young man with Alexander when he began his career of conquest, was Ptolemy. First-hand experience of battle and diplomacy brought him to early maturity and he developed a broader view of affairs than most of the self-centred rivals for control of Alexander's empire. Intelligent, good-humoured and shrewd, Ptolemy knew what he wanted from the division of the provinces carried out at the conferences following Alexander's death. It was Egypt, potentially the richest of them all and, as no doubt he had realised when he had been there with Alexander, much the easiest to defend.

The inhabited part of the country was the long narrow strip extending a few miles on either side of the Nile. Its fertility was proverbial and the native inhabitants were easy to rule. Defence was easy, because the desert and the swamps of the delta were impenetrable barriers. An invading army would have to come along the coast from the Holy Land and pass through territory not more than 48 km (30 miles) wide. Strongly-garrisoned fortresses could cope with that problem. Ptolemy set off as fast as he could from Babylon, accompanied by a small force of 2,500 troops and a number of sacred objects looted many years previously by the Persians. Returning these to Egypt would, he hoped, create a good impression. The country had been left under the control of a Greek financier called Kleomenes, to whom Alexander entrusted the raising of taxes so necessary to finance his mercenary armies. It was quickly obvious to Ptolemy that Kleomenes was feathering his own nest and creating much resentment among the population, who were complaining about unjust treatment of many kinds. Wisely, Ptolemy had the unpopular administrator arrested, tried and executed; and took control of the Treasury and used some of the gold to pay a substantial army, which he recruited and trained as fast as he could. He ousted the last of the native pharaohs, who had, in any case, lost his political power, though retaining prestige in a society dominated by a priesthood who asserted that the pharaohs were gods. The Egyptian reverence for the dead as well as the living encouraged Ptolemy to abduct Alexander's body as it made its slow journey in its golden coffin, pulled by a large team of mules, which were to take it back to Macedon. An Egyptian force intercepted the cortège at Damascus and diverted it to Alexandria, where Ptolemy ordered a magnificient tomb to be constructed. He was claiming to be the rightful successor to the Great One, with all the status and privileges entailed.

His former companions in arms were unhappy at this development, if only because it undermined the fragile façade of unity they had created. The one who felt most threatened was Perdiccas, who claimed that, by handing him his signet ring, Alexander had made him overlord of his empire, at least until his male heirs were able to take command. Only force would bring Ptolemy to heel, so Perdiccas led a huge army into Egypt, where he met his death. The troops got into difficulties crossing the Nile and Perdiccas' furious officers made him pay the penalty for leading them into an impossible position. They stabbed him in his tent. The new overlord, Antipater, confirmed Ptolemy's position and allowed him to marry his daughter. However, Ptolemy was not yet safe – he had to fight off the ruler of much of Asia Minor, Antigonos the One-Eyed, who twice attempted an invasion of Egypt, while his son, Demetrios Poliorketes, conducted the famous siege of Rhodes, which was Ptolemy's ally. In spite of these difficulties, Ptolemy was safe in his domain because of the geographical factors already mentioned. Contemporaries compared him to a tortoise which made good use of its armour and, occasionally, poked its head out to remind everyone that it was still alive.

It was a very prudent policy to make good use of the security created by a well-defended frontier to build up the prosperity of Egypt. Ptolemy encouraged agriculture by trying out new varieties of grain and new stock for animal breeding. Commerce and intellectual life were stimulated by fostering the growth of the Greek and Jewish communities. Immigration was encouraged and money from the Treasury paid for the establishment of the Museum at Alexandria. This was the Home of the Muses, where poets, philosophers, mathematicians and scholars of all kinds worked and lived free. Their keep was paid for by the state. A natural development was the building of the Library to house their reference books. Eventually it contained thousands of papyrus rolls which, had they survived, would have provided us with an immense amount of information about the ancient world. Religion was such a strong political force in Egypt that Ptolemy made sure to have it working for him. As well as adapting pharaoh-worship to his needs, he fostered the cult of Sarapis, a god who might have been invented for his purposes. Portrayed as a mature bearded man, resembling Zeus, Sarapis wore a distinctive symbol on his head. This was a corn-measure, the container in which grain was placed when the harvest was assessed. Fertility was stressed in another way by giving Sarapis a consort. She was Isis, the ancient goddess of the Nile. Egyptian and Greek culture were fused in these deities, whose worship seems to have been a cohesive force during the three centuries of Ptolemaic rule.

There had been no indigenous coinage in Egypt before Alexander's conquest and, when he established a mint at Alexandria (the town he founded and named after himself), he was providing the country with an essential element in the Greek way of life. Ptolemy continued the coinage, making gradual changes from Alexander's standard types. His first innovation was to give the portrait on the coins an elephant-skin headdress, instead of the lion's scalp worn by Alexander in his pose as Hercules (206). Next, he removed Zeus from the reverse and substituted Athena in a fighting pose (207). Finally, he put his own name in place of Alexander's. In 311, Alexander's surviving heir was murdered and the nominal unity of the empire was ended. Several provincial rulers, including Ptolemy, began to call themselves king (Basileos).It is possible that the Ptolemaic Era is dated from this event, though there is a theory that the conversion of the coinage from the Athenian to the Phoenician weight standard, which occurred in 305 BC marks the beginning of the dating system for coins. It is confusing to have more than one method in use at the same time. Several Ptolemies recorded the year of their reign on the reverses of their coins and a few used numbers over a hundred, obviously referring to one of the Eras observed in the Greek world. The subject is still a difficult one and detailed coin descriptions wisely refer to the 'annual sequence mark' instead of the date. Ptolemy put his own portrait on coins (208) and began a long series of issues that changed little over the centuries. The Egyptians certainly liked tradition and continuity. Gold was minted as a matter of policy rather than the result of a crisis, as was the case as far as other Greek mints were concerned. Tetradrachms were the usual silver denomination, though smaller coins sometimes appeared. Bronze was more important in Egypt than elsewhere, so there was less need for small silver when transactions could be paid for with a different metal. Moreover, the mints produced great quantities of bronze coins for everyday use. They have survived well in the dry sands, providing modern collectors with very impressive specimens. Zeus was on the obverses and an eagle, the badge of the dynasty, occupied the reverses of silver and gold as well as bronze (209). Compared with the magnificient portraits produced for the Seleukid Empire, Ptolemaic counterparts are less well executed. However, the details to be found on similar, and comparatively common, coins add much interest. Apart from the baffling dates, there are artists' initials, marks of value and the letters that identify the mint towns. Alexandria was the most important one and there were others outside Egypt, including Tyre, Sidon, Joppa, Gaza, Askalon, Damascus, Ptolemais and Salamis in Cyprus.

At eighty-four, Ptolemy died in his bed, the only one of Alexander's successors to do so. He had married three times and handed on the throne to a son of his youngest wife. This Ptolemy – all males took the regal name – is called Philadelphos, the Peacelover. Though this title is a little uncomplimentary, because ancient historians preferred successful generals, we, who know so much about the consequences of war, emphasise other aspects of his reign and restore his reputation. He continued to develop the Egyptian economy and set out to make Alexandria a truly magnificent city. The streets were laid out systematically, there were many public buildings, the harbour was extended, the lighthouse built and so on. His capital soon became the largest city in the ancient world, with about half-a-million inhabitants. Every trade and craft was to be found there and, of course, a very large coinage was required for their commercial needs. Ptolemy II provided it, along lines that were becoming traditional. The new development of greatest interest to the modern collector is the portrait coins of his queen, Arsinoe II (210). This forceful lady had been married twice before when, in her forties, she returned to Egypt and took the honoured place which the king's sister could expect. Within a short time, she had driven the queen into exile and supplanted her, thus continuing an old Egyptian custom that the pharaohs should marry their sisters. Who else was fit to be the wife of a god? Arsinoe dominated Egyptian politics for about seven years until she died. Ptolemy perpetuated her memory by minting splendid portrait coins that show her 'veiled'. This descriptive term is traditional, but fails to convey the meaning that the dead peson whose coin portrait follows this convention is, in fact, wearing a shroud. The impressive ceremonies associated with Arsinoe's burial have given rise to one numismatic hypothesis that, from it (270 BC), was dated a different Ptolemaic Era.

Ptolemy Philadelphos was a good diplomat, who negotiated treaties with the neighbouring Seleukid Empire and maintained strict neutrality in the fighting between Rome and Carthage. When he died, his son, Ptolemy III, Euergetes, the Benefactor, found that it was high time to launch a campaign. His sister, Berenike, had been the second wife of Antiochos II and, at his death, she was attacked by supporters of his first queen and grown-up sons. For a time, Berenike held out in her palace near Antioch, sending urgent calls for help to her brother. He led an army to her rescue, arriving too late. Berenike and her baby son had been killed. The furious Ptolemy resolved to teach the Syrians a lesson. First, he allowed his troops to plunder Antioch and, then, he led them deeper into the Seleukid territories, eventually reaching Babylon and the new eastern capital, Seleukia-on-the-Tigris. He was away for five years and hurried back to Egypt on receiving the news that a succession of low Niles had caused several years of hardship and, consequently, there was trouble brewing. The treasure he brought back with him must have helped restore the situation. We know very little of the events that took place in the last twenty years of his reign. Peace gave the chroniclers little to record and, presumably, Ptolemy Euergetes had had enough of campaigning, preferring to concentrate on restoring his country's prosperity. If this was, indeed, the case, he earned his title, the Benefactor. The principal numismatic interest of his reign lies in some striking gold pieces (211,212). There are four portraits on each. One royal pair are probably Ptolemy II and Arsinoe II, and the other, Ptolemy III and his queen, who was called Berenike and ruled the country very competently while he was away. She also appears veiled on some big silver pieces, special issues probably associated with her funeral (213).

The fourth Ptolemy came to the throne at the age of twenty-four. Preferring his pleasures to the business of politics, he left the conduct of government to his chief minister, Sosibios. Like so many officials in similar positions, Sosibios has received a bad press because of his self-seeking policies, though, on the other hand, his conduct of government was not by any means disastrous and he did remarkably well as the director of the defence preparations to cope with an invasion by Antiochos III of Syria. He recruited and trained an army, even including Egyptian soldiers, as well as the usual Macedonians. They met the invaders at the border and defeated them, leaving the young king to glory in the success which was really due to his minister's efforts. They had saved the country from the Seleukids, but had one unfortunate result. Some of the Egyptian troops retained their arms and became a kind of guerrilla force, lurking in the more inaccessible areas and working to drive out the Ptolemies. Apparently, this was almost a nationalist movement, directed against foreigners who could not even speak Egyptian. The only Ptolemy who did learn it was the famous Cleopatra and she was also the only one capable of winning the affection of her subjects. The language of the court and the civil service was, of course, Greek, as it was throughout the territories conquered by Alexander until, sooner or later, the native languages reasserted themselves. Ptolemy IV has left us some good coin portraits of himself and his queen (214,215). On the gold, he wears a crown of rays and carries a trident, doubtless posing as the victor in the war with the Seleukids. Another attractive coin is the tetradrachm that shows Sarapis and Isis in much the same style as the royal couples on earlier gold pieces (216). Ptolemy IV continued the custom of marrying his sister, another Arsinoe, who appears on a gold 8 drachma piece. She might have been a capable regent for their young son, but Sosibios poisoned her.

Ptolemy V, called Theos Epiphanes, a title conferred at his coronation, when the priests announced that he was a god come down to earth, was only five when he inherited the throne. Sosibios was in control and, after him, some other officials and generals, though their personal ambitions led them to neglect the defence of the outlying territories, which fell to the Seleukids. As he grew to manhood, this Ptolemy seemed to care for little but hunting though he was, at last, beginning to take an active interest in politics at the time of his premature death at twenty-eight. Among the coins struck in his name are some attractive portraits. His own, and a reissue of one supposed to be the founder of the dynasty, followed traditional lines (217,218). An interesting variation on well-established themes was the adaptation of the head of Isis on the bronzes to become a portrait of his queen (219), Cleopatra I, a Seleukid princess who proved a capable regent for her children, though her brother, Antiochos IV, was to invade Egypt, and left only when warned off by the Romans. She died young, leaving affairs of state in the hands of ministers whose provocative policies led to the attack by Antiochos IV. One of them, Eulaios, put his initials on the coins.

They were minted in the name of Ptolemy VI, Philometer (Son of a Beloved Mother) who, like his father, was only about five when he came to the throne. We have few details, but there must have been a faction at court that wanted his younger brother to be king. Rivalry between the two sides was intense and Philometer had to take refuge in Rome, which was becoming so strong that other powers took care not to give offence. The Senate ruled that Philometer should have Egypt and Cyprus, leaving only Kyrenaika, on the north African coast, for his brother. Philometer had a long reign and, as he matured, he grew more competent. His diplomacy involved the marriage of his daughter into the Seleukid royal family, who passed her from one husband to another until, widowed for the third time and mother of eight children, she was, for a time, Queen of the Empire. Dislike of a woman on the throne and suspicion of the Egyptian connection led to rebellion against Cleopatra Thea, with the result that her father had to lead an army into Syria to support her. In the ensuing conflict, Ptolemy VI was killed. His coins followed the usual pattern, the silver carrying a portrait of the first Ptolemy, and only some uncommon didrachms minted in Cyprus feature Philometer (220). Even then, he is in the guise of Dionysos, the wine god, who wears a head-dress of vine leaves or ivy. A new departure was to put two eagles, instead of one, on the bronzes. Possibly, this was to indicate that Philometer and his brother were the joint kings of Egypt, as they could have been regarded before the Roman diplomatic intervention.

The brother's chance came in 145. This thoroughly nasty character, who eventually grew so fat that his subjects referred to him as Physkon – 'Big Belly' – was waiting in Kyrenaika with an army ready to take advantage of the situation arising from Philometer's death while away campaigning. The mercenaries he had with him changed sides and joined the Seleukids, leaving his widow almost defenceless in Alexandria. She fled with her children, one of whom was styled

Ptolemy VII, to Memphis, and maintained a precarious authority there as regent, whle her brother was in control of Alexandria. The relations between the Ptolemies are difficult for us to understand. This Cleopatra was the widow of her elder brother, obviously wanted power herself and, eventually, agreed to retain it by marrying her younger brother. When she became pregnant, he had her young son killed, who was, of course, his nephew, too. Next, Physkon (officially called Euergetes, though what benefits he brought his people are difficult to establish) became infatuated with his niece, who was now his step-daughter. The result was that he took her as his wife and had two queens, referred to as Cleopatra the Wife and Cleopatra the Sister. This situation lasted for fifteen years and, not surprisingly, the two queens hated each other. Dislike for Physkon spread to the people, who grew so troublesome that he felt it wise to leave Egypt for Cyprus, taking his Wife and her children with him. He was determined to regain the throne and assembled his mercenaries in readiness for the right opportunity. Insanely jealous of his sister, he murdered the son she had borne him, had the body cut up, embalmed, beautifully packaged and sent to her as a birthday present. Physkon got back to Egypt in 129, drove out his sister, who took refuge with her daughter Cleopatra Thea in Syria, and ruled for another twelve years. It was unintentional, but one result of his devious goings-on was to confuse numismatists. Since he counted the years of his reign from his original bid for power, they overlap with his brother's and the result is that it is impossible to separate the issues.

Cleopatra the Wife survived her husband and, at last, wielded the power she had apparently always sought. For sixteen years, until her death at sixty, she dominated politics, though nominal authority rested with her sons, Ptolemy Soter II, the ninth Ptolemy and the tenth one, called Ptolemy Alexander. Not surprisingly, they conspired to do away with their formidable mother. After about ten years, the elder of the two had to go into exile in Cyprus to avoid arrest and was eventually acknowledged as king of the island, striking coins which have ΠΑ on them. Subsequently, these letters appeared on coins minted in Alexandria, so they are not an infallible guide to identification. The Queen Mother's death may have been a natural one, though Ptolemy Alexander was accused of poisoning her. He ruled in his own right for eighteen years, growing like his father, corpulent, drunken and extravagant. Such a man could not retain his subjects' loyalty indefinitely and, in 88 BC, they rebelled. He was murdered on board a ship bound for Cyprus and his brother found that he could at last leave this island kingdom and return to the Egyptian throne. His second reign lasted eight years and the coins from it can be identified by the regnal years, which go up to thirty-six, because, like all deposed monarchs, he reckoned from the first time he could claim the throne. Otherwise, his coins are very much like his father's.

The numbering of the Ptolemies in modern books is not consistent at this point. The reason is that the succession to the throne was in a confused state. There was no legitimate heirs. A young man, who called himself Ptolemy Alexander, the second man to bear this title, got Roman support and became king of Egypt. He was, apparently a son of Ptolemy X (hence, the name Alexander) by his first wife, about whom we know nothing. He was obliged by Egyptian custom to marry the queen, daughter of Ptolemy IX and, therefore, his aunt, or perhaps his step-mother or even his cousin. Records of these personages who had the same names can be very confusing. We can rely on the story that, a few days after the unwelcome wedding, he had his bride put to death and the Alexandrian mob were so incensed that they broke into the palace and tore him to pieces. Though he never had time to issue any coins, we shall, however, follow the practice of calling him the eleventh Ptolemy.

The twelfth one was the son of a concubine of whom Ptolemy IX had been fond. Wisely fearing for his safety after his father's death, his mother had taken him away from Egypt, where close relatives of the reigning king often had a short life, and was given hospitality at the court of King Mithradates VI of Pontos. He was now the claimant to the Egyptian throne, but everything depended on permission from Rome, the empire of which had expanded to the point when it might easily engulf Egypt. This expansion involved power struggles between men who have become much better known than the Ptolemies, largely because we have the works of the Roman historians. In the year 80 BC, which our survey has now reached, the ruthless Sulla was dictator. He had backed the unsuccessful Ptolemy, Alexander II, and the Senate, unwilling to offend him, was reluctant to approve the new candidate for the Egyptian throne. Nevertheless, he held a coronation and then made sustained efforts to obtain formal recognition from Rome. Had he been a more forceful personality, he might have been able to make something advantageous out of his depressing situation, but he spent his time, as so many Ptolemies had done, in pleasure-seeking. His fondness for music earned him the derisive nickname Auletes, the Flute-player, instead of Neos Dionysos, 'the New God Dionysos', which he used officially. Such an unprepossessing king could not afford to be an oppressive tax-gatherer or to lose further ground to the Romans. Nevertheless, they took Cyprus and the exasperated Alexandrians drove out Auletes. His daughter Berenike, murderously effective like her predecessors, reigned in his place. She took a husband who was a distant cousin and, finding he did not come up to expectations, she had him strangled within a week. Then she married a young man from the court of Pontos, where she had been well treated as a girl. They made a capable royal pair, but Auletes got his kingdom back. First, he offered Julius Caesar, who was hounded by creditors, a big bribe to be paid when he got hold of the Egyptian treasury. Caesar persuaded the Senate to support Auletes and then had to find the troops to make good his claims. The proconsul of Syria was similarly bribed and sent three legions to conduct Auletes back to Alexandria. He saw to it that his daughter and her husband were killed, leaving him in control until his death about four years later. His coins followed the familiar pattern, growing more debased, rather like the dynasty (221).

A last flicker of hope came in the form of Auletes' seventeen-year-old daughter, *the* Cleopatra to us and Cleopatra VII in the royal line. Her story has given rise to so much fiction and film that it is almost impossible to make a balanced assessment of her. We do not know, even, what she looked like, though the prominent nose given her by the coin portraits has become the feature that tradition emphasises (222). As for romantic love, it is very unlikely that such hard-bitten characters as Julius Caesar and Mark Antony had much time for it. They were far more interested in the riches that Egypt might bring them. Caesar found Cleopatra at Alexandria confronted by armed enemies who claimed to be acting in the name of her brother, who was aged about fifteen. He helped her win the struggle, during which the fierce fighting led to the death of that young man and the burning down of the Library. When the situation was calm, Cleopatra did as Ptolemies were expected to do and went through a marriage ceremony with an even younger brother. Officially, the two were the thirteenth and fourteenth Ptolemies, though it was Cleopatra who was in command. When Caesar had made her pregnant, she went to live in a magnificent villa in Rome and the boy born to her was named

Caesarion – the fifteenth and last male Ptolemy. Her hopes of becoming consort of the first emperor of Rome were dashed when Caesar was murdered. She quietly went back to Egypt and was soon sent for by Antony, who wanted her wealth and ships in his confrontation with Octavian, the future Augustus. For a time he left her to marry Octavia, sister of his rival, who temporarily made peace (223). Then, he ruined his reputation through unsuccessful campaigns against the Parthians and returned to Cleopatra. She seems to have expected that the two men could arrange a division of the Roman world, but could not prevent the final decisive battle when their galleys fought off Actium, a cape in western Greece. She made matters worse by fleeing from the scene and encouraging Antony to follow her. After deserting his men like that, there was no hope for Antony, who was in turn deserted when Octavian's forces reached Alexandria. He committed suicide, leaving Cleopatra to try the effectiveness of her charms on Octavian. He was unimpressed and informed her that if she did not also commit suicide she would be dragged through Rome in his victory triumph. Whether there was a snake is doubtful, but it is reasonably certain that Cleopatra and her maids were found dead in their apartments. They had put on their finest robes and jewellery before taking poison. Octavian had Caesarion killed and, though the three children that Cleopatra had by Antony were looked after by Octavia, the two boys vanished from history, as so many youthful princes had done. No rivals, even potential ones, were allowed to live to threaten Octavian, who declared Egypt to be his personal property and so it remained, passed on to successive emperors. The Ptolemaic coinage came to an end and it was replaced by a plentiful and distinctive currency minted by the Romans. If collectors would like a portrait of Cleopatra, there are several bronzes, one of which shows her as Aphrodite, Goddess of Love. However, these are usually in poor condition and most people prefer one of the denarii or tetradrachms that were minted to pay her mercenaries. These silver pieces have her head on one side and Antony's on the other (224,225).

Ptolemy I, Soter, 305–283 BC.
206 Tetradrachm. Alexander the Great with an elephant-skin head-dress; Zeus and his eagle. **207** Tetradrachm. Athena has been substituted for Zeus. **208** Tetradrachm. Ptolemy's portrait and eagle. **209** Large bronze coin, Ptolemy II, Philadelphos, 285–246 BC. Zeus and eagle.

210 Dekadrachm. Portrait of Queen Arsinoe II and double cornucopia.

Ptolemy III, Euergetes, 246–221 BC.
211 Gold oktadrachm. Portraits of himself and his queen, and his parents. **212** Gold tetradrachm. Similar. **213** Gold oktadrachm. Queen Berenike II.

Ptolemy IV, Philopater, 221–204 BC.
214 Gold oktadrachm. His portrait with crown of rays; radiate cornucopiae. **215** Didrachm. His portrait and eagle.

216 Tetradrachm. Sarapis and Isis.

Ptolemy V, Epiphanes, 204–180 BC.
217 Tetradrachm. Portrait believed to be his own.   **218** Tetradrachm. The portrait is probably an idealised one of the founder of the dynasty.
219 Bronze coin. Queen Cleopatra I as Isis.

Ptolemy VI, Philometor, 180–145 BC.
220 Didrachm minted in Cyprus. Portrait of Ptolemy as Dionysos.

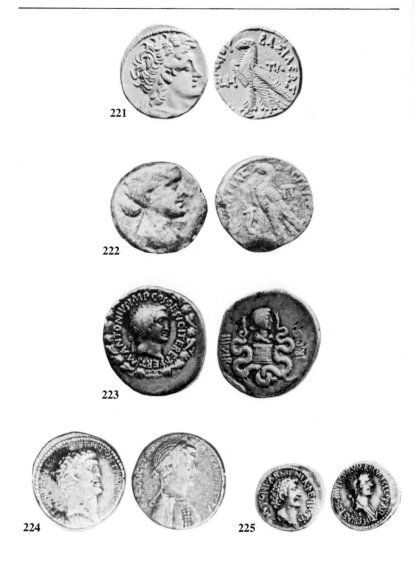

221 Portrait tetradrachm, Ptolemy XII, Neos Dionysos (Auletes), 80–58 and 55–51 BC. **222** Bronze coin, Cleopatra VII, 51–30 BC. With her portrait. **223** Cistophoric tetradrachm. Mark Antony and Octavia. Probably minted at Pergamun. **224** Tetradrachm with portraits of Mark Antony and Cleopatra. **225** A similar denarius.

THE SMALLER HELLENISTIC KINGDOMS

Among the kingdoms formed from Alexander's empire, the Seleukid, Ptolemaic and Macedonian were obviously the most powerful. Several smaller kingdoms emerged, either immediately after Alexander's death or at times when weaknesses at the power centre of one of the 'big three' allowed them to do so. These kingdoms produced interesting coins, some of which have on them portraits of very colourful characters. What follows is a review of the more important developments as far as coin collectors are concerned.

XVIII. EPEIROS UNDER KING PYRRHUS

Among the numerous Greek warriors, few have left such a curious reputation as King Pyrrhus of Epeiros. As far as the Romans were concerned, he was the first commander from Mainland Greece whom they encountered in battle – and they were impressed. They admired not only his tactical skill but also his chivalry. Indeed, few people who met Pyrrhus failed to succumb to his personal magnetism. On the other hand, he proved to be an inept and autocratic ruler of the empire he created. Moreover, although he won most of his battles, his losses were usually so heavy that it was his side that was placed at a disadvantage by the outcome of the fighting. Such a costly triumph is still sometimes called a Pyrrhic victory.

Epeiros, now divided between the states of Albania and Greece, is a mountainous region that has always been difficult to rule. Its fiercely independent people do not take kindly to outside interference and are not inclined to submit to rulers who bring no obvious benefits. The young Pyrrhus found this out at an early age, when his father was deposed in one of the numerous coups that were the chief feature of Macedonian politics. After a time, the young lad was made nominal ruler by another coup, only to lose his throne again as he reached his later teens. After this, he fought under Alexander's old general Antigonos and, after several adventures, found himself a prisoner of war in Egypt. Being of royal blood, Pyrrhus was well treated and invited to attend Ptolemy's court, where his good looks and personality won him admirers among the ladies. He soon married Ptolemy's daughter and persuaded his father-in-law to provide him with an army to restore himself to the throne. He was successful and was even invited to rule the neighbouring kingdom of Macedon. However, the tribes there proved too unruly and he was obliged to return to Epeiros.

To honour his homeland, he minted a splendid coin (226). Apart from bearing Pyrrhus's name, it publicises the Oracle of Dodona, the chief claim to fame that Epeiros could make among the Greek states. This very ancient oracle was the most important known to the Greeks of the Homeric Age though, by Pyrrhus' time, it had been eclipsed by the Oracle of Delphi. At Dodona, grew a grove of sacred oak trees. People who came to consult the oracle listened to the movement of the wind in the branches, a procedure that was made easier by means of bronze vessels suspended in the trees in such a way that they clashed together. Priestesses interpreted the messages and supervised the temple. It was dedicated to Zeus, father of the gods, who is shown wearing a wreath of oak leaves on this tetradrachm. On the reverse is his consort. Known in Epeiros as Dione, she seems to have been the goddess of the region's earliest inhabitants. The invading Greeks identified her with Hera and believed her to be the mother of Aphrodite. She is seated in state on her throne and holds a sceptre. Her other hand lifts her stephanos, the large shawl which was the principal garment of Greek women. Great care went into the making of these shawls and poets lovingly described their designs. A bride covered her head with her stephanos on her wedding day and there may be a hint, on this coin, that the oracle unveiled herself when she spoke her secrets.

Pyrrhus' opportunity to establish an empire arose because of warfare in southern Italy. There, the native peoples and the independent Greek cities of Magna Graecia were fighting desperately to avoid being overwhelmed by the Romans. After years of campaigning, the Romans had reached the Adriatic coast of Italy, defeated the Gauls in the north and were preparing to deal with the 'foot' of Italy. The inhabitants of Tarentum (as described in the chapter devoted to this city), sensing the seriousness of the situation, launched a surprise attack on the Roman fleet anchored in their splendid harbour. After this declaration of war, they sent an embassy to Pyrrhus to ask for his help. He was willing to come only on his own terms which were: supreme command of their troops; the right to keep a garrison in Tarentum; and that the city should pay all the costs of the war. Such payment might have been relatively easy for Tarentum, which was a very prosperous trading centre, the currency of which, the 'horsemen', circulated throughout Italy, Sicily and Greece.

In accordance with his agreement, Pyrrhus crossed to Tarentum in 280 BC with 20,000 infantry, 2,000 archers, 500 slingers, 3,000 cavalry and 20 elephants. The latter caused great excitement. They became associated with Pyrrhus to such an extent that some Tarentine coins, struck while he was in Italy, bear a little elephant as a mint-mark (61). Not content with this army, which was quite large by the standards of the time, Pyrrhus used the 'horsemen' to recruit mercenaries from among the Italian tribes. However, the inhabitants of Tarentum refused to enlist. Annoyed at such behaviour on the part of those who had invited him to lead them, Pyrrhus proceeded to treat Tarentum as an occupied city. He argued that, since its citizens had broken their promises, he was no longer bound by his own pledge to leave as soon as the Roman threat had been averted.

The Romans controlled a large part of Italy and found it relatively easy to raise troops, so they soon had two large armies. One kept the Lucanians and Samnites from joining Pyrrhus, while the other advanced against him. They met near Herakleia in a fierce battle. Early in the day, Pyrrhus was unhorsed by a cavalry charge. His troops began to waver when their leader disappeared from view and he was obliged to go bare-headed among them so that they could recognise him and take heart. As Pyrrhus was leading the infantry, his lieutenant, who had put on the general's helmet to divert attention from the real commander, was struck down. Finally, the elephants were sent in. At the sight of them, the raw Roman militia began to panic and suffer heavy casualties. If the Romans had devised a VC, they would have instantly awarded it to the man who prevented their annihilation. He was Gaius Minucius, First Hastate (Principal Spearman – a senior NCO) of the Fourth Legion, who stepped between an elephant's legs and speared it in the stomach. The wounded animal ran amok and created great confusion among Pyrrhus' troops. Taking advantage of the situation, the surviving Romans escaped, leaving about 15,000 of their comrades on the battlefield. Among them was Minucius. 4,000 of Pyrrhus' veterans also lay dead. In numerical terms, he had won the day, but these veterans were irreplaceable, whereas, the Roman militia had many potential recruits.

Three Italian tribes now joined Pyrrhus, but the others would not go over to him. Thus, his position was precarious and he had to act quickly to gain advantage from his victory. Therefore, he opened negotiations, demanding guarantees of freedom for the cities of Magna Graecia and the restoration of their lands to the dispossessed Italian tribes. His ambassador had almost convinced the Senate that they should accept these terms, when a blind and aged member rose to speak. He was the ex-consul Appius Claudius, who had emerged from retirement to proclaim the doctrine that Rome would never consent to negotiate while foreign troops remained on Italian soil – a principle that the Senate adopted and always adhered to as far as Pyrrhus was concerned.

He marched towards Rome and found no welcome in any of the cities he reached. The only friendly cities in Italy were in the south and thither he had to withdraw to spend the winter. At the Saturnalia (the Christmas season to us), he released his prisoners on parole – a chivalrous gesture, made partly because he could scarcely feed them, but they kept their word and did not take up arms again. Meanwhile, the Senate was assembling a large army and, incidentally, ordering the first large coin issues it ever authorised in order to meet the expenses of next season's campaign (228,229).

The two sides met at the battle of Ausculum in the Spring of 279 BC. Once again, after a fierce fight, the elephants (only nineteen in number, thanks to Minucius) won the day. The Romans were driven back and took shelter in their fortified camp. They had suffered 6,000 casualties, twice as many as Pyrrhus' army, but they were ready to fight another day. The hostile confederacy was still in being and, although he held the field of battle, Pyrrhus was obliged to return to Tarentum. The Romans were feeling confident of eventual victory and were prepared to prolong the war in a way which Pyrrhus, who was used to the short campaigns and frequent truces typical of the Greeks, found disconcerting. He recognised his duty to protect his allies but was looking for an excuse to leave Italy, when events seemed to favour him at last.

In Sicily, the Greek cities were threatened by a dangerous Carthaginian advance. The Carthaginians had been struggling for years to control the island and now that its natural leader, Agathokles, ruler of Syracuse, was dead, they seized their chance. Pyrrhus had taken a daughter of Agathokles as his second wife and, to him, the Syracusans offered the crown, on condition that he drove away the Carthaginians. It seemed that an empire was his at last – Epeiros and the Greek cities of Italy and Sicily could be turned into a powerful political unit. However, his enemies realised this, too, and made an alliance against him.

For some time, the Carthaginian fleet prevented him from crossing the straits to aid Syracuse and, when at last he got there, the Romans gradually wore down the resistance of the cities he had left behind. One by one, they surrendered, while Pyrrhus concentrated on securing Sicily. He made use of the facilities in Syracuse to build a fleet and almost succeeded in driving the Carthaginians from the island. However, he soon showed that his military prowess was not matched by statesmanship. Apparently unaware of the fierce determination to preserve their independence shown by the Sicilian cities, Pyrrhus appointed his courtiers to rule them, showed scant respect for local dignitaries and confiscated their property to pay his troops. He may have acquired this oriental approach to kingship while at the Egyptian court, but it was totally unsuited to Sicily (227). Next, he made another mistake. Without finishing off the Carthaginians, Pyrrhus returned to Tarentum to protect his few remaining Italian allies against the Romans. Thereupon, the Sicilians invited back the Carthaginians, in the belief that they could not possibly be worse than Pyrrhus, whom this decision left as a mere adventurer without a kingdom. The extensive Carthaginian coinage for Sicily is described in another chapter.

With the money he had seized from the Treasury of Persephone at Locris – an act of sacrilege, of course – Phyrrhus managed to raise an Italian army, which met the Romans near Beneventum in 276 BC. These inexperienced troops let him down. A division intended to take the Roman flank got lost in a forest during a night march and failed to appear on time. His elephants were panicked into charging the opposite way to that which he planned and his army was scattered. The Romans captured 1,300 prisoners and four elephants, the first seen in Rome. Pyrrhus' treasure was put to good use, financing a splendid aqueduct to bring much-needed water supplies to the growing city. Pyrrhus himself was obliged to return to Epeiros, where he continued a rather hopeless career through several campaigns, finally, meeting the soldier's death that he probably sought, in an insignificant street fight at Argos in 272 BC. In the same year, Tarentum surrendered. Shortly afterwards, the Romans controlled all Italy. It had been a hard struggle, yet they never ceased to honour Pyrrhus as a gallant adversary. Perhaps they, like us, regretted that his sense of decorum made him refrain from putting his portrait on his coins – no one now knows what he looked like.

226 Tetradrachm. Zeus and Dione.   **227** Bronze issued in Syracuse by Pyrrhus. Head of Hercules; Athena.

Romano-Campanian coinage minted by the Romans to finance the campaigns against Pyrrhus, 275–270 BC.
228 Didrachm. Heads of Mars and a horse.   **229** Didrachm. Head of Apollo and horse.

XIX. PERGAMUM

A few miles inland from the western coast of Asia Minor and opposite the island of Lesbos is a natural citadel, the site of Pergamum (Bergama, on modern maps). The city was of ancient foundation and its inhabitants liked to compare it with the great Troy. Its earliest coins, issued about 310 BC, feature the Palladium, the huge wooden statue supposed to confer divine protection on Troy as long as it stood within its walls. There was no Palladium at Pergamum, but the protection of several gods brought remarkable prosperity for a time.

The city was the treasure house of Lysimachos, Alexander's general who obtained Thrace after his leader's death. While fighting Demetrios the Besieger for control of Macedonian territory, Lysimachos left Pergamum in the safe-keeping of the eunuch Philetairos, a court official. For a time, Lysimachos was victorious but, after a few years, he succumbed to another rival for Alexander's empire, Seleukos I, ruler of Syria and the East. In 281 BC, after Lysimachos fell in battle, Philetairos paid homage to Seleukos and was confirmed in his position as governor of Pergamum. He put Seleukos' head on his tetradrachms and, for the reverses, he retained Lysimachos' device of the seated Athena holding Nike, the goddess of victory, crowning the ruler's name. However, Philetairos replaced the name Lysimachos with his own – an indication of his virtual independence. After a successful reign, he was succeeded in 263 BC by his nephew, Eumenes I, who adopted his uncle's portrait for Pergamum's coins and kept the reverses unchanged (230). Eunuch or not, he was given credit for founding the Attalid dynasty, who ruled the city until it came under Roman control (231). For a century and a half, Pergamum prospered, reaching its greatest magnificence in the reign of Eumenes II (197–159 BC). He succeeded in dominating eastern Asia Minor, built or enlarged his city's temples and founded a library intended to surpass that of Alexandria, the most famous in the ancient world. As a result of such activities, Pergamum acquired a reputation for statuary and made the discovery of parchment (originally called *charta Pergamena*).

Not all Pergamum's rulers added to their subjects' happiness. The last of the dynasty, Attalos III, was a cruel tyrant who exterminated many political opponents, causing much hostility. In his more studious moments he wrote treatises on gardening, including the cultivation of poisonous plants that might prove useful to one in his position. On his death-bed, in what was probably a final act of revenge against his ungrateful subjects, he drew up a will leaving his kingdom to Rome (133 BC). This was one of the most valuable legacies in history and was a god-send to the leading Roman politician, Tiberius Gracchus, who used Pergamum's revenues to finance his schemes of social reform, based on the purchase of estates from the rich so that the poor could be granted smallholdings at the republic's expense. Moreover, the feuding Roman politicians now had a most lucrative provincial governorship to tempt players in their game of power politics.

Pergamum became the capital of Roman Asia Minor and its coin types were made standard for the province. These were the cistophoric tetradrachms, soon to become the best-known and most numerous of the coins produced in the eastern Empire– a development which has ensured that they survived in sufficient numbers to be readily available to present-day collectors (232–235). First issued as early as 200 BC by the Attalids, whose standard coins remained the Philetairos types, the cistophoric tetradrachms proved to be an acceptable coinage for a large area. Under Roman rule, they were produced by twelve mints, of which Pergamum was the chief. Consequently, these coins bear a wide variety of city and magistrates' names. (Among the latter is the only numismatic reference to Cicero, who once was pro-consul of Cilicia in Asia Minor.) The name 'cistophoric tetradrachm' is derived from the *cista mystica*, or sacred casket, on the obverse. This object was used in the worship of Dionysos, god of wine, whose temple was among those at Pergamum. The casket contained a serpent, which was released at the climax of the religious ceremony, and it can be seen on the coins emerging from the casket. Serpents were sacred to Dionysos, who, according to legend, had once been obliged to roam the earth in human form and convince mankind of his divinity, introducing them to wine and the frenzy that came over those who first experienced its effects.

On one occasion, he was captured by pirates, who intended to sell him into slavery, but he halted the galley by turning the oars into snakes and causing ivy to entwine itself around the vessel. An ivy wreath surrounds the cista mystica on these tetradrachms and one was also placed on statues of Dionysos. Another object used in his temple is also found on some of these coins. This is the thyrsos, a staff topped by a pine-cone and entwined with ivy or serpents.

Similar to this device is the caduceus, badge of the Royal Army Medical Corps and originally carried by Asklepios (Latin *Aesculapius*) the god of medicine, and patron of doctors. Many cities honoured him, as is scarcely surprising, and Pergamum was among them. The city contained a temple dedicated to him and also a famous medical school. The most renowned of its graduates was Galen, physician to the emperors Marcus Aurelius and Lucius Verus, and author of medical textbooks that were highly regarded until the sixteenth century. Well before his time, Pergamum had issued small bronze coins featuring the head of Asklepios as the obverse and the caduceus as the reverse. The snakes on the cistophoric tetradrachms are probably a reference to medicine as well as wine, for snakes were sacred to both Asklepios and Dionysos. The god of medicine was first worshipped by the Romans when a plague struck their city in 293 BC and they believed that Asklepios had made his appearance in the form of a serpent. The serpent was believed to know the secret of rejuvenation because it could slough its skin and, moreover, snakes sought out medicinal herbs for Asklepios to cure the sick.

At Pergamum, men might find the means of healing their bodies but, according to the author of the Book of Revelation, their souls would be in danger and he warned the city of the wrath to come, for it contained 'Satan's throne'. Towards the end of the first century AD, when he was writing to encourage Christians facing persecution by the Romans, the chief architectural feature of Pergamum was a spectacular temple of Zeus and this is what he may have had in mind. However, Pergamum was the first city to pay divine honours to the Roman emperors and failure to do so was the principal reason why the Christians were put to death. Collectors with a feeling for history will seek the bronze coins issued at Pergamum in the names of Tiberius and his wife Livia. Their busts are found on the obverses and the reverse designs show a temple containing a statue of Augustus – a memento of a crucial time for Christianity and a direct link with the Bible.

230 Tetradrachm, Eumenes I, 263–241 BC. Portrait of Philetairos; Athena holding shield. **231** Tetradrachm, Attalos I, Soter, 241–197 BC. Portrait of Philetairas; Athena crowns his name.

Cistophoric tetradrachms.
232 Pergamum mint, 200–133 BC. **233** Apameia mint, 189–133 BC.

234 Tralles mint, 155–143 BC. 235 Ephesos. *c.* 103 BC.

XX. BITHYNIA

In the valleys along the south-west part of the Black Sea coast lived people whom Herodotus had considered wild and savage. Even the Persians had found them difficult to rule and Alexander had bypassed them. Communications across the ridges of highland were difficult, with the result that Bithynian life retained its fierce independence and distinctive customs for a great many years. Eventually, some of the chieftains grew sufficiently powerful to call themselves kings and mint coins in the best Greek style, though it is very probable that skilled die-cutters were brought in from elsewhere. These minor kings even had their own Era for dating coins. It began in 297 BC, when the otherwise almost unknown Zipoetes officially adopted the title 'King'. His son, Nikomedes I (c 279–255 BC) made himself a force to be reckoned with, by incorporating into his army the invading Gauls, whom we have already briefly encountered as being responsible for the death of Ptolemy Keraunos, the assassin of Seleukos, on the visit to Macedon. Having extended his territory, Nikomedes founded a new capital, the port named Nikomedia after him and now called Izmid. As at Alexandria, immigrants were welcomed and this city rapidly grew to be a great commercial centre.Nikomedes' silver pieces show him as a shrewd, capable man. He chose for the reverses a seated god and goddess to whom we could give the conventional Greek identifications of Ares and Artemis, though they are more probably local deities. Later silver has on it Zeus, crowning the king's name, and this is believed to be an adaptation of a well-known ancient statue, which stood in the impressive temple built at Nikomedia.

The king who gave orders for it was Prusias (236), grandson of Nikomedes and an ally of Philip V of Macedon in his war with the Romans. Consistent with this foreign policy was hospitality for Hannibal, who had been obliged to leave the Seleukid Empire. He was hunted down and forced to commit suicide by the Romans, whose implacable hostility would not let an old man quietly end his days in a comfortable villa with a view of the Black Sea. Connivance at this infringement of convention seems more appropriate to Prusias II, the weak son of his similarly named father. Though allowances should be made for the difficulties of acting independently while under the shadow of Rome, it is difficult to find anything good to say about Prusias II, whom the Greek historian Polybius described as absolutely lacking the qualities expected in a king. His portrait coins (237) show him wearing a winged diadem, presumably implying descent from Perseus, the mythical hero, who was lent a magic helmet, winged sandals and other useful objects by the divine beings who wished to be rid of the Gorgons. Monstrous self-indulgence, and the paranoia that sometimes accompanies it, gave Prusias good reason for suspecting his son of plotting against him. In the ensuing uprising, he met his death at the altar in Zeus' temple.

The son, the second Nikomedes, had for several years been his father's representative in Rome and favoured very pro-Roman policies. He was a welcome ally, whose power and prestige were suitably boosted while, at home, he was a popular ruler. Though Bithynia was obviously a client kingdom, it was permitted to maintain a mint that produced a further series of good portraits of Nikomedes (238,239) and his two successors, who also took his name. Fortunately, all the coins are dated in a continuous series, so we can separate the three kings. They quarrelled with neighbouring Cappadocia and Pontos, though they also managed to grow rich from a thriving trade in agricultural products and slaves. The Romans kept the peace by intermittent diplomatic and military campaigns. On one of the latter, the young Julius Caesar, then a junior officer sent by his commander to the court of Nikomedes IV with a request for the loan of his fleet, secured it in return for services that earned him the scornful nickname 'Queen of Bithynia', which his enemies remembered for the rest of his life. Nikomedes had no legitimate male heir, so he willed his kingdom to Rome. It was probably the best way of securing protection for his subjects.

Prusias I, c. 228–185 BC.
236 Tetradrachm. His portrait and the statue of Zeus.   **237** Tetradrachm,
Prusias II, *c*. 185–149 BC. His portrait with a winged diadem.   **238** Portrait
tetradrachm, Nikomedes II, Epiphanes, 149–128 BC.   **239** Similar
tetradrachm, Nikomedes III, 128–94 BC. Attributed to this reign by the date in
the Bithynian Era.

XXI. PONTOS

The river valleys to the south-east of the Black Sea were, like Bithynia, inhabited by people of non-Greek origins, who maintained their identity under Persian rule. The kings of the area used the royal name, Mithradates, an allusion to their semi-divine ancestry, which involved the god Mithras and the Persian emperors. Their dynastic badge was the star and crescent that had its origin in some ancient religion and the gods used on coins may be the asiatic Mên, Ma and Anaitis rather than the Greek deities they resemble.

Rare and expensive tetradrachms (240) give us portraits of the earlier Pontic kings but, here, attention focuses on the only one whose coinage is readily available to collectors.

This is Mithradates VI (120–63 BC), an extraordinary character, who managed to impose his will on much of Asia Minor, making even the Romans treat him with respect. A legend in his own lifetime, Mithradates had a hazardous boyhood, hiding in the mountains to escape from the Regent, his mother, Laodike. In his late teens, toughened by his way of life, he was able to seize power with the help of Laodike's enemies. She was imprisoned and put to death, a younger son was killed and a daughter taken as wife by Mithradates, who was imitating the Ptolemies through marrying his sister. He then proceeded to live as an oriental despot, generous to his friends but hard-hearted, and even murderous, towards anyone who displeased him. Shrewd and intelligent, speaking several languages, he achieved various diplomatic and military coups, and survived numerous setbacks. By 97 BC, his domination of neighbouring territories had become so formidable that the Romans intervened to force him back to his original frontiers. Determined that this should never be allowed to happen again, Mithradates trained a huge army and equipped himself with the necessary financial resources by minting great quantities of gold and silver coins. They show him as a young god with flowing hair (241,242). Pegasos, on the reverse, is an allusion to descent from Perseus and the wreath that encloses the design relates to Dionysos, whom Mithradates claimed to resemble. In 88 BC, the Bithynians, with Roman support, invaded Pontos and Mithradates struck back hard. He defeated the army and recaptured all the Roman possessions in Asia Minor. The isolated garrisons were easily overcome. Mercenary troops changed sides and the Greek elements welcomed Mithradates everywhere as a deliverer. The flatterers may well have seen in him a new Dionysos – he certainly did not discourage them. Marius Aquillius, the avaricious Roman consul whose personal ambitions provoked the war, was handed over by the citizens of Mytilene on the island of Lesbos and, after being dragged in disgrace from city to city, he was sentenced to an appropriate death by having molten gold poured down his throat. Secret orders were sent out to all city governors that, on a particular day, every resident Roman – man, woman or child – was to be killed and their property confiscated: 80,000 people are said to have perished. Immense sums flowed into the treasury and one result was a large coin issue. Since mints were established in Ephesos and Pergamum, some reverses show a stag in place of Pegasos (243,244). Mithradates' armies crossed into Greece, where he was similarly welcomed. One coin that perpetuates the occasion is the New Style Athenian tetradrachm with his name on it. Thrace, Macedon and several important islands fell under Mithradates' control, though Rhodes held out with its accustomed tenacity. There was even an invitation sent from the Italian cities that resented Roman rule, but he wisely declined it.

Meanwhile, the Senate, faced with the most successful enemy that had appeared for many years was taking counter-measures. The renowned Sulla led an army that drove Mithradates from Greece and obliged him to make peace. He was lucky to keep his kingdom and would not have done so if Sulla had not been anxious about the machinations of rivals for power in Rome. Revenge for the massacre had to be confined to the execution of Mithradates' leading supporters in many cities and a very heavy levy on the others to meet the costs of the campaign.

Relations remained strained for the next few years, while the power struggle for control of Rome continued, allowing Mithradates to restore his armed forces. Hostilities recommenced in earnest when

Nikomedes left Bithynia to the Romans and the prospect of such unwelcome neighbours caused great alarm to Mithradates. He declared war and, once again, there was an anti-Roman rising, involving massacres, though on a much smaller sale. After initial victories, Mithradates was driven to take refuge with King Tigranes of Armenia, only to recover the lost ground when the Roman troops mutinied. Three years later, Pompey crushingly defeated him and obliged Tigranes to surrender. Mithradates, now growing rather old and no longer the man whose appetite for food, wine and women had become proverbial, prepared to have another attempt at regaining power. From his base in the Crimea, he assembled yet another army and made plans to link up with the Thracians, Scythians, Celts and other wild peoples in the Danube region, who would descend in great strength on the Roman possessions.

However, Mithradates, the great hater, was also hated and his supporters deserted in ever-increasing numbers. Eventually, his son Pharnakes informed him that he must die. Characteristically, he retired to his palace, ordered the deaths of his womenfolk – wives, concubines and daughters – and then took poison. When that seemed not to work, he ordered a mercenary to cut off his head. The body was given honourable burial on Pompey's orders, though there was much rejoicing at the death of this implacable enemy, who had met his end in the sixty-eighth year of his life and the fifty-seventh of his reign. Pompey, who was at Jericho when the good news reached him, marched back to Pontos, destroyed all the fortifications and crushed any remaining opposition to Roman rule.

240

240 Tetradrachm, Pharnakes I, 185–159 BC. His portrait and a male deity, possibly Mên.

Mithradates VI, Eupator, the Great, 120–63 BC.
241 Tetradrachm. His portrait and Pegasos.   **242** Bronze coin. His portrait in a helmet; Pegasos.   **243** Tetradrachm. His portrait and a stag.
244 Drachm. Similar.

XXII. CAPPADOCIA

The high, central plateau of Asia Minor was one of the areas fought over by Bithynia, Pontos and Rome. Its kings did their best to maintain their independence, though they scarcely had the resources to do so against a strong enemy. From about 280 BC to the reign of Augustus, they struck silver drachms in large quantities, which make a comparatively inexpensive portrait series, though biographical details are sketchy.

The royal name was Ariarathes, first borne by the satrap who was able to assert his independence from the Seleukid Empire. His successors usually married a Seleukid princess, though it was wise for them to ally with Rome in order to avert conquest by their neighbours, which was always a possibility. Neglect of this strategy and aid given to Antiochos the Great in 188 BC resulted in a huge indemnity having to be paid to Rome. The coins minted for the purpose are dated to the thirty-third year of the reign of Ariarathes IV and are the commonest Cappadocian coins (245). His son (246) died fighting for the Romans against Aristonikos, a pretender to the throne of Pergamum. His queen, Nysa, is reputed to have done away with five sons (not necessarily her own, for it was customary for a harem to be maintained) in order to secure her position as regent for the young Ariarathes VI (247). Scarcely had he reached manhood, when he was murdered by an ambitious noble and the throne passed to his infant son (248). His mother, the widowed queen Laodike, was daughter of Mithradates VI of Pontos and soon became the wife of Nikomedes III of Bithynia, who took control of Cappadocia, driving out the boy king. Mithradates intervened, restored him to the throne and, later, killed him to make way for his own son, who continued the custom of calling himself Ariarathes (the ninth, in this case). Disliked by his subjects, he was deposed in 89 BC by the Romans fighting against his father. Some rare tetradrachms modelled on those minted in such large quantities for Mithradates show the son's portrait backed by Pegasos, a break with tradition, for almost all Cappadocian coins have Athena on their reverses. This Ariarathes died during the first Mithradatic War and was replaced by one of the nobility chosen by his peers. He was called Ariobarzanes and assumed the title Philoromaios, Friend of the Romans (249). They stood by him, and restored him to the throne at least six times after he was driven from his kingdom by Mithradates or Tigranes of Armenia, or both, acting together. In 63 BC, Pompey obliged him to abdicate in favour of a son who publicly protested his reluctance to take such a troubled crown (or rather, a diadem). He took his father's name and, after a reign of about ten years, was murdered in a palace coup organised by the Parthians. His eldest son (250) met a similar fate because he refused to help Cassius in the civil war following Caesar's death. A second son was executed by Mark Antony for backing the other side. The replacement was Archelaus (251), whose status apparently depended on his position as high priest at the principal temple of the Mother Goddess, Ma, at Coinana. Though he remained faithful to Antony, Archelaus was later confirmed in his position by Augustus and given more territory to administer. He reigned for over fifty years, outliving Augustus himself. When he died, Tiberius replaced him with a governor in keeping with the new status he gave Cappadocia, which ceased to be a client kingdom and became a Roman province.

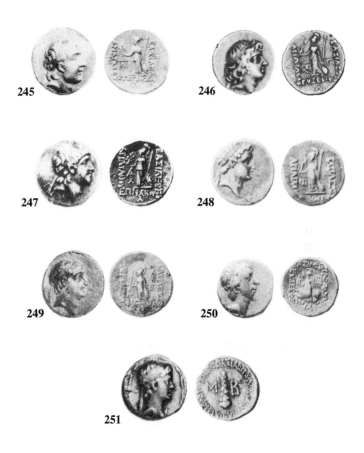

Drachms with portraits of the Cappadocian kings and Athena on the reverses.
245 Ariarathes IV, Eusebes, 220–163 BC. Year 33.   **246** Ariarathes V,
Eusebes Philopater, 163–130 BC.   **247** Ariarathes VI, Epiphanes
Philopater, 130–116 BC.   **248** Ariarathes VII, Philometer, 116–101 BC.
249 Ariobarzanes I, Philoromaios, 95–63 BC.
250 Ariobarzanes III, Eusebes Philoromaios, 52–42 BC.
251 Archelaus Philopatris Ktistes, 36 BC–AD 17. Reverse; Club.

XXIII. ARMENIA

This was another mountainous area that proved difficult for the Persians to rule. It was situated in the southern Caucasus, the extreme east of Asia Minor and, depending on the fortunes of war, extended at times as far as the headwaters of the Tigris and Euphrates. We have a few bronze coins minted by earlier kings, but the only Armenian ruler likely to appeal to modern collectors is Tigranes II, 'the Great', (c. 97–56 BC).

He had been brought up as a hostage at the Parthian court, where he gained the friendship of the king, who restored him to his own country as a long-term ally. However, Tigranes was well able to look after his own interests and, as soon as a disputed succession in Parthia provided the opportunity, he started extending his kingdom eastwards and, also, into the Caucasus. He made an ally of Mithradates of Pontos and married his daughter. By this time, Tigranes was beginning to call himself 'King of Kings' and to be seen in public wearing purple robes and a high tiara, which is his head-dress on coins (252). The image of an oriental potentate, successor to the Persian Emperors, was completed by his having numerous slaves, who attended him wherever he went. Though it is easy to dismiss this as affectation, the people in the Seleukid Empire were so impressed that, in 83 BC, they invited Tigranes to take the throne and give them good government, something they could not expect from the exasperatingly selfish Seleukids, whose energies were entirely taken up with opposing each other. Tigranes had little difficulty in taking over most of the Seleukid territory and his next step was to turn against Cappadocia, hoping to add that to his kingdom but, by becoming so powerful, he aroused the apprehensions of the Romans.

Meanwhile, he had used the mints of Antioch and Damascus to provide himself with a silver coinage. As mentioned previously, he is unmistakable, in an Armenian tiara with his face clean-shaven in the Greek fashion, in contrast to the Parthians who wore long beards. The reverse design shows the personifications of one or other of these cities. The inhabitants were probably glad to submit to Tigranes, who, as far as we know, ruled quite well for fourteen years, until the Romans obliged Mithradates to seek refuge with him and then proceeded to treat him as a hostile power. They demanded that he hand back Syria to the young Seleukids, who had taken refuge in Rome. Lucullus led an army into Mesopotamia, eventually capturing Tigranocerta, the new capital Tigranes had built. The king was pursued into Armenia, but guerilla warfare and the cold winter led Lucullus' troops to declare they would go no further, so he had to withdraw. His position became worse when Mithradates led successful attacks on the Roman forces elsewhere in Asia Minor. Tigranes was saved for a while, but the arrival of Pompey, who made Syria a Roman province and forced Mithradates to escape to the Crimea, marked the end of his dominance. Without fighting a battle, he made peace, handing over to the Romans all his territories except Armenia, and became a client king. His decision may have been arrived at through realism or faint-heartedness. Nevertheless, it permitted another generation of Armenian kings to occupy the throne before the Romans turned the kingdom into a province of their expanding empire.

Other post-Alexandrine kingdoms are Thrace, Parthia, Bactria and those in northern India. All will be found in later chapters.

252

252 Tigranes II, 83–69 BC. His portrait wearing an Armenian tiara; the Tyche of Antioch with the river-god Orontes swimming.

THE COINAGE OF THE NON-GREEK AREAS

'Greek' coins were minted in a great many places that were affected by Hellenisation. This term implies the veneer of Greek culture that concealed the non-hellenic origins of the rulers and upper classes, in states where the native people spoke a different language, originated from a different part of the world, worshipped their own gods and conducted their affairs with scant regard for what happened on the Greek mainland. We have already seen that dynasties of Macedonian origin provided Egypt and Asia Minor with coinage. The people who used it may well have been unable to understand what the inscriptions meant though, on the other hand, Greek was the lingua franca of the Eastern Mediterranean world, as the travels of St Paul clearly demonstrate. It would certainly be possible to call the Ptolemaic and Seleukid empires 'non-Greek areas', Even if their coins give a contrary impression. However, the groups of 'Greek' coins surveyed in this section emanate from territories that were not dominated by Greek-speaking conquerors and where there was no need to pretend to be part of the greater Greek community. Commercial needs obliged the authorities to mint currencies that were, to a greater or lesser extent, similar to what was already in circulation, though the cultural influences behind them were very different.

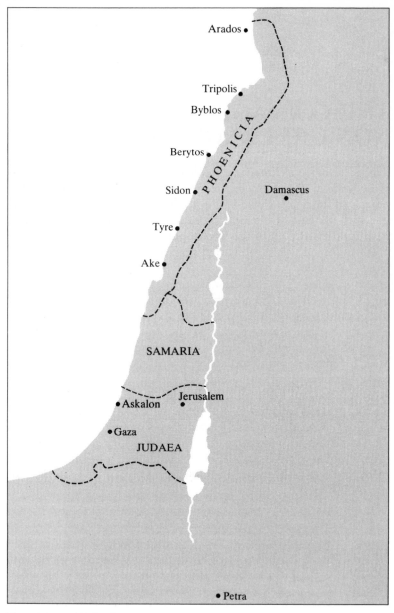

Phoenicia and Palestine

XXIV. THE PHOENICIANS

The Phoenicians inhabited part of Syria and the Holy Land, a coastal strip about 192 km (120 miles) long and 32 km (20 miles) wide between the sea and the mountains, whence they got timber for their ships. The Bible classes them among the Canaanites, ie the tribes established there before the Israelites arrived. Their cities were Tyre, Sidon, Berytos, Tripolis and Byblos. The greatest was Tyre, which owed its commanding position to its off-shore island site. Being the most southerly Phoenician city, Tyre made contact with the Israelites and we find Hiram, its king, supplying Solomon with materials for his temple, a merchant fleet manned by Phoenician crews and the luxuries that characterised his reign. Many years later, King Ahab married a Tyrian princess who brought with her the worship of Baal. His wife was, of course, Jezebel, whose career and sticky end are recounted in the saga of Elijah.

From such references, it becomes clear that the Phoenicians were pioneer traders, whose hey-day was in the remote centuries before 700 BC, when they had a monopoly of Mediterranean trade. At various times, they founded colonies in North Africa, Sicily, Sardinia, the Balearics and Spain. Here, Gades (Cadiz) was beyond the Pillars of Hercules on the Atlantic coast, a region unknown to the Greeks. The Greek historian, Herodotos, records the story of a Phoenician expedition that circumnavigated Africa, starting from the Red Sea and returning through the Straits of Gibraltar. It took three years, mainly because the crews had to beach their ships, sow crops and wait until harvest time. Herodotos is sceptical about the whole thing and gives as his reason the very details that confirm the truth of the story as far as we are concerned. When the ships set out, the sun was on their left, but later it was on their right – ie it shone from the south at first as it always does in the northern hemisphere but, after they crossed the equator, it appeared to the north of them. Sea power, commercial enterprise, monopolies of distant markets and precious metals from the Spanish mines, made the Phoenicians very prosperous and they are especially remembered for their metalwork, glass and dye – the famous Tyrian purple, made from shellfish. Unlike their contemporaries, they were not empire builders – that is, with the exception of Carthage, which far outgrew its mother city. Such Phoenician colonies as were established were intended as trading posts. There were few close links between the Phoenician cities, each of which had its own king and did not necessarily cooperate with its neighbours. An instance of their attitudes is provided in the foundation of Tripolis (262) by Tyre, Sidon and Arados. So that none should claim greater honour, the new town was built in three separate sections, a little apart from each other, each with its own walls.

The Phoenician coins of greatest appeal to collectors were issued in the fifth and fourth centuries BC, when the cities paid allegiance to the Persian Empire. They are thick silver pieces with a pronounced oriental look about them. Nearly all feature a galley (253–259), a warship, to remind everyone of Phoenician sea-power, and there are various other political and religious designs. For example, Sidon portrayed the King of Persia killing a lion with his dagger (254) and, on another coin, riding in his chariot, while the Egyptian pharaoh follows on foot as a humble attendant (255). Tyre shows its god Melkart riding a hippocamp (256) (a mythological creature, half horse, half fish, connected, of course, with the concept of sea-power) and, on the reverse, is the owl of Athena holding under its wing the crook and flail – symbols of Egyptian kingship (257). The hippocamp appears on the coins of Byblos (258), also, while on those of Arados there is a fish-tailed bearded god, an oriental triton.

This distinctive coinage was ended by the conquests of Alexander the Great. After his defeat of the Persian Emperor at Issus, all the Phoenician cities submitted to him, except for Tyre, the obstinacy of which was ill-judged. Alexander proceeded to make an example of her, thus discouraging other cities from opposing him. Tyre was besieged and, after long, heroic resistance, the city was captured, the surviving defenders slain and the women and children sold into slavery. The cities that had surrendered, Sidon, Ake, Arados and Byblos, became mint towns for Alexander, striking the silver pieces that show Hercules in his lion's skin and the enthroned Zeus on the reverse. Sidon's coins can often be distinguished by the letter Σ under Zeus' throne and, sometimes, they have a date letter.

After Alexander's death, the Seleukid dynasty in Asia Minor and the Ptolemies in Egypt struggled for control of Phoenicia. As a result, we have third-century tetradrachms of the standard Egyptian type, showing the head of Ptolemy and an eagle on the reverse, accompanied by the first letters of Sidon and Tyre (which had been rebuilt). This city was recovered by Antiochos the Great and, in the second century BC, he and his successors minted there, producing tetradrachms bearing excellent portraits of themselves (260,261). All dated their coins in the Seleukid era, which began in 312 BC when Seleukos I captured Babylon (266). The commonest and best-publicised Tyrian coins are the tetradrachms, sometimes called shekels, issued during the first centuries BC and AD (263–265). Common in the Holy Land at the time of Jesus' ministry, they are said to be the coins referred to as 'the thirty pieces of silver'. This identification is largely supposition but, if they really were paid to the betrayer of Christ, it would be appropriate. The god on the obverses appears to be a very virile Hercules, but is, in fact, a hellenised version of Melkart who, centuries before, was Baal – a Hebrew generic term for pagan deities – in whose name Jezebel tried to exterminate the Jewish religion. These shekels have an eagle on the reverse. After Pompey's conquest of Asia Minor in 64 BC (which incidentally is the beginning of the Pompeian era, by which coins of some cities in the area are dated), the eagle should be considered to be Roman rather than Egyptian. Thus, it would be symbolic of the authorities who put Jesus to death. These shekels were the last substantial coinage issued by the Phoenician cities for, as previously explained, it was the custom in the Roman Empire that the central mints struck gold and silver and the provincial cities could issue only bronze as essential small change.

253 Arados. ¹/₁₂ stater, 400–350 BC. Bearded deity and galley. **254** Sidon.
Shekel, *c*. 425 BC. Galley in front of the city walls; the king killing a lion.
255 4-shekel piece, fourth century BC. Galley; king in his chariot.
256 Tyre. Double shekel, 400–360 BC. Melkart riding a hippocamp;
owl with the crook and flail of Egypt. **257** Double shekel, *c*. 425 BC.
Dolphin over the waves; the owl incuse. **258** Byblos. Double shekel,
fourth century BC. Galley manned by three warriors; hippocamp beneath
it; lion attacking a bull. **259** Sidon. Half-shekel, *c*. 400 BC. Galley with
sails; an archer.

260 Tetradrachm, Demetrios II. Minted at Tyre. **261** Tetradrachm, Antiochos VII. Minted at Sidon. **262** Tetradrachm, first century BC. Minted at Tripolis. Heads of the Dioskouroi; Tyche of the city. **263** Tetradrachm, 107–106 BC. LK = Year 20 of Tyre's independence from the Seleukids. Melkart and eagle.

264

265

266

264 A similar coin. 57–56 BC. **265** Half-shekel, AD 36–37. **266** Arados. Tetradrachm, date OMP = 111 BC. Tyche of the city and Nike.

XXV. CARTHAGE

Britain's first contacts with the classical world are usually said to have been established through Carthaginian merchants, who came in search of tin, and such a venture would certainly have been in keeping with the traditions of the second-largest city of the ancient world. Founded in the ninth century BC, a hundred years earlier than Rome, Carthage began her existence as an outpost of the Phoenician port of Tyre. She quickly outgrew the parent city and began to dominate a large part of the southern and western Mediterranean. Her strategic position on the North African coast opposite Sicily enabled her to control the straits: she subjugated the peaceful inhabitants of what were then the great grain-growing areas along the North African coast and colonised southern Spain and parts of Sicily. The Carthaginians' Semitic origins and customs made them obnoxious to the Greeks and Romans, who deplored their oppressive government, harsh justice and, above all else, their practice of sacrificing children to the god Moloch and his consort Tanit. Also offensive by Greek standards was the excessive devotion paid by the Carthaginians to commerce. If families became rich, they scarcely needed further entitlement to honour and power in the city. Wealth also enabled the citizens to defend themselves, for they preferred to employ mercenaries instead of serving in a citizen militia, such as was normally found in Greek cities. Some guide to the resources available can be obtained from Strabo's statement that, at the time of her destruction in the Third Punic War against Rome, Carthage contained 700,000 people. Even when allowances have been made for the exaggeration to which ancient authors are notoriously prone, we still have a description of a commercial centre of prodigious size, built upon the twin foundations of agricultural wealth and its merchants' galleys.

For many years, Carthaginian goods must have been bartered – a deduction based on the fact that the city had no early coinage. Eventually, Carthage was obliged to produce coins but these were not primarily for trade: they were to pay mercenaries fighting in Sicily. Some of the many prosperous cities on the island were under Carthaginian control and others owed allegiance to Syracuse, her great rival for control of Mediterranean commerce until both were eclipsed by Rome. The first round of the conquest between the two cities was fought in 480 BC, when the Carthaginians launched a great invasion of Sicily, where they were heavily defeated at the battle of Himera and their campaign collapsed. The occasion was marked by the issue of the famous dekadrachms, featuring a victorious four-horse chariot with Nike, goddess of victory, flying above it. These were struck by order of Gelon, tyrant (as the ruler was called) of Syracuse, from the captured silver originally intended to pay the Carthaginian army, which, if it was paid off at all, was paid in bullion, because there was still no Carthaginian currency.

The first Carthaginian coins were produced during the next invasion of Sicily. This time (in 409 BC), the invaders were much more successful and, among other triumphs, utterly destroyed the town of Himera to avenge their officers' grandfathers. The rank and file, mercenaries of many nations, must have been accustomed to payment in coin for, at this date, every city of any consequence was striking its own currency. The Carthaginians followed suit and struck gold and silver for their men. The gold bears an uncertain female head and a horse on the reverse. The silver (267) depicts the horse being crowned by Nike and, on the reverse, is a date palm. Some of these coins bear Phoenician inscriptions, New City of Carthage and The Camp, leaving no doubt concerning their purpose (268,269).Within a few years, more coins made their appearance. They had the head of Arethusa copied from the superb Syracusan tetradrachms engraved by Euainetos at the orders of Dionysos, the tyrant of the period. On the reverses, instead of the chariot of the originals, is the horse or horse's head with palm tree (270). Once more, the Phoenician inscriptions tell their tale. The Carthaginians had imitated Dionysos and he promptly proceeded to imitate his imitators, by producing similar coins. These are of better style, for he had in his employ some of the finest engravers of the ancient world and, if doubt remains when comparing specimens, his coins can be distinguished by the absence of any inscriptions. Dionysos' coins induced whole units of the Carthaginian army to desert and, after the invaders left Sicily, the two almost-identical currencies continued to circulate for many years. Consequently, they are more readily available to collectors than the first Carthaginian issues (or Siculo-Punic coins as they are called). Later still, in the fourth century BC, the Carthaginians in Sicily became familiar with the plentiful tetradrachms of Alexander the Great, which were spreading westwards. Once again, they were provided with an imitative coinage: tetradrachms with an obverse head of Hercules, similar to Alexander's, and the horse's head for the reverse, instead of the seated Zeus (271).

In about 300 BC, Carthage at last acknowledged the increased sophistication of world trade and produced a regular coinage. Its weight standard was Ptolemaic and, thus, she encouraged the creation of a single currency area stretching from Cyprus, through the Holy Land, to Egypt and, thence, along the north African coast as far as the Carthaginian colonies in Spain. All the Carthaginian coins, gold, silver and bronze, feature the familiar horse, sometimes accompanied by a palm tree on the reverse, and have as the obverse a head of Tanit or Persephone (272–274). This goddess, also known as Kore or Proserpina, controlled the earth's fertility. According to legend, she spent six months of the year on the surface of the earth and six months in the underworld, whence she was recalled with the aid of sacrifices, such as were carried to horrifying lengths at Carthage. Persephone is usually depicted wearing a wreath of corn ears, together with elaborate earrings and a necklace. Many of the coins that bear her portrait were made from silver produced by the Spanish mines developed by the Carthaginians in the third century BC. This was the century of the Punic Wars which ruined Carthage. In the first (265–242 BC), she lost Sicily to Rome and, in the second (218–201 BC), the famous Hannibal ravaged Italy, only to be defeated in the end. Naturally, his fourteen-year campaign there has left a numismatic record. However, we lack coins bearing his name or portrait, and most collectors will be content to leave the serious specialist to distinguish Hannibal's imitations from the Roman Janus-head silver pieces or to read his influence into the issues of the Bruttians, his chief Italian allies. After Hannibal's defeat, Carthage retained but a shadow of her former greatness, and the crudity of her silver and bronze indicates the fact. The same coinage types were issued until 146 BC, when the Roman Senate resolved to destroy Carthage forever. Despite her weakened state, she put up heroic resistance, which all her citizens must have known was hopeless from the start. Defeat was inevitable and the work of destruction was completed by levelling the site and ploughing salt into the ground, to the accompaniment of a solemn curse on any who tried to rebuild there. Nevertheless, the Romans eventually resettled the site themselves, for the great double harbour (now silted up) and the fertile grain-lands were too valuable to leave unoccupied. As Colonia Carthago, the new city grew to be, once again, the largest city in north Africa, until it was destroyed by the Arabs in AD 698. Roman Carthage issued a few bronzes as early as the reign of Tiberius and, in the later empire, became a mint town. Even so, these coins are poor specimens compared with the products of the independent and prosperous Carthage, the golden age of which occurred before she had any coins at all and of which the new lease of life was anticlimactic.

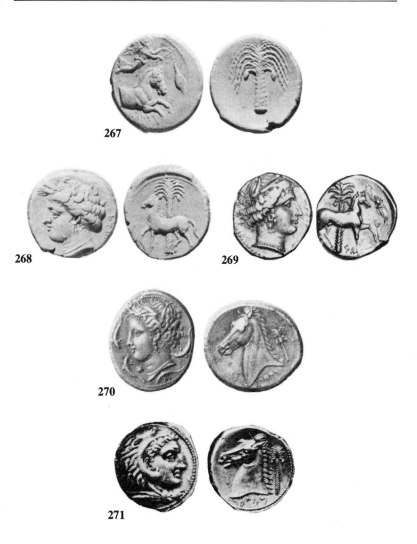

267 Tetradrachm, late fifth century BC. Half-horse crowned by Nike; barleycorn; palm tree with dates. **268** Tetradrachm, mid-fourth century BC. Female head wreathed with corn; horse and date-palm. **269** Similar tetradrachm. Nike crowning horse. **270** Tetradrachm, 350–325 BC. Head of Arethusa or Tanit; horse's head and palm. **271** Tetradrachm, 325–300 BC. Heads of Hercules and a horse; palm tree.

272 Electrum stater, 310–290 BC. Tanit and horse.
273 ¼ stater, 221–202 BC. Similar designs.
274 Large bronze, third century BC. Tanit, horse and palm tree.

XXVI. JEWISH COINS

The Jews have always been distinguished from other peoples by their faith. For thousands of years, it has enabled them to survive against countless oppressors, from the Pharaoh to the Führer. Only recently, has a Jewish state been established and, for most of their long history, the Jews have been a subject people. Recent Israeli coin issues confirm the fact that political independence is essential if the Jews (or any other nation) are to have their own coinage. In ancient times, the Jews had sufficient independence only in the first and second centuries BC and AD, and we shall survey the coinage of this period here.

The series began in 138 BC, when the High Priest, Simon Maccabeus, received permission from Antiochos VII, the Seleukid King of Syria, 'to coin money for the country with thine own stamp' (I Maccabees 15:6). At the time, the Jews were enjoying a certain amount of freedom, which had been won in a bitter war against an earlier Syrian monarch, Antiochos IV (175–164 BC), whose divine pretensions and hellenising policies had provoked a revolt among the Jews. They had been forbidden to worship, to observe the Sabbath, circumcise their children or even to possess a copy of the Scriptures. Hellenisation entailed forcible acceptance of Greek customs, involving alien practices, ranging from the public nudity at baths and athletic contests to idol worship. Antiochos chose the title 'Epiphanes', which meant 'God Manifest', and he saw himself as the incarnation of one of the classical deities that he expected his subjects (of whom the Jews were a small minority) to venerate. Most inhabitants of the Seleukid Kingdom humoured him, but he met bitter resistance in the Holy Land. Led by the family known to us as the Maccabees, the Jews conducted a prolonged guerrilla war, which ended in the establishment of a semi-autonomous government headed by the High Priest. This Jewish state was not strong enough to throw off Seleukid

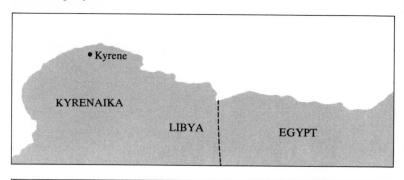

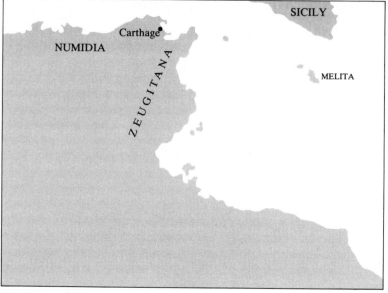

Carthage and Kyrene

rule completely and token tribute was paid. However, most of Antiochos Epiphanes' successors were content to remain in the capital (Antioch) and allow the Jews to control their own domestic affairs.

As one would expect, the earliest coins issued under the authority of the Jewish High Priests bore no royal portraits and made no reference to classical deities. Such themes would have been totally unacceptable on religious grounds and the Jews never portrayed their own god. The second commandment prohibited the manufacture of idols and, to the more scrupulous, this included any representations of human beings or animals. Consequently, the designs for coins had to be unexception-able – a palm, flower, anchor or cornucopia, for instance – and such devices were usually subordinated to the inscriptions. All the coins of the high-priestly series were intended for local use and were insignificant bronze pieces. In this instance, the Seleukids seem to have followed a policy similar to that of the Roman Emperors, who centralised the issue of gold and silver, and allowed provincial mints to strike only in base metals. The best known Jewish coins from this period (138–37 BC) are those issued by Alexander Jannaeus (103–76 BC). The obverse shows an anchor and the reverse a flower, each surrounded by an inscription. At first, they were about the size of a farthing but, as they were imitated by generations of workmen, they became smaller, more irregular and badly struck. Eventually, these misshapen pieces of metal lost what little artistic merit the original design had possessed and the inscriptions became debased into meaninglessness (276,277). However, they will always retain interest for numismatists because these (or, perhaps, the small bronzes of the first century AD) are the 'widow's mites' so aptly described by Jesus, when he contrasted her devout poverty with the lavish gold and silver donations given to the Temple by the men of affluence but shallow faith.

In 37 BC, as a result of the exploits of Mark Antony, the Jews found themselves under Roman rule. The Romans sometimes entrusted outlying provinces to client kings, who were supposed to enjoy public support while remaining loyal to the Emperor. Their choice for King of the Jews was Herod, known to history as 'the Great'. He ruled from 37 to 4 BC and kept a firm grip on his turbulent subjects, who could never fully accept him because of his Idumean (Arab) blood. Although he rebuilt the Temple, the Jews were not deceived by his nominal conformity to their religion. They realised that Herod was a pagan and a hellenist, and that his first priority was to retain Roman friendship. His taxes and fortress-building placed heavy burdens on his people and, as he grew older, his suspicions of secret enemies reached the level of insanity indicated by the story of the murder of the children born at the same time as Jesus. Herod's heirs, also, feature in the Bible. Herod Antipas (4 BC–AD 40) ordered the execution of John the Baptist and interrogated Jesus. Herod Agrippa I (AD 37–44) imprisoned Peter, executed James and met a horrible death caused by intestinal worms which, in the opinion of the author of *Acts*, were sent as divine retribution. Finally, there was Herod Agrippa II (AD 48–100), before whom Paul was tried. The powers and territory administered by the members of the Herodian dynasty varied according to the vicissitudes of fortune and of Roman policy. Thus, the titles used on their coins indicate their status. Herod the Great called himself 'King' (Basileus) (278) but Herod Antipas was only 'Tetrarch', ruler of the fourth part of his predecessor's kingdom (279). Herodian coins followed the pattern of the earlier Jewish issues – small coppers with simple devices (a bunch of grapes, ears of barley or a ceremonial umbrella) and an inscription which included 'Herod' or 'Agrippa' in Greek letters (280).

At the same time as this coinage was being produced, another similar one circulated alongside it. This was authorised by the Procurators of Judaea, Roman officials responsible for the administration of Jerusalem and its surrounding district, the most troublesome part of the Holy Land. In any other part of the Roman Empire, the official coinage would incorporate a portrait of the ruling emperor, but this would not be suitable for Jerusalem. At the entrance to its Temple sat the money changers who ensured that no coin bearing Caesar's head (a 'graven image' and, moreover, the portrait of someone to whom divine honours were often offered) should be brought into the building and, thus, defile it. Consequently, the Procurators respected Jewish feelings and saw to it that their coins followed the acceptable pattern. They featured some unexceptionable device with the emperor's name in abbreviated form and, sometimes, his regnal year. Among the insignificant little coins (281–284), collectors must prize those of Pontius Pilate who, of course, condemned Jesus to death. The traditional date of the crucifixion is AD 30. Thus, coins bearing the name of Tiberius and the letters IΣ are particularly desirable. IΣ are the Greek numerals 16, ie the sixteenth year of the reign of Tiberius, which we would refer to as AD 29/30. Unfortunately for numismatists, neither Pilate, nor any of the Procurators, put their own names on their coins: they were not senior enough to have the authority to do so.

Florus, the last of the Procurators, carried oppression to extremes and plundered the Temple treasury. At this, the Jews rose in open rebellion (AD 66). Most of Judaea was taken over: some small towns inhabited by emperor-worshipping gentiles were burned and hope of establishing a new Zion possessed the insurgents. However, their optimism was ill-founded. The Jews could not make up in courage what they lacked in numbers and resources. 60,000 legionaries, under the command of Vespasian, soon appeared on the scene and the rebellion was doomed. To mark their independence the Jews had issued their own coins. The small coppers were continued (285). New designs for them featured an amphora and the year of the new era (years 1–5). For the reverse, a vine leaf was chosen and around it was written in Hebrew 'The Deliverence of Israel'. Collectors can acquire these pieces fairly cheaply, but the silver shekels of the Jewish Revolt cost hundreds of pounds (286,287). On their obverse is a sacred chalice and, on the reverse, a three-budded lily. The significance of these symbols is obscure, but the inscriptions 'Shekel of Israel' and 'Jerusalem the Holy' leave us in no doubt concerning the aspirations of the Jewish leaders. Faced with Roman military might, Jerusalem endured a five-month siege. During it, Vespasian left to be installed Emperor at Rome. Meanwhile his son, Titus, completed the conquest of the Holy Land. Thousands of Jews were killed or enslaved and, inexorably, the legions closed in on their last stronghold near the Dead Sea. It was the hill-top fortress of Masada, the precipitous slopes of which made it almost impregnable. Starvation slowly weakened the defenders and the Romans spent months building a great ramp up which they could climb to enter. When all was lost, the Jewish survivors burnt their possessions and then drew lots. The twelve men selected killed first their companions and then each other, the last falling on his own sword. Next morning, the besiegers entered a silent fortress, marvelling at the resolution of those who preferred death to submission. Masada has been recently excavated. Among the finds were a number of shekels lying where they had been tossed on that fateful night in AD 73. Masada can be found on a modern Israeli commemorative coin, for it has become a symbol of heroic resistance. Recruits to the Israeli forces are taken there to be sworn in. Their courage is expected to be as great as that shown by their ancestors.

Following Roman tradition, Vespasian and Titus commemorated their victories by issuing coins (294). Their designs vary. The commonest shows a Jewess seated in the attitude of mourning under a palm tree. The simple but expressive legend reads Judaea Capta. The Jews had been defeated, but they still had the will to resist. Two generations later, in AD 132, they rose again. Led by Simon Bar-Kochba, a mysterious figure whose name, 'Son of a Star', serves to disguise his true identity, the rebels occupied Jerusalem and established strongholds in remote areas. A few of these mountain caves served as hiding-places for the Dead Sea Scrolls. Somewhere else, coins were minted. Their designers chose the vine-leaf and chalice again, also using other religious symbols. Some dies were struck on Roman denarii, satisfactorily obliterating Caesar's image (288–292). Larger coins bear Simon's name and a star. The most impressive (and the most expensive) of all coins from the Second Revolt are the shekels (293). Their obverse features a building, probably the 'Screen of the Tabernacle' and, on the reverse, is a bunch of twigs, the lulab used in the ritual of the Feast of the Tabernacles. Their inscription 'Deliverence of Jerusalem' refers to a brief period of success. Hadrian, the emperor of the time, a firm, efficient soldier and administrator, overcame the rebellion comparatively easily. He razed Jerusalem to the ground (AD 135) and refounded it, a few years later, with a new street-plan and a new pagan name, *Aelia Capitolina*. A large commemorative bronze coin shows him with an ox-team, ploughing the symbolic first furrows of the new settlement. Another bearing its name shows the deities Jupiter, Juno and Minerva in the Temple of Jupiter Capitolinus, which stood in the centre of Rome. Nothing now remains of Herodian Jerusalem, but the massive wall of the Jewish Temple, the 'Wailing Wall', too strongly built for Titus, Hadrian or anyone else to destroy, still stands in witness to Jewish resolution. No one can possess the Wailing Wall, but many coin collectors have the opportunity to acquire specimens of the ancient Jewish coins – a series as evocative as anyone could wish.

Small bronze coins, sometimes called prutahs.
275 Issued by Alexander Jannaeus 103–76 BC. Anchor and wheel (or flower). **276** Another example, more debased. **277** Another. John Hyrcanus II, 67–40 BC. Cornucopiae and inscription. **278** Herod I, the Great, 37–4 BC. Caduceus between cornucopiae; Hebrew legend.
279 Herod Antipas, 4 BC–AD 39. Crossed cornucopiae and sacred candlestick. **280** Herod Agrippa I, AD 37–44. Ritual umbrella and three ears of barley.

Coins of the Procurators of Judaea
281 Pontius Pilate, AD 26–36. Three ears of barley bound together; sacred vessel. **282** Antonius Felix, AD 52–60. Crossed palms and Greek inscriptions. **283** Palm tree and crossed shields. **284** Palm branch and inscription.

285 Bronze of the First Revolt, AD 66–70. Amphora and vine leaf.
286 Shekel of the First Revolt, Year 2. Chalice and lily.   **287** Half-shekel,
Year 3.   **288** Denarius of the Second Revolt, AD 132–135. Vine leaf and an
ewer.   **289** Similar coin. Vine leaf and lyre.   **290** Similar coin. Inscription
and ewer.   **291** Inscription and lyre.

292 Bronze coin. Palm tree and vine leaf.   **293** Shekel. Façade of the temple; star; lulab.   **294** Sestertius of Vespasian commemorating the suppression of the First Revolt.

XXVII. THE ETRUSCANS AND BRUTTIANS

Before the Romans became totally dominant, there were several non-Greek peoples in Italy. Not much reliable information is available about any of them, though two have been chosen to serve as examples in this chapter.

First we have the Etruscans. Their origins, history and fate are obscure, though a great many antiquities from their tombs appear on the market. Tomb robbers, using television equipment to see inside the underground caves excavated by the Etruscans to hold the dead and their possessions, have developed the plunder of archaeological sites into a fine art and present a difficult problem to the Italian authorities. Difficulties of another kind are emerging, as supposed Etruscan objects are subjected to dating tests based on radioactivity. Even some of the prized exhibits in our great museums are proving to be fakes. So, in spite of the efforts of many scholars, we are not very much nearer an understanding of the Etruscans. Their language has yet to be translated, their alphabet is dubious and such historical records as we have were the work of the Roman writers who had little real understanding or love for the Etruscans.

One reason for this attitude was the belief, possibly true, that the ancient kings of Rome, expelled for their dictatorial policies to make way for the Republic, had been Etruscans. Another factor was the tendency to ascribe views and habits considered superstitious or decadent to Etruscan influence. The Latin authors accepted the statements of the Greek historian Theopompus, who wrote in the fourth century BC. He said that the Etruscans had their women in common, and gave plenty of details about their dress and habits, even to the fact that mothers did not know who were the fathers of their children, so the children were brought up communally.

Elaborating on this sort of information, writers such as Horace dwelt on the supposed ability of the Etruscans to live especially well. Details of their dinner parties are lovingly preserved. We are told about the dishes, the music, the wine, the dancing girls and so on. Even those modern scholars who are inclined to be sceptical are intrigued by the numerous sarcophagi that depict couples reclining together on couches. Their clothes are elaborate and, in the cases where the paint survives, were brightly coloured – an expensive luxury in the ancient world. Another unusual aspect of Etruscan life is the position of women, who were treated on equal terms with men. They ate and drank together, shared family responsibilities and seem to have formed what we would call good companionate marriages. No wonder historians have long been intrigued by these people and there are a great many theories about them, few of which have much to support them, apart from ingenuity.

By the time the use of coinage became general in Italy, the Etruscan state had passed its peak. Like other shadowy peoples, such as the Umbrians, Latins and Sabines, they were slowly yielding to Roman domination. Rome, of course, was in the process of expanding from a collection of villages on seven hills, to world domination. The Etruscan territory was called Etruria and is now Tuscany. It lay north of Rome and stretched between the Apennines and the coast. The principal port, Populonia, is believed to have been the mint town and was also a base for privateers, though in this, as in much else, the Etruscans received more than their fair share of condemnation. According to some Greek writers, every pirate in the eastern Mediterranean was an Etruscan, a people whose only invention was the grappling iron to secure their prey. Agriculture, cattle breeding, wine growing and even silver mining kept the standard of living high. Nevertheless, signs of hostility against the southern cities have been seen by some scholars in the design of Etruscan coins. They seem to have copied them from pieces circulated in Attica or Asia Minor, rather than Magna Graecia, their prosperous neighbour. On the other hand, the practice may not have had such implications. One aspect of Etruscan coinage that is certainly unusual is the retention of a blank reverse long after this feature, which is usually found on the very earliest coins, had disappeared elsewhere.

Typical examples of Etruscan coins are silver pieces from the mint Populonia. First, is a didrachm bearing a grotesque head (295). Usually known as a gorgon, after the hideous monster whose glance turned men to stone, such a device appears in several parts of the Greek world, in Macedon, for example, or Eretria. A satisfactory explanation of the choice has still to be given. A hostile monster seems an inappropriate city badge, though it could have been the head of some other mythical beast, the image of which guarded the gates, as was arranged in south-east Asia in more modern times. Another didrachm shows the gorgon replaced by a male head wearing a lion's skin. This puts us in mind of Hercules, who slew the dreaded Nemean lion with his bare hands and used its skin for his cloak, treating the skull as a helmet. The most famous coins showing Hercules like this were minted in great quantities by Alexander, who saw himself as the new Hercules and took care that his own features should be recognisable on the coins. However, Alexander always appeared in profile and this Etruscan coin shows Hercules full face. Moreover, Alexander's conquests did not extend as far as this. Were the Populonians using the design to portray themselves? The X on each side of the head or below it is taken as an indication of value and has been equated with twenty (XX) hemilitrae (half-litras, originally Sicilian weights or coins of about 7 grains). Numerous Roman republican denarii have a single X to denote the value, as does our third Etruscan example, which this time features a young male head (296). Quite likely, this is Apollo, god of the sun, protection, music, civic life and much else, who would be an appropriate choice for a people who are supposed to have perfected the art of living. Dates for these coins are speculative. We have to rely on style, since there is no connection with identifiable events or personages. They may all be safely placed in the fifth or fourth centuries BC and, certainly, before 268, when Rome was in a position to claim a monopoly of silver coinage in Italy. Though this does not appear to have been strictly enforced, it certainly applied to the northern parts of the peninsula, which were provided with a distinctive coinage that we call Romano-Campanian. It was the forerunner of the flood of republican denarii that soon superseded it and is identifiable by the distinctive legend Romano, ie 'of the Romans', as opposed to the usual Roma – Rome – that became standard. One example (228) shows Mars and a horse's head and is a didrachm, a denomination suited to commerce with the Greek cities and worth twice as much as the denarius, which was to become the staple currency of Italy and of the Roman Empire.

One of the few mints that escaped the Roman ban on silver issues was the one used by the Bruttians, the other group of people we are considering here. They were the native inhabitants of the toe of Italy at the time when the cities of Magna Graecia were founded. Driven from their best land, they retreated to the hills, preserving a distinctive way of life. We know little about them except that they were bilingual, retaining their native language, as did the Etruscans, yet managing to speak enough Greek to trade with the cities. Obviously, the spread of Greek culture would be expected to eliminate any distinctive qualities of the Bruttian way of life, given time. However, in 356 BC, they were able to stage a 'come-back' and throw off Greek domination. We know few details of the affair, though the impression is that the sturdy hill-men, who had been in a state of semi-serfdom, rebelled against their masters and established their independence, which they were able to retain until the end of the third century.

The political situation made it difficult for the Bruttians to develop their state. At first, it was touch and go whether their old enemies, the Greek cities, would reconquer them. Then, the growing power of Rome made itself felt. With a few exceptions, the southern Italian cities resisted Roman domination. As already recounted, when Tarentum was endangered, she invited King Pyrrhus of Epeiros to come to her aid. He crossed the Adriatic with his army, and waged an apparently successful campaign. However, his victories cost him such heavy losses that he was unable to reap the expected benefits and, eventually, had to retreat to Sicily. The Bruttians had joined other states opposed to Rome and, among other consequences, it is possible to see some indication of their alliance in their new coins. The third-century pieces feature Zeus and a foot-soldier (302). In Epeiros, there was a famous shrine of Zeus and the device of the infantryman may reflect a determination to resist aggression. So, too, may Ares, Victory and the Bruttian patron goddess (303,304). Then we have a coin with the head of Amphitrite, wife of the sea-god Poseidon, and, on the reverse, Poseidon himself (297), possibly an indication of aid coming from overseas – and, finally, there is a drachm that shows the winged bust of Nike, the goddess who brought victory, while on the reverse a young man (could it be Pyrrhus?) crowns himself with Nike's wreath (298–300). Evidence of a certain sophistication in production methods is seen in the mint-marks, which include a bull's skull, an eagle and an altar. Unfortunately, as is the case with many mint-marks, we simply do not have the key to interpreting them.

After ten years of resistance, the Bruttians were obliged to submit to Rome in about 272 BC. The details of the settlement are not clear, though it was obviously not unconditional surrender because, as previously mentioned, they retained the right to coin silver. Some authorities would place the coins described here in the second half of the third century. Towards the end of that period, the Bruttians' last chance to retain their independence came in the form of Hannibal's army. As is well known, he crossed from Carthage, on the North African coast, and campaigned for several years against the Romans. Although he won many victories, he never seemed to have fought the decisive battle. The Romans did not know when they were beaten. Moreover, although they had allies in Magna Graecia, many of the Italian towns closed their gates to the Carthaginians. If they welcomed them, they would, it was believed, be exchanging domination by Rome for a worse fate.

A Bruttian city that rejected Hannibal was Petelia. It would be more accurate to call it a walled village, and it was so small that it really did not stand a chance. Nevertheless, with despairing courage, its citizens put up what resistance they could, obliging Hannibal to undertake a siege which, predictably, did not last long and had only one possible outcome. In memory of the stand taken by these humble people there is nothing apart from the few bronzes issued in the town. It was too small to run to a silver coinage. One of its coins has a portrait of Demeter, the fertility goddess, and Zeus hurling his thunderbolt (301). No one knows the details of its production and, unfortunately, it is unlikely to have been a warning to Hannibal not to take the Petelians for granted, though this would have been appropriate. As the war swept to and fro across Italy, Hannibal made a secure base in the hills of Bruttium. Indeed, he held out there for four years (207–204 BC). Eventually, he evacuated his surviving troops, not because he was defeated, but because the Romans had sent an invasion force under Scipio to Africa, and Carthage itself was threatened. Hannibal received orders to return and defend the capital. He left his former allies defenceless and the Romans, understandably, took their revenge. Everyone who had not been their undoubted friend suffered in some way. The Bruttians lost territory, and also status: they became second-class citizens with no right to bear arms and, certainly, no special privilege to strike any more coins.

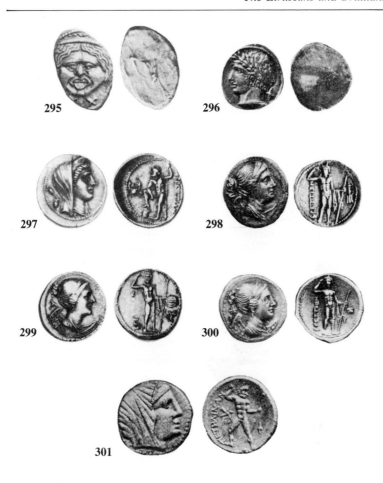

295 Etruscan didrachm, *c.* 300 BC. Gorgon and blank reverse. XX value.
296 Another. Apollo?

Bruttium.
297 Didrachm, third century BC. Poseidon and Amphitrite.   **298** Drachm of
the Bruttian League, 215–205 BC. Head of Nike; Horned youth crowning
himself; mint-mark, incense-burner(?)   **299** Similar coin. Mint-mark,
chariot wheel.   **300** Similar coin. Mint-mark, cap(?)   **301** Petelia. Bronze
coin. 280–216 BC. Head of Demeter; Zeus hurling a thunderbolt.

302

303

304

Bruttian League.
302 Bronze coin. Zeus and warrior.   **303** Bronze coin. Head of Ares;
Victory crowning a trophy of arms.   **304** A similar coin. Mars and Hera
Hoplosmia, the patron goddess of the Bruttians.

XXVIII. THRACE

The 1976 exhibition of treasure from Thrace, and accompanying programmes about it on television, were, to most of us, an introduction to a much neglected area of the ancient world. The neglect is scarcely surprising because there are few historical records of what went on there and the names of its rulers, occasionally given in the record of a treaty, tell us very little. An exception to this generalisation is Lysimachos, one of Alexander's generals, who built up a substantial empire, but the exception tends to prove the rule.

Thrace was part of the Balkans, coinciding approximately with modern Bulgaria, the European part of Turkey and the part of Greece on the north coast of the Aegean. The two cities on that coast, Abdera and Maroneia, were of some importance as trade centres and served as gateways to the interior, where Greek culture and civilised life were by no means well established. An indigenous way of life seems to have existed, capable of adaptation to absorb invading influences – Greek, Celtic or Macedonian.

Archaeologists steadily reveal more and more about Thrace and, in recent years, the Bulgarians have made great efforts to rediscover as much as possible about their national heritage. Coins have not been neglected and a new standard work has been translated into English entitled *Coins of the Ancient Thracians*, by Y Youroukova. If you enjoy a scholarly detective story, this is good value for money and will take you along the unfrequented paths in ancient numismatics. The author relies on evidence from coin hoards discovered in Bulgaria and is very cautious in accepting as genuine unusual speciments in the collections of the world's greatest museums. She always gives her reasons. For instance, take the case of the earliest Thracian coins, rare staters showing a chariot of archaic style above which is an eagle or a wheel. The reverse is the triskeles, the three legs, most familiar to us as the badge of the Isle of Man. Although some of these staters are genuine, others, outside Bulgarian collections, bear the names of totally unknown and improbable tribes. Nineteenth century forgers copied the genuine specimens to produce novelties for eager collectors and deceived many experts of the day. Of course, our knowledge of coins has advanced greatly since then.

More accessible are the coins produced by the Orescii tribe at the end of the sixth century BC (305). Long famous for their lack of modesty, they show a naked man in an appropriately aroused state carrying off a young woman. They are usually catalogued as a satyr and nymph who, students of the classics would know, frequently got up to that sort of thing. Perhaps they are: the gods often appeared on coins produced in the Greek world. On the other hand, they probably represent the fertility cult of Dionysos, who was widely worshipped and whose portrait appeared on Thracian coins in later centuries when production techniques improved. An early date is often indicated by lack of a reverse design. Here, as in many other cases, we simply have the mark of the punch, referred to as an incuse. At the time they were produced, there was probably stable government in Thrace or an alliance of its various tribes – either hypothesis would explain the need for a considerable quantity of coinage.

Early in the fifth century BC, we hear of the kingdom of Odrysae which produced the gold and silver articles shown at the exhibition. However, it did not mint many coins. Its silver was copied from the issues of the coast towns. The eagle on the obverse was used by Olynthos and the horse by Maroneia. The latter had smaller denominations, featuring half a horse, and this was copied too (308). Indeed, the close resemblances suggest that coins were ordered from the mints established in those cities. Odrysae made an impression on the Athenians when it drove back an invading army from its neighbour Macedon. Later, in 400 BC, a royal personage known as Seuthes II attempted to gain the Thracian throne. He approached Xenophon, leader of a mercenary force whose adventures are described in the 'Persian Expedition', and offered his daughter's hand in marriage to the commander, promising every man a wage of one tetradrachm per month, plus his keep. Eventually, he failed to honour the bargain. He paid only one talent (26.192 kg of silver), 600 oxen, 4,000 sheep and 120 slaves. Not bad, one might think, but remember that this had to be shared among 10,000 men.

Possibly, all Greek cities on the Thracian coast paid tribute to Odrysae. If this was so, a sufficiently large supply of coinage would come into Thrace (306,307) and there would have been little need to produce a coinage of its own. Some rare little bronze pieces record the names of otherwise unknown kings and we are left with a gap in our knowledge of Thrace until Philip II, Alexander's father, captured it and added it to his growing kingdom. The well-known silver and gold pieces of these two rulers circulated there (148–159) and were soon accompanied by the splendid issues authorised by Lysimachos, who made Thrace the centre of his kingdom – the first time that Thrace played a leading part in Greek politics.

Lysimachos was one of the generals who divided Alexander's Empire between them. He was awarded the governorship of Thrace and steadily extended his possessions along the coast of the Black Sea and into Asia Minor. His armies had to be paid and, therefore, a plentiful coinage was supplied. At first, the tetradrachms bearing the portrait of Alexander wearing a lion's skin, and the seated Zeus as the reverse, were retained (309). It was as if the great leader had not died or, at least, no one was rash enough to replace him.

After a few years, Lysimachos adopted new designs that announced to the world two things. First, that Alexander had joined the gods and, secondly, that his successor was Lysimachos. The gold staters and silver tetradrachms show Alexander with a ram's horn growing from his brow (310–313). This is the horn of Ammon, an Egyptian god whose temple had particularly taken his fancy. Some said that a vision there had given him the confidence to go on with his spectacular career. These portraits must have been executed by gifted engravers, for they convey the impression of nobility and indicate by the uplifted gaze that Alexander was now divine. On the reverses, Athena replaced Zeus. She holds a small figure of Victory, who crowns the name Lysimachos. The meaning of this symbolism is obvious but, at the time, it was considered presumptuous. Of course, success tends to provoke jealousy and some of the carping came from people who were displeased to see Lysimachos go from strength to strength. His coinage proved very popular and was struck at several mints in gold as well as silver. When he was able to seize Macedon, the stream of coins was augmented by contributions from Pella and Amphipolis and, for many years after his death, commercial centres in northern Greece, Asia Minor, even Rhodes, imitated them. Hence, we have another instance of variations on a basic theme. In general, coins of 'good style' are more prized than the somewhat uninspired or downright crude posthumous issues. After establishing himself firmly on the throne, Lysimachos was persuaded by his second wife, Arsinoe, sister of Ptolemy II, to put his eldest son to death on a false conspiracy charge. This mistake left no capable successor and Lysimachos' kingdom perished with him. He was overthrown by the Seleukids in his eightieth year, when he was killed in battle, game to the last.

A few years after Lysimachos' death in 281 BC, Thrace experienced occupation by the Celts, who were undertaking one of their westward migrations. They dominated the area until 216 BC and this has added to the confusion of historians. Once again, we have a few coins from unknown chieftains. Youroukova weaves some fascinating arguments about them from iconography and epigraphy – the study of coin design and inscriptions. Even so, very little is certain in the Celtic period. In the second century BC, the power of the Celts declined, as Thrace again became an area of dispute between the kingdoms of the Seleukids, Ptolemies, Macedonians and a new power, the Romans.

Coins of all four rivals probably circulated in Thrace, but the most popular silver pieces were the tetradrachms from the neighbouring Aegean island of Thasos. A typical specimen is illustrated, showing Dionysos wearing an ivy wreath and Hercules standing, holding his club (314). There are many contemporary imitations, some obviously produced by illiterate die-makers who could not understand the original Greek words on the coins. Good silver was needed in quantity in the hill country of Thrace, but there was little need for literacy there. This was unfortunate for succeeding generations – who can now tell us anything about the Thracian leaders of the time? Who, for instance, was Mostis who overstruck his tetradrachms on the standard types of Thasos? The coins place him in the last quarter of the second century BC and he may have had a long reign. Very probably, he was an ally of the Macedonian king, Mithradates VI, in his successful campaigns against the invading Romans. Another Thracian leader, Kotys, was cavalry commander for King Perseus of Macedon, and Roman histories refer favourably to his valour and efficiency, but we still have a problem – there must have been several rulers in the first century BC who were called Kotys.

The other royal name carried by a succession of kings was Sadalas. One of them backed a loser in 48 BC when he fought for Pompey against Julius Caesar at the battle of Pharsalus. A successor, called Rhoemetalces, deserted Antony for Augustus at Actium, the great victory for which Augustus struck coins in honour of his second-in-command, Agrippa. At last, unchallenged as ruler of the Empire, Augustus confirmed Rhoemetalces as king of Thrace. His reign lasted forty years, during which time he was a power to be reckoned with in the Balkans. He issued well-engraved silver coins, showing portraits of Augustus and himself on opposite sides. Similar coins, in less well executed bronze, are more plentiful (315). Others featured Augustus and his own queen, an uncommon means of flattering both parts of the imperial pair. Many coins were produced at Byzantium, as yet only a small port, unaware of the future honours Constantine would confer on it as capital of the New Empire.

The long series of Thracian bronzes reminds us that the name Rhoemetalces was borne by its last three kings. There is difficulty in distinguishing the issues made by the first two, though the designs chosen by Rhoemetalces III leave nothing in doubt. We know that he was brought up with Caligula and, therefore, that emperor confirmed him in possession of a large kingdom. In gratitude, he issued bronzes with a portrait of Caligula and reverses showing the confirmation scene. Neither ruler lasted long and Thrace became more closely incorporated into the Empire and deprived of its right to issue coinage.

Coinage of independent cities.
305 Thasos. Stater, 463–411 BC. Satyr carrying off a nymph. **306** Abdera.
Tetradrachm, *c.* 465–450 BC. Griffin and a square with inscription.
307 Ainos. Tetradrachm, 463–461 BC. Hermes and goat. **308** Maroneia.
Drachm, 480–450 BC. Half-horse and ram's head.

King Lysimachos 323—281 BC.
309 Alexandrine drachm with Lysimachos' name. **310** Gold stater. Deified
Alexander and Athena. **311** Tetradrachm. Similar designs. 'Good style'.

312 A similar coin. Style not quite so good.   **313** Late version. Debased style.   **314** Thasos. Tetradrachm, after 148 BC. Dionysos and Hercules. **315** Bronze coin, Rhoemetalces I, 11 BC–AD 12. Head of Augustus; heads of the king and queen.

XXIX. CELTIC COINS

The Celts were a group of peoples of uncertain origin, though probably from eastern France and south-west Germany, but they grew numerous and powerful, spreading across much of Europe from about 1200 BC. The Celts' arrival was not a steady stream. They came in waves and, as far as Britain was concerned, one migration arrived in the eighth century BC and another about 250 BC.

It is believed that, physically, they were of the type often associated with the Irish – sturdy, reddish-haired, freckled, blue-eyed and subject to quick changes of mood. The Celts were farmers, who provided themselves with fortified enclosures for protection. These often survive as what we call hill-forts and were referred to as *oppida* in Roman accounts. Our tendency to rely on the Latin authors (and, particularly, Julius Caesar) gives a distorted picture of the Celts, or Gauls, as they were usually called. The Romans were writing about enemies whom they considered to be barbarians and were, therefore, unsympathetic. We cannot give the other side of the picture from Celtic literature, since there was none until the early Middle Ages and, therefore, we rely upon archaeology (in which coins can be very important). From it, we know that the Celts were efficient farmers and skilled metal workers, and that they probably believed in the supernatural world peopled by extraordinary spirits who had their influence on life in this world and the next. The Celts loved to incorporate imaginary creatures into their art, which gradually developed into a most elaborate form, best-known from Irish illuminated manuscripts. These were ideal media for intricate and many-coloured interlacing scroll decorations and stylised figures. Nowadays, the Celtic languages survive only in Ireland, western Scotland, Wales and Brittany, though many place names are Celtic in origin. There is a modern semi-political movement to revive national consciousness among people from the 'Celtic' areas, and even to produce some sort of Celtic league or alliance to protect the cultural and economic interests of the areas forming the Celtic fringe of Britain and Europe. However, these activities would not have appealed to the ancient Celts, who seem to have quarrelled incessantly among themselves. Their chiefs held sway over quite small kingdoms, and the world of the average person was limited to a few miles' radius of his home – as was, of course, true of peasants for many centuries after the period we shall be considering.

Celtic coins began to appear in the fourth century BC. By the second century they had become very numerous and continued until the Romans suppressed them in favour of their own currency. There are many identifiable groups of Celtic coins, almost all of which were made for local use. They are found in areas from 80 km (50 miles) to 160 km (100 miles) in diameter, often centred on the river valleys. Plotting distributions is an important aspect of the study of this coinage and, consequently, it is very necessary to report every find of hoards or single examples. I hope that everyone fortunate enough to find a Celtic coin with his metal detector remembers this!

The models for Celtic coins were Greek or Roman issues obtained through trade or which simply appealed to their aesthetic tastes. Over the years, the imitative coins departed further and further from the originals so that, eventually, the connection was scarcely recognisable. British readers will recall that it is often pointed out that the strange designs of ancient British staters owed their origin to the coins minted by Philip II of Macedon. Older histories make much of the crudities and loss of contact with these fine examples of Greek art which seem to be apparent in Celtic coins, implying a degree of barbarism comparable to the Victorian idea of 'Darkest Africa'. This view has been reconsidered on the grounds that the Celts were competent metal workers and die-makers. If they had wished to make accurate copies of Greek coins, they probably could have done so. However, they apparently had no wish to and, instead, adapted the designs to suit their own artistic and religious conventions. This argument is the more convincing if you consider a typical Gallo-Belgic or British gold stater (316–322). What die-cutter who wanted to put a horse on his coin would carve a disjointed animal unless he intended to? Like the White Horse of Uffington, there must have been a deliberate purpose in the design and, furthermore, everyone knows that horses have only one tail – how do we account for the three-tailed breed on coins, unless they were symbolic? They could be a chief's or clan's standard or a creature from mythology, but not simply the incompetent efforts of barbarians.

The numerous groups of Celtic coins can be classified into a Silver Belt and a Gold Belt. The silver coins stretch from the coast of the Black Sea up the Danube and across northern Italy, into the south of France and Spain. Gold coins predominated in what is now Czechoslavakia, Germany, northern France and Britain. The first silver coins in the Danube area were copies of the tetradrachms issued by Philip II, who ruled Macedon from 359 to 336 BC (323–326). They had an impressive portrait of Zeus on the obverse and a horseman on the reverse. Imitations incorporated distorted heads and strange horses, setting a pattern followed by the people who copied the tetradrachms of Alexander the Great (327) and, much later, those from the island of Thasos (314,328,329). Massilia (the future Marseilles) supplied coins which appealed to the Celts in the Po valley (330,331): two Spanish towns, Rhoda and Emporion, both on the north-east coast, were the strongest influence on French coinage. The processes of imitation and alteration converted Massilia's nymph and lion into unrecognisable heads and beasts. The open rose on coins from Rhoda was interpreted as a cross, giving rise to a long series of small coins referred to by the French numismatists as *monnaies-à-la-croix* (332,333). Further up the Rhone, the denarii of Republican Rome were more popular.

In Bohemia and Germany, the gold of Alexander the Great was imitated, thus, the designs were based on the head of Athena backed by a standing Nike (Victory), whereas, further west, in Switzerland, the Rhineland, northern France, Belgium and Britain, the head of Apollo and his chariot were used because, in that area, gold staters issued by Alexander's father, Philip, predominated. In covering such a wide area, it is tempting to over-simplify the picture and, therefore, several other coinages (334), such as those of Lysimachos, king of Thrace and the Italian port of Tarentum should be mentioned as other models for Celtic coins. However, it is the variations on the theme which fascinate rather than the original inspiration. A case in point is the Armorican billon staters, used in northern France and the Channel Islands. They show infinite variations on the theme of an elaborately coiffured head and a stylised horse, and are recommended on the grounds of cheapness and investment potential, as well as interest

(335–338).

Another unusual series, though a rather undistinguished one, is the base-metal potin, or tin, coins used in Gaul and Kent (339,340). They were cast in strips, their design so simplified that the heads on them are scarcely recognisable as such. Large quantities survive, indicating their popularity as small change and, fortunately, providing the modern collector of British coins with examples of pre-Roman coinage that he can afford.

In Spain, a complex coinage in silver and bronze developed among the Celts and other peoples, generally referred to as the Iberians, who lived side by side with them. The bewildering assortment of Celtic/Iberian coins from eighty mints have been grouped systematically so that their relationship to Greek and Roman models can be clearly seen. The alphabets used when the Iberian Celts learnt the importance of a name on a coin are classified and, as a result, we have scripts originating from Phoenician letters which would, otherwise, have been incomprehensible, had not bilingual coins given us the essentials (342–344).

It is quite rare for the mint town to appear on Celtic coins though, in Britain, three were named – Calleva (341), Verlamio and Camuloduno – or, as we are accustomed to refer to them – Silchester, St Albans and Colchester. Chieftains, too, left their names for posterity by putting them on coins. Many of them will remain simply as names or even abbreviations, because there is no other written record through which we can bring them to life again. Fortunately, the British coins were among the last of the Celtic series and, consequently, the Romans, who had extended their empire into Gaul, knew a good deal about what was going on in these islands, and write about the dynasties established by Commius and Tasciovanus, not to mention the leaders encountered during the Conquest.

One leading British expert, Derek Allen, believed that there were distinct stages in the evolution of Celtic designs. First, came close imitation of the original Greek or Roman coins, then fragmentation of the components. After a time, the pieces were put together in a different, peculiarly Celtic design and, lastly, as the independent life of a Celtic tribe drew to a close, there would be new emphasis placed on Roman designs, inscriptions and so on. Possibly, this latter tendency was most marked when Celtic chiefs were allowed to remain in power as client kings, after their lands had been overrun by the Romans. The commonest element in Celtic coin design, as it is in Greek and Roman, is the human head. When they move away from Zeus, Dionysos or Athena, designs may show Celtic deities, though we are reduced to describing them simply as male or female because we do not know enough about Celtic mythology. The little heads sometimes accompanying larger ones are also a puzzle and may, perhaps, be that object of awe and veneration, the severed head, often appearing in Celtic literature.

Realistic portraits and animals do not exist. They are highly stylised and often accompanied by other miniature creatures or devices such as wheels, suns, or things which defeat description. They cannot be only doodles, because the die-cutters were working with a limited range of magical or decorative themes. Presumably, they once had heraldic or mystical significance. Horses, as already mentioned, tend to break up or grow several tails, or grow horns and even wings. Boars and bulls were less versatile but equally stylised, while other fabulous beasts may originate from lions or Massilian coins. Birds, too, vary a lot.

The weapons used for hunting and fighting were also placed on coins though, otherwise, there is little reliable indication of how people dressed or spent their time. The humdrum aspects of life, the role of coinage as a medium of exchange and the result of mass-production tend to be overlooked by the more romantically inclined collectors of Celtic coins. On the other hand, are they not products of the same culture from which evolved the long, elaborate Welsh and Irish fairy tales? Perhaps, every collector sees something different in them.

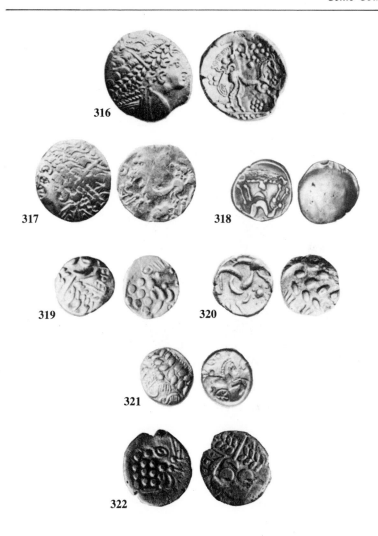

Gold Gallo-Belgic staters.
316 The Ambiani, 130–80 BC. **317** A similar coin. Less realistic.
318 The Ambiani or Morini, 57–45 BC. Horse; other side blank.

British staters
319 'Westerham' type, first century BC. **320** The Coritani, *c.*
30 BC–AD 10. **321** The Catuvellauni, 'Whaddon Close' type, *c.* 45–20 BC.
322 The Durotriges, *c.* 60 BC–AD 60.

Celtic copies of Philip II's silver tetradrachms.
323 A close imitation.   **324** More Celtic in style.   **325** Very stylised.
326 An impressive adaptation of high technical and artistic quality.
327 Celtic copy of a tetradrachm of Alexander the Great.

328 Celtic copy of a tetradrachm from Thasos.   **329** A more stylised
version.   **330** Massilia. Drachm, third century BC. Artemis and lion.
331 Celtic version of it.   **332** Gaul, Volcae Tectosages. Drachm, first
century BC. Head and cross.   **333** S.W. Gaul. Half-stater ? Head and cross.
334 Silver stater – an imitation of the coins of Larissa ?

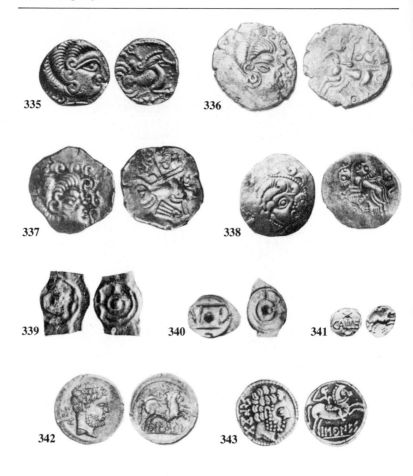

Armorican billon staters, first century BC.
335 Recognisable head and mythical creature.   **336** Disjointed head and horse.   **337** Recognisable head; Baffling reverse.   **338** Recognisable head; creature and several heads on the reverse.

339 Potin coin. N. Thames area. 50 BC–AD 50.   **340** A similar coin.
341 British gold ¹/₄ stater, Atrebates and Regni, *c.* AD 5–10. Prancing horse and mint name – CALLEV = Silchester.

Iberian imitations of a Roman denarius. Punic alphabet used. Second or first century BC.
342 Attributed to Osca.   **343** Attributed to Belsinum.

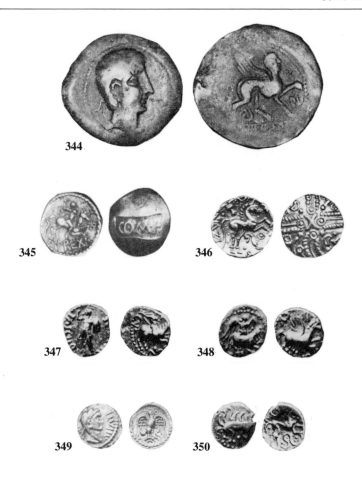

344 Iberian Celtic bronze coin. Castulo. Male head and mythical creature; Iberian legend.

British Celtic coinage.
345 Stater, Eppillus son of Commius, King of the Regni. Horseman. Eppillus Rex; COM.F. on reverse.　**346** Gold stater, Tasciovanus, *c.* 20 BC–AD 10. Horse; crescents on wreath.　**347** Cunobelin, Shakespeare's Cymbeline, AD 10–40. Small bronze coin. Horseman and warrior.　**348** Similar coin. Victory and Pegasos.　**349** Silver coin, Epatticus, AD 25–35. Head of Hercules and eagle.　**350** Coin of the Coritani, 50 BC–AD 10. Boar and horse.

THE EAST UNDER HELLENISTIC INFLUENCE

Alexander received homage from numerous chieftains or kings in the territories to the east of Asia Minor. Some had been defeated, and others thought it wise to ask for his friendship and keep their positions. Most found it politic to demonstrate a degree of Philhellenism. They may have really believed that the Greek way of life was superior and, certainly, had no doubt about it if they came from Macedonian stock. However, the break-up of Alexander's empire and the establishment of its Seleukid successor, in which the outlying provinces almost always showed a tendency towards independence, gradually weakened the Greek elements in the eastern courts. Intermarriage and invasion speeded up the process, with the result that the non-Greek cultures of these huge areas became dominant. As far as coins are concerned, it is usually possible to trace this process through the metamorphosis of series that began with splendid hellenistic portraits but ended with designs derived from a very different and obviously oriental source. The principal groups of coins in question are those minted for the Parthian, Sasanian, Bactrian and Indian kingdoms.

XXX. PARTHIA

Parthia proper was an area south-east of the Caspian Sea, inhabited by a migrant people – skilled and hardy horsemen, fierce and uncivilised (at least by Greek and Roman standards). They have left us few records and appear in the pages of classical history only when at war with the western world. Hence, our knowledge of them is often shadowy and, for it, we rely heavily on their ancient enemies and modern archaeologists. To the latter, their coins provide important evidence of dress and cultural developments which would, otherwise, be lacking. Parthian settlements known to us (as opposed to burial mounds) are so few that, at one time, it was believed that they did not live in cities at all. If this were so then, presumably, their coins were minted in cities captured as their empire was extended.

Parthia's independence was established about 250 BC, when a chieftain called Arsakes led a rebellion to free his people from rule by the Seleukids, who struggled to keep control of the huge area stretching from Syria to northern India. Soon after his victory, Arsakes died. His successors deified him as the founder of the state and he can be found on the reverses of many of their coins. At first, he is seen to be wearing the cap, cloak and trousers that characterised the Parthian. Later, as the coinage degenerated, he became a stick figure but still clearly held a bow. This was the principal weapon used by the Parthian horsemen, who won the respect of the Roman legions by their tactics. They would sweep down upon the infantry, release a cloud of arrows and and then veer away, still shooting as they turned in the saddle, thus inflicting maximum damage and avoiding hand-to-hand combat, at which the legionaries were superior.

Arsakes was succeeded by his brother, Tiridates I, who issued the first Parthian coins. His portrait is easily distinguished by its pointed cap or helmet, presumably a touch of realism, or a symbol of nationalism and hostility to the culture of the Greek world. Anti-Hellenism seems to have been strong when Parthia became independent, and to have diminished as the empire was extended and confidence grew. Presumably, the inhabitants of the captured Greek cities in Mesopotamia, such as Ecbatana and Seleukia, could be expected to remain loyal to the Parthian kings only as long as their way of life was respected.

Possession of the mints in those cities enabled their rulers to strike some handsome portrait coins, with reverse designs similar to those of contemporary Syria and Egypt. Among such issues are found the most valuable Parthian coins – large tetradrachms (354,358,360), which are scarce and untypical of the mass of Parthian coinage available to collectors. This comes from the numerous hoards buried at later periods, when life became very insecure indeed.

As the empire was extended into Mesopotamia, there were frequent clashes with the Seleukids and, later, the Romans, whose own empire came to include Asia Minor. On the eastern borders of Parthia, the situation was equally unsettled because of the frequent invasions by the Scythians, another migrant people very similar to the Parthians themselves and challengers for control of the steppe. Several Parthian kings fell in battle against them and others died violent deaths in civil war or in court conspiracies. Nearly every Parthian coin which we have in our collections was probably secreted away by someone who sensed danger and was proved only too right. The savings hoarded by the owners who were unable to return for them are rediscovered by modern farmers, building workers and archaeologists in Iran and its neighbours, and become available to us in batches, possibly after changing hands many times on their way to the dealers.

The splendid portraits of the earlier Parthian kings make us wish we knew more about them (351–360). It would be tedious to summarise our scanty knowledge of the majority of them here, particularly, since it usually amounts to measures taken to cope with invasions from east or west, conspiracies and civil wars. Building projects, law-making and the fostering of the arts were activities seldom engaged in by an essentially nomadic people.

Some of the Parthian kings who have influenced the historical developments already mentioned here are Mithradates II (353) (*c*. 123–88 BC), who restored Tigranes to the Armenian throne; Gotarzes I (355) (*c* 90–80 BC), from whom Tigranes captured extensive territories; and Orodes II (357) (*c*. 57–38 BC), whose crushing victory over a Roman army commanded by Crassus did much to establish Parthia's prestige and to complicate politics in the last years of the Roman Republic. Phraates IV (358) (38–2 BC) drove back Mark Antony but, later, established good relations with Augustus and returned to him the standards that Crassus had lost at Carrhae. Since there was no greater disgrace to Roman arms than to let a standard fall into enemy hands, the return of them through a bloodless diplomatic victory was a splendid achievement and Augustus publicised the fact by issuing numerous coins (371). Parthian coins always followed the same basic designs, though the original inspiration was weakening. Despite this, Gotarzes II (AD 40–51) actually described himself on drachms as 'Philhellene', when he should more realistically have done as his successor Vologases I (361) (AD 51–78) did and used the Parthian script which, from time to time, made its appearance in company with Greek on coins.

After a long period in which the classical historians make only brief references to Parthia, their accounts of Trajan's lengthy campaign to subdue the East bring it again into focus for a short time. Trajan advanced from Syria with a large army. Armenia and Mesopotamia surrendered after token resistance and can be seen in subjection on a splendid sestertius issued to commemorate the emperor's success. Trajan then pressed on into the lands occupied by the Parthians, capturing the major cities – Ctesiphon, Babylon, Susa and Seleukia. The Parthian king Osroes (364) fell back with his horsemen into his homeland, leaving the legions with no visible enemy against whom to do battle.

Trajan might have advanced even further east, but learnt that his lines of communication were endangered by risings in Syria and Asia Minor. Wisdom demanded withdrawal and so he set up a puppet king in Ctesiphon, commemorating his action with another sestertius. As his armies fought their way back, Trajan fell ill and died before he could reach Rome. Soon after Trajan had vacated Parthia, Osroes reappeared with his men. The Roman appointee was quickly deposed, having scarcely had time to strike a few coins, and Osroes became king again, reigning for another fourteen years.

After his death, the situation in Parthia became steadily more chaotic. The Scythians always threatened the east, while the Romans launched several campaigns from the west. Their successes or, perhaps, propaganda campaigns, are commemorated on coins of Lucius Verus, Septimius Severus and Caracalla, all of whom authorised designs suitably honouring Victory and adding 'Parthicus' to their titles.

In contrast, the coins of the Parthian kings became cruder. Their portraits are stereotyped and difficult to identify (361–370). An interesting innovation of this period is the full-face portrait, but what these designs merit for originality is counterbalanced by the low standards of workmanship (368–370). As royal control over the Parthian empire weakened, there were revolts among the subject peoples, particularly, the Persians, who had memories of former greatness to inspire them. Finally, in four years of civil war, King Artabanus was killed and his son Artavasdes captured (367). He was the last ruler of the Parthian Kingdom, the coinage of which, already but a pale copy of its former magnificence, came to an abrupt end in AD 224.

The feudal relationships within Parthia allowed for the establishment of semi-independent kingdoms, which are referred to by the general term 'sub-Parthian'. We know very little about their history but, since they produced attractive and intriguing portrait coinages, it is helpful to show how they fitted into the picture (372–377). There were three of them – Persis, historic home of the Persians and Sasanians, north-east of the Persian Gulf; Elymais situated between Babylon in the West and Persis in the east, with its capital at Susa; and Characene in the Tigris-Euphrates delta. We can scarcely date a single reign for certain and lists of kings are very conjectural, even more so, because it is not always easy to read their names in the scripts used on their coins. Vigorous portraiture is these coins' main attraction and the larger silver pieces are popular among collectors, in spite of the impossibility of ever knowing much about the personalities of these monarchs.

Drachms or tetradrachms with portraits of the Parthian kings. The standard reverse design shows Arsakes with his bow.
351 Arsakes I, *c.* 238–211 BC. Issued by Tiridates.   **352** Mithradates I, *c.* 171–138 BC.   **353** Mithradates II, *c.* 123–88 BC. Wearing a tiara.
354 Diademed portrait.   **355** Gotarzes I, *c.* 90–80 BC. Wearing a tiara.
356 Phraates III, *c.* 70–57 BC.   **357** Orodes II, *c.* 57–38 BC.

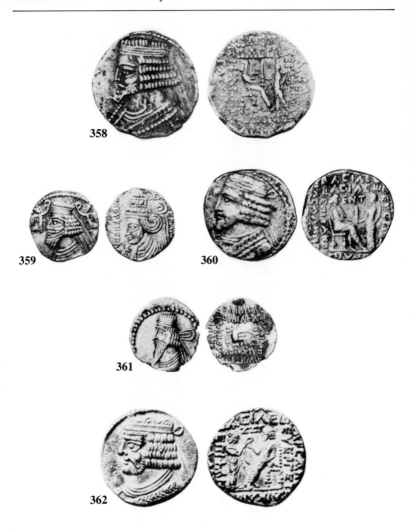

358 Phraates IV, *c.* 38–2 BC. Tyche presents the king with a palm branch.
359 Phraates V, sometimes called Phraataces, 2 BC–AD 4. His portrait, crowned by two figures of Nike; portrait of his mother, Musa, on the reverse.
360 Vardanes I, AD 40–45. Tyche presents the king with a palm branch.
361 Vologases I, AD 51–78.   **362** Vardanes II, AD 55–58. Tyche presents the king with a diadem.

363 Vologases III, AD 105–147. King receiving his diadem from Tyche.
364 Osroes I, AD 109–129.   **365** Vologases IV, AD 147–191.
366 Vologases VI, AD 208–228.   **367** Artabanus IV, AD 216–224.

Full-face portrait drachms.
368 Darius, *c.*70 BC.   **369** Vonones II, *c.* AD 51.   **370** Vologases V, AD 191–208.
371 Denarius minted by Augustus to commemorate the return of the standards captured by the Parthians.

The 'Sub-Parthian' Kingdoms.
Persis.
Bagadates I, third century BC.
372 Tetradrachm. His portrait; fire-altar before which he stands.

Elymais.
373 Tetradrachm, Kamnaskires IV, first century BC. Portraits of the king and his father, Kamnaskires III ?   **374** Drachm of similar design.   **375** Portrait tetradrachm, possibly Kamnaskires III.

Characene.
376 Tetradrachm, Tiraios II, *c.* 61–48 BC. His portrait and Hercules.
377 Tetradrachm, Attambelos I, *c.* 44–40 BC. Similar designs.

XXXI. THE SASANIANS AND THEIR COINS

One of those arbitrary dividing lines convenient to historians separates the Parthians from the Sasanians and usually leads to the latter's omission from books about Greek coins. There are certainly grounds for treating them as a phenomenon of the early mediaeval world. On the other hand, dealers and auction houses frequently list Sasanian coins alongside Greek and, for this reason, they are included in this book.

The Sasanian dynasty ruled Persia during the four centuries from the fall of the Parthians to the invasion of Central Asia by Islam (AD 224–651). Europeans knew little about them, and even less about their coins, until the interest taken in Persia since the Second World War led to a reappraisal in the West of many aspects of life in the East. Even the names of Sasanian kings have been spelt in different ways, making some of them unrecognisable to the novice. For example, the man called Chosroes in Gibbon's *Decline and Fall* should now be called Xusro, because that form is much closer to the sound made by the original letters. Such changes have come about through the researches of contemporary scholars, the most prominent of whom, as far as coins are concerned, is Robert Gobl of Vienna, whose work has become generally accepted as a convincing reassessment of the Sasanian series and is heavily relied upon here.

Tradition has it that the founder of the dynasty, a certain Sasan, was the high priest of a temple to the goddess Anahit, that stood in the small town called Stakhr near Persepolis. This little place had its own king, who claimed authority over several neighbouring towns, or villages, as we should call them. Sasan made a royal marriage – not difficult in the circumstances – and one of his grandsons became a city governor. Like many others at the time, this young man set about winning himself a kingdom. His name, Ardaser, meant nothing to the

Parthian overlord Artabanus, for he was only another ambitious princeling but, as time went by, he was able to send the heads of his neighbours to be placed on Anahit's altar. In AD 224, Ardaser had himself proclaimed emperor. With remarkable energy and determination, he was able to master not only Artaban but other potential rivals among the nobility. For many, the threat of having one's head placed on the altar was probably sufficient. An added incentive to support the new emperor took the form of a campaign against Rome and a revival of the Persian claim to Asia Minor.

The new emperor lost no time in minting coins. Prestige necessitated it and, of course, he needed funds. At first, his portrait closely resembled his Parthian predecessor's but, instead of Arsakes, the mythical founder of their dynasty, he placed on the reverses a rendering of the, by now famous, altar. It had a perpetual fire burning on it and, in the course of time, fire became a central feature of worship in Persian religion. Its later form is known as Zoroastrianism and is regarded as one of the world's great religions. However, in the Sasanian period, a multitude of gods was acknowledged. Their symbols, not all of which are fully understood, were worked into the crowns of the Sasanian kings and it is by these crowns that we can most easily distinguish them. Gobl provides an invaluable table of the various crowns and we have no space to reproduce it here. However, our illustrations show some of them (378–389). We can pick out wings, stars, crescents, the sphere that probably represented the sun, earpieces, pendants and so on. It is believed that each king had at least one distinctive crown designed for himself and incorporated his favourite religious symbols. Not surprisingly, as one ruler followed another, the crowns became more and more elaborate, even fantastic. It is as well for us that this custom was followed, because the inscriptions on Sasanian coins are extremely difficult. A particular letter can mean different things. Words are abbreviated by writing letters only once if they are used for two successive words. Then, if this is not enough, Gobl gives his opinion that the mint workers were illiterate.

Craftsmen migrated to Persia from Asia Minor and brought Greek and Roman artistic traditions. They had been moving east since the great days of Athens, and Persian coinage reflects their influence. The early Sasanian portraits are quite lifelike but, after half a century or so, they became stereotyped, presumably, because skill and classical influence declined. Contemporary Roman coins suffered a similar change and it is possible that the mint workers were following a trend set by the greater coin producer. On the other hand, the Sasanians differed from the Romans in that they produced large quantities of silver. Though gold and bronze coins do exist, the mass of Sasanian coins are silver drachms, light, thin coins made from comparatively large flans. The design is set in a circle which is smaller than the flan, leaving a border that, in successive reigns, grew wider and wider. Ornaments were provided for it, a star and crescent being the rule, and there are, sometimes, inscriptions. Because the coins are so thin, the phenomenon known as the 'dead spot' occurs (393). This is an area, usually in the middle of the reverse, where the design is not properly reproduced. The explanation is that, in normal coins, there is enough metal to fill all the indentations in the dies, both obverse and reverse. But, in the case of very thin coins, the metal is insufficient to fill the places in the dies where the design has been cut most deeply. So, when a flan was struck, the metal was forced into the obverse, the royal portrait, and there was not enough of it to fill the reverse die behind it. Where this happened, there is a blurred impression of the reverse die or even none at all. The designs of all Sasanian coins are basically similar – the king's crowned portrait backed by the fire altar – though almost every die has slightly different details. The varied crowns are obvious. The altars also vary in design. Sometimes, there are attendants and, in some reigns, one of them is the king himself. On others, his bust is shown in the flames. Presumably, bronze busts were made and endured the fire in a way that the heads of enemies did not, but this point is uncertain (383–384).

Unfortunately for collectors, the Sasanian kings refrained from commemorating historical events, apart from their accessions, by issuing special coins. A spectacular triumph was the capture by Ardaser's son, Sapur, of the Roman Emperor Valerianus. He had spent his whole reign fighting invaders, the Franks, Alemanni, Goths and, finally, the Persians. On the whole, he had been successful and, although nearing seventy, he led an army eastwards. He crossed the Euphrates and marched on until halted near Edessa. There, the elusive Persian horsemen appeared in thousands and surrounded the Roman legions. They tried to cut their way out but casualties were too heavy and there was no hope for an army cut off from its supplies. The unfortuante Valerianus had to surrender – the only Roman emperor ever to do so. To celebrate, Sapur cut huge pictures and inscriptions into the cliffs, where they remain to this day. He dragged Valerianus around with him in a cage and used him as a mounting block when he got on his horse. Had the campaign gone the other way, Sapur would have been treated similarly at the Roman triumph, although his body would probably not have been stuffed and displayed in a temple for many years, as was Valerianus' by the Persians.

Much of the Sasanian history consists of intricate dynastic struggles that are now of little interest. However, when the ruler was strong, Persia was a great power. The most successful king was Xusro I (AD 531–537), who stabilised internal politics, treated the nobility so considerately that they became personally loyal to him, improved the administration, followed an efficient and humane tax policy, encouraged learning and did much else that, eventually, made him the Wise King of Persian fairy stories. A significant contact with the west was made in AD 529, when Christian Byzantium closed the Academy at Athens. Xusro invited the expelled philosophers to take up residence in Persia and bring their books with them. His relations with Byzantium were usually good and he was not the only Sasanian king to receive a secret annual tribute in return for fending off the fierce tribes who lived beyond the Caucasus, ready to invade Asia Minor if they got the chance. His grandson, Xusro II, carried Sasanian power to its peak. In murderous campaigns, the Byzantines at first prevailed sufficiently to destroy the sacred central fire shrine and then they were forced back. In about seven years (AD 610–616), the Persians overran most of Asia Minor, Damascus, Jerusalem, Gaza and even Egypt. Persia was very much a world power at this point but, a generation later, the Sasanian empire had collapsed. A new and very formidable foe had appeared – Islam, the warrior's religion. Its followers embarked upon a series of conquests that, in the west, took them to Spain and, in the east, to India. The Sasanians were driven back and back, surrendering more and more territory. When Merv fell, the remnants of the royal family were obliged to seek refuge with the Chinese emperor and gradually faded out of history.

Coinage very similar to the Sasanian was continued until the end of the eighth century in the area south of the Caspian called Tabaristan (390–392). Its Arab rulers, known as the Ispahbad dynasty, minted coins similar to those their subjects had been used to for centuries. An important difference is that the standard denomination is the half-drachm and not the full drachm, otherwise, we might think their coins were Sasanian. However, the mint workers must have been even less educated. The king's portrait becomes stylised to the point of being unrecognisable as a human face and the altar's attendants turn into two pillars. Eventually, this coinage was superseded by the Abassid types, silver dirhems with Arabic inscriptions on both sides. It was doomed, if not politically, then religiously, because of the Islamic prohibition against making representations of created beings, human or animal or even plants. There are still fire worshippers in Persia, though life there is changing rapidly. The bulldozers uncover Sasanian hoards, and tourists and students bring them to Britain, where most dealers in ancient coins have a few Sasanian pieces in their lists. They are still cheap and, if you are attracted, here is a field with plenty of scope for research.

A representative selection of coins. All have the fire-altar on the reverse.
378 Drachm, Ardaser I, AD 224–241.   **379** Hemidrachm, Ardaser I.
380 Drachm, Sapur I, AD 241–272.   **381** Drachm, Varhran I,
AD 273–276.   **382** Drachm, Varhran II, AD 276–293. The king and queen
face a smaller bust – their son.   **383** Gold stater, Hormizd II, AD 303–309.

384 Drachm. Hormizd II.   **385** Gold stater, Sapur II, AD 309–379.
386 Drachm, Yazdgard II, AD 438–457.   **387** Drachm, Xusro II,
AD 591–628.   **388** Drachm, Kavad II, *c.* AD 628.

389 Drachm, Xusro V, AD 631–633.

Kingdom of Tabaristan.
390 Hemidrachm, Sa'id Ibn Da'laj, AD 773–780.   **391** Hemidrachm,
Sulaiman, AD 784–789.   **392** Hemidrachm, Abdallah Ibn Kantaba,
AD 792.   **393** Drachm of an unknown king AD 475–575? showing the 'dead
spot'.

XXXII. BACTRIA AND INDIA

Bactria was the region that now comprises northern Afghanistan and the adjoining parts of Russia. In Alexander's time it was called 'Paradise on Earth', a land flowing with milk and honey that contained a thousand cities. Tales of the wonders to be found in Merv, Bokhara and Samarkand were to fascinate the West in centuries to come and, in the fourth century BC, such fortified towns were the strongholds of a local aristocracy. Used to feudal relationships, they submitted to Alexander and soon married their daughters to the officers he left behind in command of garrisons which reputedly numbered 3,000 cavalry and 10,000 foot soldiers. They and their descendants were an island of Greek civilisation in a sea of oriental culture. Our records of what went on there are very scanty because great distances separated Bactria from Athens, Alexandria or Rome, where historians wrote the kind of accounts of their times that have been preserved. Bactria was nominally part of the Seleukid Empire, though, like other eastern territories, it broke away from that unwieldy state.

The decisive move was made by a mercenary officer serving as a governor in Bactria. He is known to us as Diodotos I, having made himself king while his overlord, Antiochos II, was engaged in a campaign against Ptolemaic Egypt. The exact date is disputed, for even the creation of the new kingdom was not recorded accurately by a contemporary. Governors were always rebelling and Bactria, however fertile, was a very long way from the Mediterranean, the theatre of war in which the struggles between Seleukids, Ptolemies, Macedonians and Romans were fought out. Modern historians assign Bactrian independence to 250 BC or thereabouts. Confusion also exists about the reign of Diodotos. His son of the same name succeeded him and no one knows which of them reigned the longer or which issued the first Bactrian coins. They were needed for two purposes, to help commerce and to serve as propaganda. No self-respecting king would long allow the coins which bore his former suzerain's portrait to circulate without, at least, a supplementary supply of pieces showing his own features and titles. The Bactrian kings were most fortunate in having available Greek die-engravers of remarkable skill. Their coin portraits are among the best ever produced and have always been keenly sought by collectors. All the heads are full of character and the care taken over them is exemplified in the silver tetradrachms of Euthydemos (394,395). They were issued at intervals during his forty-year reign and show him growing older and more experienced.

Unwilling to innovate too fast, he used as his reverse design the seated Hercules found on Seleukid silver minted for Syria. Possibly, there is another reason for his choice. It might have been wise for him to maintain good relations with the Seleukid kings who were, if they so chose, capable of putting a substantial army into the field. There was, probably, ample warning of the advance of a great host under the command of Antiochos III. Polybius, the Greek historian, relates how he conducted a two-year siege of Bactria, which had been amply provisioned by Euthydemos, and how a compromise was eventually reached. Euthydemos kept his throne but had to lend his calvalry and elephants to Antiochos, who found them invaluable when he penetrated into India. This story demonstrates how we have a record of events in Bactria only when something that was of importance to the Mediterranean world happened there. The later kings tend to be mere names in an unfamiliar list (405–412). However, coin collectors will always be interested in the unusual. Square coins are uncommon and, for this reason if no other, we note the names of Apollodotos (160–150 BC), for issuing square silver drachms, and Euthydemos II, for beginning a series of square copper and copper-nickel – very modern, we might think – lesser denominations that have been echoed by many of the currencies produced for Indian states in later centuries.

One of the drachms appropriately pairs an elephant and a Brahmin or Zebu bull (402). The copper coins are not uncommon in poor condition but, as is so often the case, difficult to obtain in a desirable state. They kept their Greek flavour, with representations of Hercules, Apollo, Athena and other deities, backed by their attributes or the royal portrait. Another unusual feature of Bactrian coins is the headgear worn by the kings. One, Antimachos, wears a flat circular hat of Macedonian origin (398); and another, Eukratides I, wears a large helmet (400). It was probably made of bronze, though some have suggested it was a solar topee, anticipating by many centuries what the Victorian soldiers and explorers wore. Eukratides came to power after a civil war and tried to establish his dynasty a little more firmly by honouring his parents, whose portraits he placed on the reverses of some of his coins. Although he reigned sixteen years, his family piety did not save him from a regrettable end – murder by his son, Plato (401). In turn, Plato was killed by his brother Heliokles (407). He is the last of the line of Bactrian kings we shall mention, apart from those involved in the establishment of a kingdom in India. He was probably still on the throne when Bactria was overrun by nomad tribes from the northern steppes and the coin series came to an end.

An even more remote outpost of Greek civilisation was the state set up beyond the Khyber Pass in north-west India. We know of three Greek armies that penetrated that far – Alexander's in 326 BC; Seleukos' in 302; and Antiochos' in 206. They won battles but they were too small in numbers, too far from base and, probably, insufficiently motivated to establish themselves permanently. India was a well-populated country with an ancient culture much older than the Greek. At the time of these invasions, the coinage in circulation consisted of small, irregular strips of silver, covered in punch marks (413–415). Recently, many of them have come on the market at modest prices. Known as puranas, they offer combinations of many signs – the sun, elephant, cow, chariot, horse, bull, jackal, tree, tiger, lion and symbolic devices, such as the swastika. As yet, archaeology has been unable to explain the signs, and it will be many years before we find out.

More successful in occupying part of India was the Bactrian king Demetrios I (205–171 BC) (396). He won several victories against the Indian kings and celebrated by placing his portrait on his coins, complete with elephant-head hat and backed by a standing Hercules in the act of placing the laurel crown of victory on his own head, while holding a second crown in his other hand (397). Demetrios made his relatives sub-kings and encouraged his subjects to infiltrate across their eastern border, so that the new conquests would have enough Greek-educated inhabitants. In time, it became the last independent Greek state. All the others had fallen to the barbarians or the Romans. Our records of what went on there are extremely scanty – it would be more accurate to speak of small shifting kingdoms rather than one unified settlement. The king about whom we know most is Menander (160–145 BC). He features in a Buddhist text that honours him for his conversion to that religion and portrays him as a great warrior, philosopher-king and saint, whose ashes were divided between several cities that competed for the honour of preserving them. He ruled the Punjab and produced large quantities of bilingual coins – Greek around his portrait and Kharoshti on the reverse, around a standing Athena (403, 404).

In spite of the obvious Indian influence, standards were kept up. The dignity and poise of this remarkable man are conveyed in dies that accurately show him aging as the years went by. He looks as if he could well have conducted a debate with a Buddhist sage and, also, brought prosperity to his people. As evidence of it, his coins are found in widely scattered hoards hidden along the trade routes. His religious conversion made him Indian rather than Greek and his successors became progressively more so.

The last Indian coins that have any trace of Greek influence were minted by the Kushans, a group of tribes that succeeded in dominating the Punjab by stages from about 100 BC to AD 50. Their gold pieces carry titles such as the Persian Shaonana Shao instead of the Greek Basileus Basileon, which both mean King of Kings (416–419). In place of the Greek deities, we have Shiva, Buddha or a king seated cross-legged in the familiar Indian pose. One of these coins shows the king in Indian armour, backed by the four-armed Shiva holding the traditional sacred objects. Obviously, coin designs had developed to a point where we can appropriately end our survey of the Indo-Greeks' contribution to numismatics. After the 1st century AD, there were no Indo-Greeks left!

394 Tetradrachm, Euthydemos I, 230–190 BC. Youthful portrait and Hercules. **395** Similar coin. Older portrait. **396** Portrait tetradrachm, Demetrios, *c.* 205–171 BC. With Athena. **397** Tetradrachm, Demetrios. The king wearing an elephant-skin head-dress; standing Hercules.

398 Tetradrachm, Antimachos, *c.* 171–160 BC. The king wearing a kausia; Poseidon standing. **399** Drachm of similar design. **400** Tetradrachm, Eukratides, 171–135 BC. The king wears a helmet; the mounted Dioskouroi are on the reverse. **401** Tetradrachm, Plato, *c.* 150 BC. His portrait; Helios driving the chariot of the sun. **402** Square drachm, Apollodotos I, *c.* 160–150 BC. Elephant and humped bull.

403 Tetradrachm, Menander, 160–145 BC. Athena; bilingual legends.
404 Drachm, Menander. King in a heroic pose with a spear.   **405** Drachm,
Antialkidas, *c.* 145–135 BC. King wearing kausia; Zeus holding Nike.
406 Tetradrachm, Antialkidas. King in a heroic pose; riding an elephant on
the reverse.   **407** Portrait tetradrachm, Heliokles, 135–110 BC. Zeus with
thunderbolt.   **408** Square drachm, Philoxenos, *c.* 110–80 BC. King on
horseback; bilingual legends.   **409** Tetradrachm, Archebios, *c.* 80–60 BC.
King in helmet; standing Zeus.

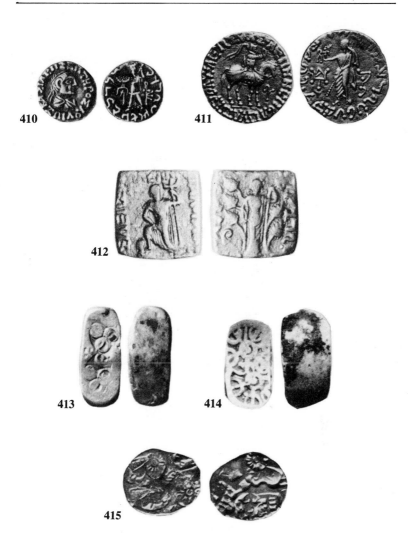

410 Drachm, Zoilos II, 75–50 BC. Athena; bilingual legends.
411 Tetradrachm, Azes I, Indo-Scythian king, *c.* 90–40 BC. King on
horseback; Zeus holding Nike; bilingual legend.   **412** Square bronze coin,
Azes I. Poseidon; female between trees.   **413, 414 & 415** Puranas, third to
first century BC.

416 Kushan gold stater, Kanishka, *c.* AD 120–150. Standing king and goddess. **417** Kushan gold stater, Huvishka, *c.* AD 150–180. King and goddess. **418** Another. King and moon goddess. **419** Another, Kipanada *c.* AD 330–360. King and goddess.

THEMATIC COLLECTING

Many collectors prefer to avoid the limitations imposed by
concentrating on individual cities or states, and widen their scope
through collecting on a thematic basis. 'Thematic collecting' is a term
frequently used in philately and the activity has long been popular as
far as ancient coins are concerned, though it may not always be
described as such.

Frequently, people 'discover' Greek and Roman coins through an
interest in travel, mythology, literature or, of course, ancient history.
They then put together selections of coins related to their own
enthusiasm. The possibilities are limited only by one's imagination and
the depth of one's purse. Popular choices include: deities and
personifications of the virtues; soldiers, arms and armour; animals and
plants; buildings and statues; coins connected with the Bible;
head-dresses and clothes; women on coins; mythological or fabulous
creatures and so on.

It is not possible to cover all themes adequately, so this section is
limited to two of them. They are both likely to have a broad appeal and
will, it is hoped, serve as an introduction to thematic collecting and,
also, to Greek religion and literature. If Roman coins are occasionally
mentioned, this will remind readers that the Roman Republic began as
one of the 'Greek' cities and evolved into something much greater.
These themes are Religion and Seafaring.

XXXIII. GREEK RELIGION

Any account of Greek religion tends to involve concepts that are familiar to modern man, but were not to the ancients. They needed to explain the unknown and to account for storm and shipwreck, disease and death, or the outcome of battles. Every event could be attributed to intervention by a god, goddess, satyr, nymph or some other supernatural being, and it was necessary to keep such creatures well-disposed towards one. The very timid must have felt insecure in a world where each hill, valley, wood, river, island or rock had its guardian spirit. Of course, most people lived their lives in very restricted areas with which they were familiar and where they had only a few supernatural beings to deal with. Nevertheless, anyone who had travelled and encountered religious cults unfamiliar to him was obliged to rationalise and to explain them as variations on religions he knew. As a result of this process, gods of distant lands that originally had no connection with those worshipped in Greece itself were identified as Apollo, Dionysos, Athena and so on. Toleration for almost all beliefs was general. There were no exclusive orthodoxies (apart from Judaism) and the hospitable spirit of polytheism broke down cultural barriers. In the course of time, the multitude of stories told about the gods became systematised into sagas, taking account of all kinds of local variations and making sense of apparent contradictions.

Robert Graves has shown us that the Greek myths incorporate a great many historical facts, remembered in terms of one national god winning an advantage over another, a hero killing a monster or a supernatural occurrence explaining an otherwise unbelievable traveller's tale. Syncretism, the process through which religions merge into one another, eventually led to the emergence of the twelve Immortals who lived in their palace on Mount Olympus and of the Heroes, whose exploits delighted generation after generation. By the time that the Schools of Philosophy had developed in the fourth century BC, there were highly respected people who no longer believed in the ancient gods and left their views in writing. On the other hand, it was rash to do something in public that appeared to offend the gods. Most people still had some kind of faith, though we have no means of measuring its strength. Convention obliged the inhabitants of every city to observe the festivals associated with its religion and to regard at least one deity as their patron. He or she would be placed on the coins, usually with objects called 'attributes' that enabled anyone who handled such money to recognise who it was. Sometimes, the personification of the city assumed a god-like form. Coins from Alexandria, Antioch, Damascus and, outstandingly, Rome have on them female figures that may remind us of Britannia or Marianne though we think that, to contemporaries, they were much more 'real' and, certainly, more venerated. Alexander and his successors, who put their own portraits on coins and relegated the gods to the reverses, were, nevertheless, inclined to retain them – the principle of the Divine Right of Kings has a long history. The modern tendency to treat the Greek gods as embodiments of various principles or moral requirements may satisfy the needs of dramatists, but is too abstract a concept to fit well with coin design.

The lines of research opened up by collecting on a religious theme are best indicated by considering a representative selection of the numismatic gods and other mystical creatures in some detail. (It is not intended to describe every eligible coin. Collectors will quickly find their own favourites.)

XXXIV. ATHENA

Like most of the major classical deities, Athena represented several strands of primitive religion which gradually merged together. Traditionally, she was the daughter of Zeus, the father of the gods, and of Metis, the wise counsel. Zeus swallowed his pregnant wife, with the result that he was smitten with an intolerable headache. The only cure was for another of the gods to split open his head to release whatever might be causing the pain. Out leaped Athena, fully grown and fully armed. This story is Greek mythology in its most elaborate form. Another origin of Athena's cult seems to be indicated by Herodotos and Plato, who identified her with the Libyan goddess Neith, who had a temple at Sa'is. Each year the priestesses there battled against each other for the office of high priestess. Possibly, this is the origin of the legend that Athena accidentally killed Pallas, one of the three nymph daughters of the river god Triton, among whom she grew up. Athena is often given the forename Pallas, which means 'maiden' or 'youth'. It may be connected with this legend or it may simply be a reference to her chastity, which set her apart from the other Olympian gods, who were well-known for their contrary preferences.

Athena's fierce defence of her chastity was taken by the Athenians, whose particular patron she was, (96–102) as a symbol of their city's invincibility. Her head appears on nearly all their coins and, also, on those of many other cities. Athena became honoured as the defender of citadels; the best fighter of all the gods; and the wisest general and the most merciful.

The Sybarites relied on her, (47–51) though she proved unable to save them in their struggle against Kroton. When they returned to Italy and refounded their city, the head of Athena on its coins is probably an acknowledgement of help from the Athenians rather than the goddess, though who could separate her from her city?

Corinth and her colonies issued a great many silver pieces which show Athena in a helmet so characteristic that is is known as 'Corinthian'. When pushed to the back of the head, it uncovered the face and if pulled forward it acted as a visor (117–129).

The fountain on Corinth's citadel sprang from a rock where, it was believed, Pegasos' hoof struck the ground. The reverse of a Corinthian coin usually shows Pegasos, who is linked with Athena in another way. It was she who provided the Corinthian hero, Bellerophon, with the golden bridle that enabled him to catch and tame the flying horse. Athena was a great patron of heroes. Apart from Bellerophon, there was Hercules who undertook prodigious labours; Perseus, who fought the Gorgons; and Odysseus whose wanderings are familiar from the pages of Homer. In the Trojan War, from which Odysseus was returning, Athena helped the Greeks and brought them victory. Troy, like other Greek cities, treasured Athena's statue – the Palladium – in its citadel and, before the Trojans could be defeated, it had to be stolen by two daring Greeks. In later centuries, palladia gave many Greeks confidence in divine protection and several of these statues have survived to show us how the ancients imagined Athena to look. She is always shown fully armed, with spear and shield, wearing the aegis – a goat-skin surcoat, with Medusa's head fixed across the breast (207).

Another aspect of Athena is revealed through the concept of her as patroness of wisdom, the intellectual and moral side of human life and, in particular, the useful arts. She is credited with the invention of the olive tree, flute, trumpet, earthenware pot, plough, rake, ox-yoke, horse-bridle, chariot and ship – articles of greater use to mankind than those provided by any other deity. As one might expect, there is little indication of this side of her nature on the numerous Greek coins depicting Athena (520). The propaganda value of a state's coinage usually demanded a more warlike goddess.

For example, we see her on a coin (426,427) of the Thessalian Confederacy, formed in Eastern Greece during the period 191–146 BC, when the area was involved in a power struggle between the Romans and the kings of Syria and Macedon. She is shown with spear and shield, about to attack the enemy. In this posture, the goddess is usually called Athena Promachos, 'she who fights in the foremost ranks'. No doubt the cities of Thessaly needed all the help that they could possibly get!

Lysimachos of Thrace preferred a seated Athena, who is

the numismatic ancestor of our Britannia (310–313). She holds a miniature figure of Victory, presumably handing it to the king – a device favoured by the Roman Emperors, among whom Domitian stands out as particularly fond of Athena, or Minerva, as he would have called her.

Athena can be found on many of the coins described in other chapters. This is a representative selection of those that might be chosen for a thematic collection and which are not mentioned elsewhere in this book.

420 Side. Stater, 400–375 BC. Athena standing, holding her owl and resting her other hand on a shield; Apollo with a laurel branch by an altar.
421 Paeonia. Drachm, King Audoleon, 315–286 BC. Athena, three-quarter face, wearing triple-crested helmet; trotting horse.   **422** Velia. Didrachm, 350–281 BC. Athena wearing crested Athenian helmet ornamented with a griffin; lion walking.   **423** Syracuse. Gold stater, Agathokles, 317–289 BC. Athena wearing a crested Corinthian helmet ornamented with a griffin; thunderbolt.

424 Lebedos. Tetradrachm, second century BC. Athena wearing triple-crested helmet wreathed with olive; her owl, between two cornucopiae.
425 Bithynia. Bronze coin, Prusias I, 228–185 BC. Head of Apollo; winged Athena crowning the king's name.   **426** Thessalian Confederacy. Double Victoriatus, 196–146 BC. Head of Zeus; Athena Itonia brandishing her spear and holding a shield.   **427** Drachm. Head of Apollo with similar reverse.

XXXV. DIONYSOS AND HIS COMPANIONS

Mankind has always prized intoxicating drink and often attributed supernatural powers to it. In ancient Greece, the vine was thought to be the gift of Dionysos. His cult originated in Thrace, an area of northern Greece that put him on many coins. One of the finest is a broad-flanned tetradrachm of a type struck after 148 BC, when the Thracian silver mines passed from the control of the Kingdom of Macedon (which had just been overrun by the Romans) into the possession of the city of Maroneia. Dionysos is shown as a young man crowned with ivy and, on the reverse, he holds a bunch of grapes (428).

Coins of this type were produced in large quantities and proved popular with the barbarian Celts of the Danube basin, who imitated them with more enthusiasm than artistic skill. Dionysos was popular everywhere and, as his cult gradually absorbed those of earlier deities, a very complex mythology developed. Consequently, he is depicted in various ways, sometimes as a bearded mature man, but more often (and nearly always on coins), as a gentle effeminate youth with flowing hair and a rather vague expression. The cast of his features is in keeping with his habits and his upbringing (429,430).

According to legend, he was the son of Zeus, who fathered him by a daughter of the King of Thebes. To save the child from his jealous wife, Hera, Zeus entrusted Dionysos to the nymphs who brought him up in the fields and mountains. As he neared manhood, he discovered the vine and the process by which wine was made. The discovery is associated with his tutor, Silenos, originally a rustic deity and, later, renowned as an old man of great wisdom. He was envisaged as ugly and pot-bellied, perpetually drunk and in need of support. Thus, he sits precariously upon an ass clutching his wine-skin from which he was never parted. Grotesque he might be, but he was venerated for his powers of prophecy. Knowing everything about the past and the future, Silenos would fall into the power of any mortal who could catch him in one of his not infrequent drunken slumbers and bind him with chains of flowers. In this state, he would be obliged to tell his captor anything he wished to know. Worshippers often tried to make use of Silenos' powers, but he is not often seen on coins. Some of the best come from Naxos and show him with a wine cup, backing the head of Dionysos wreathed in vines, on the obverse. He is to be found reclining on the back of his donkey on coins from Mende, famous for its wine (431).

The festivals in honour of Silenos and Dionysos were closely linked and were the most boisterous of the religious year. There was always plenty of music and merry-making. Wine was available to all, and everyone was expected to drink freely in acknowledgement of the gods' generosity. Those who did not become intoxicated were sometimes considered sinful in not showing their gratitude sufficiently. Participants in the processions disguised themselves and wore masks. Those on coins would probably have been worn by someone who personated Silenos himself (432–434). Most people would simply disguise themselves in order to avoid being recognised in their uninhibited capers. Masks were always worn by the actors in Greek drama and some authorities maintain that this custom derives from the Dionysian festivals. The cult was particularly strong in Phrygia, a province of Asia Minor where Cybele, the Asiatic mother-goddess, had many followers. The two religions may well have been the reasons for St John's strictures on the city of Laodikeia which, in the Book of Revelation, is denounced for lack of faith.

When Dionysos came to Phrygia, Cybele is said to have initiated him into her mysteries. Such an experience typifies in legend the merging of various beliefs with the Dionysos cult. He is supposed to have roamed the world, bringing the blessing of his discoveries to all mankind. The best-known of his adventures concerns his kidnapping by pirates who thought, from his appearance, that he was a king's son and intended to ransom him. Only the pilot of their ship recognised his divine nature and urged the crew to release him. They insisted, however, in tying Dionysos to the mast, only to see the ropes fall from his arms. Soon, a vine began to grow upon the mast. It entangled itself in the rigging and made steering impossible. Then, as a final gesture, Dionysos turned himself into a lion, which terrified the crew so much that they leapt madly overboard. Only the pilot survived to tell the tale.

Madness often affected those who opposed Dionysos and, sometimes, those who took part in his worship. Such an association of insanity with alcohol can be found in the myths of many cultures. In Rome, the Dionysian rites once provided an opportunity for uninhibited excesses of every sort; so much so that a curb had to be placed upon them. In 186 BC, a senatorial investigation reported that they had become really out of hand. The high priestess's head rolled and other prominent citizens were punished for allowing matters to degenerate so badly. After that, the festivities were drastically altered. Instead of a riotous orgy, they became a solemn procession known as the Liberalia. ('Liber Pater', (435) or Generous Father, was another name for Dionysos who may, in fact, be more familiar to readers by an alternative Latin name – Bacchus.) At the Liberalia, boys who had reached their sixteenth birthday received the toga of manhood and, shortly afterwards, a custom connected with the agricultural year took place. Little metal masks of Dionysos were hung in the Roman vineyards. They spun in the wind and, wherever they looked, they were supposed to ensure a good crop.

The vineyards and the countryside were the dwelling places of Dionysos' companions – the nymphs, centaurs and satyrs who shared his tastes in drinking and love-making. Closely associated with the satyrs was Pan, half man, half goat. He was the shepherd god, sometimes to be found in the open country playing the reed pipes which he invented. His cult began in Arcadia in the Peloponnesus, where he amused himself by giving travellers sudden frights, known as panics. Gradually, he was worshipped further afield. Pantikapaion in Thrace, and Megalopolis, a town in Arcadia that never grew large enough to justify its name, gave us the clearest representations of Pan, though his temple was erected at Athens, in gratitude for his supposed help at the Battle of Marathon and, like nearly every known god, he was eventually worshipped in Rome (436–438).

428 Maroneia. Tetradrachm, after 148 BC. Head of a young Dionysos; on the reverse, he stands holding a bunch of grapes and two wands.
429 Metapontum. Stater, 400–350 BC. Head of Dionysos wreathed with ivy; ear of barley.   **430** Larissa. Hemidrachm, 400–344 BC. Similar portrait of Dionysos; wine amphora.   **431** Mende. Tetradrachm, 465–424 BC. Silenos reclining on the back of an ass and holding a wine cup.   **432** Naxos. Litra, 530–490 BC. Head of bearded Dionysos and a bunch of grapes.   **433** Katane. Litra, 413–404 BC. Head of Silenos and thunderbolt.

434 Roman Republican denarius, minted about 91 BC by the moneyer,
Decius Silanus. Mask of Silenos and chariot. **435** Roman Republican
denarius, minted about 78 BC by Lucius Cassius. Heads of Liber and his
female counterpart, Libera. **436** Arcadian League. Stater, 370–280 BC.
Head of Zeus; Pan seated on a rock and holding a club. **437** Triobol of
similar design. **438** Pantikapaion. Tetrobol, fourth century BC. Head of Pan
and a lion.

XXXVI. HERCULES

The most widely venerated mythological hero of the ancient world who appears on the coins of many cities is Hercules, familiar to everyone as the famous strong man. According to Homer, he was the son of Zeus, who fathered him on Alcmene, wife of Amphitryon, king of Thebes in Boeotia, a territory on the north side of the Gulf of Corinth. While still in his cradle, he coped successfully with his first adversary, Hera, the jealous wife of Zeus, who sent serpents to kill the baby, but the infant strangled them and survived (439,440).

Collectors interested in Victoriana will have seen bathroom fittings, medicine bottle labels and the like, which show a baby clutching snakes. To the purveyors of iodine or strong carbolic, this device symbolised the defeat of disease and, in using it, they alluded to the classical belief that Hercules was the protector of mankind from illness or danger. However, in this role, the Greeks and Romans pictured him as a grown man.

He developed his massive strength partly as the result of an accident that occurred when he was in his teens. His earthly father, Amphitryon, provided Hercules with the very best tutors in every subject that formed early Greek education – wrestling, archery, chariot-driving, fighting as a foot soldier, singing and lyre-playing. The lad usually excelled but, one day, his music teacher, Linus, criticised him. Hercules lost his temper and struck out with his lyre, killing his tutor. To prevent a similar occurrence, Hercules' father sent him to tend his cattle and, thus, gave him the opportunity to toughen himself in the open-air life.

While working as a shepherd, Hercules performed his most famous exploit – the killing of the monstrous lion with his bare hands. In the earliest versions of the legend, it was simply a menace to the flocks: later, it became identified with the Nemean lion, the removal of which was one of Hercules' twelve labours. This theme was used by Herakleia in Lucania, a city which was one of at least nine dedicated by their founders to Hercules and, in this case, the coinage was particularly apt (442). The obverse shows Athena, the goddess who came to Hercules' aid several times. On her helmet, is a small figure of Scylla, the monster who lived in a cave on the Italian side of the Straits of Messina and menaced mariners. However, the menace that Hercules had just disposed of was skinned and he afterwards wore the skin as his usual garment, with the skull as his helmet. According to the early legends, our hero returned in triumph to the court of a neighbouring king, Thespius, and claimed his reward. It was the king's fifty daughters, each of whom Hercules honoured in a single night, thus demonstrating his superhuman strength in another way.

Hercules was destined to lead a turbulent life. He married young, but became insane (441) and murdered his wife and children, thinking them enemies. When he came to his senses, he consulted the Delphic oracle on how to expiate his terrible crime. Her orders were that he should serve Eurystheus, King of Tiryns (a coin-issuing city on the Peloponnesian coast), for twelve years. This king made life difficult for Hercules, setting him the tasks that form his famous labours in the final versions of classical mythology. The wanderings involved in the performance of these tasks took him all over the Greek world so that, eventually, there was scarcely a region that had no claim to some connection with Hercules.

First he killed the Nemean lion. Wearing the lion's skull helmet, Hercules appears on the abundant silver coinage issued by Alexander the Great (153–160). It was customary to show Hercules as a bearded man in the prime of life, but these coins show a younger man. Such a choice might be appropriate, in that the original lion legend featured him as a youth. However, it is generally agreed that what Alexander was really doing was placing his own portrait on coins and, thus, becoming the first of the world's rulers to do so. The implications of a royal appearance in the guise of Hercules are obvious. So are those of the reverse, which shows Zeus holding an eagle, the symbol of power. Zeus was Hercules' father and these coins imply that he was Alexander's too. All three, Hercules, Zeus and Alexander, ruled over and protected their subjects, bringing them great benefits and earning their gratitude and worship.

Some of Hercules' remaining labours involved the destruction or capture of other fearsome or remarkable creatures, such as the nine-headed hydra (on the coins of Phaistos in Crete) (443,444), the stag of Arcadia (which had golden antlers and bronze hooves), the Erymanthian boar, the terrible birds of prey that lived in the Stymphalian marshes, the great bull sent by Poseidon to ravage Crete, the man-eating mares belonging to Diomedes of Thrace, the oxen that were the property of Geryon, a three-bodied monster who lived on a fabulous floating island and, finally, Cerberus, the many-headed guardian of the lower world, who was hauled up to the surface of the earth and, later, released to resume his duties. In achieving all this, Hercules made good use of his favourite weapons, a huge club and a bow which shot poisoned arrows. These make their appearance on numerous coins, either in Hercules' hand or on their own. Collectors find them on Roman republican denarii, Alexander's bronze coins and later tetradrachms of Macedon, including those issued when it was under Roman rule (445–449).

The other three labours were the cleansing of the Augean stables, the seizure of the girdle worn by the queen of the Amazons and the fetching of the golden apples of the Hesperides. The stables of Augeus, king of Elis, housed 3,000 oxen which had not been mucked out for thirty years. Hercules cleansed the establishment in a day, by diverting two rivers through it. While in Elis, he founded the Olympic games. One would expect some of the coins of Olympia to feature Hercules, but this is not the case. Most of this series, which is one of the most beautiful ever struck, bear a head of Zeus or his eagle (450–452). His was the principal temple on the site of the games and it contained a magnificent statue, which was one of the wonders of the world. Hercules' adversaries, the Amazons, are hard to find on ancient coins (454). Interesting early representations of them appear on the staters of Soloi in Cilicia (453), but the side showing the Amazon kneeling over her bow is usually weakly struck. We shall look in vain for the golden apples of the Hesperides and may have to be content with one of the numerous coins issued in the names of the imperial ladies of Rome, who chose to show Venus holding a golden apple. We might add portraits of the two emperors, Commodus and Maximianus who saw themselves as Hercules – or even extend the thematic collection based on Hercules to include the pillar dollars of Spanish America. These show the pillars set up by our hero at the Straits of Gibraltar, when his wanderings took him to these limits of the known world.

439 Thebes. Stater, 395–387 BC. Boeotian shield; infant Hercules strangling snakes. **440** Kroton. Stater, 360–330 BC. Head of Apollo; infant Hercules strangling snakes. **441** Kroton. Stater, 360–330 BC. Head of Hera; Hercules reclining, holding the cup of wine that made him insane.
442 Herakleia. Didrachm, 370–281 BC. Head of Athena in crested helmet ornamented with Scylla; Hercules fighting with the Nemean lion.
443 Phaistos. Stater, 330–322 BC. Hercules holding bow and club; hobbled bull. **444** A similar coin. Hercules fighting a giant snake (the Hydra).
445 Praisos, Crete. Stater, 350–325 BC. Hercules with his bow; flying eagle.
446 Thasos. Drachm, 411–350 BC. Head of bearded Dionysos; Hercules shooting with his bow.

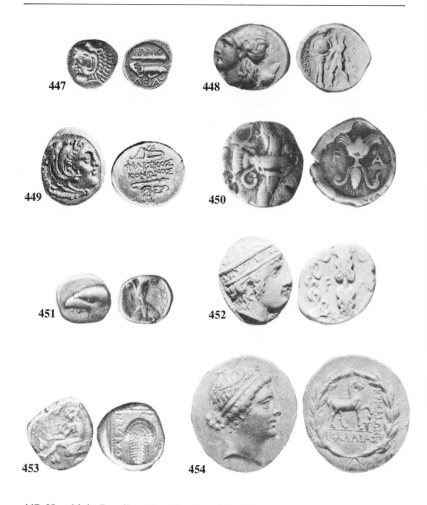

447 Herakleia Pontika. Hemidrachm, 394–364 BC. Head of Hercules; his club and bow-case. **448** Herakleia Pontika. Stater, 345–337 BC. Head of a young Dionysos; Hercules, with his club under his arm, erecting a trophy of arms. **449** Erythrai. Bronze coin, 200–133 BC. Head of Hercules; his club and bow in a case. **450** Olympia. Stater, 471–452 BC. Eagle and snake; thunderbolt. **451** Olympia. Drachm, 421–365 BC. Eagle's head and thunderbolt. **452** Olympia. Stater, 421–365 BC. Hera, wife of Zeus, and thunderbolt. **453** Soloi. Stater, 430–390 BC. Amazon and bunch of grapes. **454** Kyme. Tetradrachm, second century BC. Head of Kyme, the Amazon, founder of the city; a horse in a wreath with a single-handled vase.

XXXVII. SOME MONSTERS: MEDUSA, MARSYAS, PEGASOS AND THE CHIMAERA

Medusa is familiar to us from the story of Perseus. She was one of three terrible sisters called the Gorgons. At one time, she had been a beautiful girl, so beautiful as to attract the amorous attentions of Poseidon, who turned himself into a horse, an animal that he is supposed to have created, to carry her off. He fathered monstrous twins, one of whom was Pegasos, and Medusa gave birth to them in a temple of Athena. This act of desecration so angered the goddess that she turned Medusa into a monster, with wings, brazen claws, enormous teeth and venomous snakes where her hair had been. One glance from this terrifying creature would turn a man to stone.

After numerous heroes had suffered this fate, Perseus set out to kill Medusa. He was befriended by Athena, who lent him a mirror so that he could creep up on the sleeping monster without looking directly at her. Perseus cut off the Gorgon's head and placed it on his shield to use as a weapon against his enemies. Having satisfactorily turned them to stone, he returned the head to Athena, who is shown in statues, and a few coins, with it on her shield or breastplate. Several early coins, notably those of the Etruscans, bear the head of Medusa (295). She was, for some unknown reason, considered appropriate for small denominations and can be found used in this way on, for example, silver coins of Selge, Parion, Kelendris, Apollonia Pontika and bronzes circulated in other cities (455–458).

When Medusa was beheaded, her body gave out a plaintive wailing sound, and such was the only noise Athena could produce when she made herself a flute and tried to play. The other gods laughed as she puffed out her cheeks to blow her instrument and she was so humiliated that she threw away the flute with a curse. In due course, it was found by the satyr, Marsyas. (Satyrs had the torso and head of a man, but below the waist they were goat. They became companions of

Dionysos and are associated with freedom, loose-living and sexual adventures.) Marsyas learnt to play the flute most beautifully, with the result that he became insufferably conceited and, eventually, challenged Apollo, the god of music, to a contest. It was agreed between them that the winner should do what he liked with the loser and that the verdict should be given by a jury. After the contestants had performed, the Muses, who dominated the jury, voted for Apollo and only one of its members supported Marsyas. Then Apollo seized the satyr, tied him to a tree and flayed him alive. The offending jurist, King Midas, was punished by being given the ears of an ass.

The best representations of a satyr are on the coins of the island of Thasos, which probably used the mime in which a satyr carried off a nymph during its annual fertility rites. Some early Macedonian coins are based on the same theme. Marsyas himself is portrayed on a Roman denarius that apparently shows the statue of him erected in the forum (459–461).

Medusa and Athena are connected with another creature and another series of coins. The creature is the winged horse, Pegasos, and the coins are those of Corinth, which were produced to the same basic design over a long period. As mentioned in Chapter 12, Pegasos, the offspring of Medusa and Poseidon, was caught by the Corinthian prince Bellerophon, another of Athena's protégés (462). She gave him a golden bridle, which he slipped over the head of the wonderful animal while he was drinking at the famous fountain of Pirene, situated on the Acrocorinthos. This is the only mountain in the territory of Corinth and, hence, Pegasos became the badge of the city. He had given the city its water supply and, thereby, enabled the Acrocorinthos to be turned into a citadel. Another fountain associated with him is the Hippocrene, sacred to the Muses and the inspiration of poets. It gushed forth when Pegasos struck the rock with his hoof as he galloped through the air. He carried his master, Bellerophon, to various adventures until success turned the latter's head. Bellerophon tried to ride Pegasos up to heaven, something which no mortal should have the conceit to attempt. A wrathful Zeus sent a gad-fly to sting Pegasos, making him rear and throw his rider to his death. But Pegasos flew on into the sky, there to become a constellation.

The winged horse may seem appropriate for the ambitions of Mithradates VI of Pontos, whose career is outlined in an earlier chapter. Some coins from other sources have only the forepart of

Pegasos on them. This design was favoured in the part of Asia Minor called Mysia, though examples also come from places as remote from it as Sicily (464).

Close to Corinth, was the tiny state of Sikyonia, the coins of which often featured a chimaera (463). This fire-breathing monster had the forepart of a lion, the hindquarters of a dragon and a goat's head rising from its back. Its father was the huge lion of Nemea and its mother the nine-headed hydra of Lerna, both eventually killed by Hercules. These two districts adjoined Sikyonia, where their offspring was conceived. Hence, it was appropriate for the citizens to adopt the chimaera as their symbol on coins.

Another association with the chimaera was made through Bellerophon, the local hero who was able to kill it with the help of Pegasos. Bellerophon flew above it and shot his arrows in comparative safety (462). Legend places this incident in Lycia, part of Asia Minor where the chimaera's ravages were, presumably, not a subject of local pride, for there are no numismatic references to it from that part of the Greek world.

The chimaera, Pegasos and Bellerophon can be seen all together on small silver pieces from Corinth and bronzes from her colony Akarnania.

455 Selge. Trihemiobol, third century BC. Gorgon with long hair; head of
Athena.   **456** Parion. Hemidrachm, 350–300 BC. Gorgon and bull.
457 Apollonia Pontika. Drachm, *c.* 400 BC. Head of Gorgon, an anchor and a
crayfish.   **458** Neapolis in Macedon. Hemidrachm, 411–348 BC. Head of
Gorgon; female head, hair in 'pony-tail'.   **459** Roman Republican denarius.
Moneyer: Lucius Censorius, *c.* 82 BC. Statue of Marsyas, carrying his skin;
head of Apollo.   **460** Thasos. Stater, 463–411 BC. Satyr and nymph, with
striking crack.   **461** Thasos. Trihemiobol, 411–350 BC. Satyr with wine cup;
wine amphora.   **462** Corinth. Stater, fifth century BC. Head of Athena;
Bellerophon riding Pegasos.   **463** Sikyon. Drachm, 360–330 BC. Chimaera
and dove.   **464** Skepsis. Diobol, *c.* 350 BC. Forepart of Pegasos and palm
tree.

XXXVIII. THE NON-GREEK GODS

The fusion of religions in the ancient world created a situation in which there were non-Greek elements in most cults, even those of the Immortals. However, numismatic conventions led to the deities worshipped in most local shrines being shown as one or other of the Olympians. There are exceptions and they certainly add interest to a collection based on the religious theme.

Some of the non-Greek gods have already been encountered in earlier chapters. For instance, there is Tanit, the Carthaginian goddess (272–274). The unsqueamish Romans could not stomach the human sacrifices made to her and it is possible to see in her features on some coins the cruelty involved in the practice of flinging children into the red-hot mouth of her huge bronze idol. On the other hand, the same association with fertility gave rise to different portrayals of her in the guise of the kindly Ceres with corn-stalks in her hair. Another god with a strong preference for sacrifices was the Phoenician Baal, involved in the story of Elijah. He appears, bearing a strong resemblance to Hercules, on coins from Tyre, where he was worshipped under the name of Melquarth or Melkart (263–265). Sarapis, the god given to the Egyptians by the Ptolemies to serve as a unifying force, may have been a deliberate invention for political purposes, though his worship soon became popular and flourished for centuries (216). Ammon, who sprouts ram's horns from his head, had a famous temple at Siwa, which Alexander visited when in Egypt. We do not know how seriously he took his self-identification with this god, though Lysimachos' portrayal of the dead king with Ammon's horn makes us wonder whether he did, in fact, believe it (310–313). Ammon can also be found on coins from Kyrene in North Africa, where he served as a protector of the flocks of sheep (465–467).

If we extend the list of non-hellenic gods encountered on coins, we become involved in the religions of Asia Minor. In Karia, the double axe was a symbol of great significance. Several coins show a male deity carrying one (469,470). He is usually assumed to be Zeus, though the reason why he exchanged his customary thunderbolt for this weapon is not clear. The double axe is a major feature of the design on drachms from the Aegean island, Tenedos, where they apparently had a two-faced god. The Roman version is familiar to us. He was Janus, the patron of new undertakings, journeys, doorways and the beginning of the year, which is still named after him. However, the Tenedian coins show a god with a male and a female face, such as is unknown elsewhere. Reconstructions of the palace at Knosos in Crete imply that the double axe was painted on the walls, though it is not shown on the coins. The labyrinth is, of course, and perhaps this maze had a place in some ancient religious cult (473,474).

Asia Minor had its own earth-mother, sometimes called Ma and more often Cybele. Originally the goddess of caverns and mountains, she came to be seen as the earth itself. She ruled over the wild beasts and, therefore, has two lions to accompany her on coins. A legend that she had a son by the king of Phrygia accounted for her cult there or, perhaps, it was the other way about – the cult came first. Cybele is more easily found on Roman coins than Greek. There was probably an element from her cult in the famous Ephesian Artemis – Diana of the Ephesians, as the Bible calls her. Her statue bore no resemblance to the chaste goddess of hunting and the moon, familiar from Greek myths. It was, instead, a semi-human figure with many breasts to indicate fertility. This statue features on several coins from Phrygia, Lydia and, of course, Ephesos (475).

The male deity in Asia Minor was called Mên. Associated with the moon, he usually has a crescent behind him on coins and also holds a pine cone, presumably, a phallic symbol. In his other hand, he usually carries a sceptre to show his authority and, like other gods, he was worshipped as a giver of oracles. Very recognisable in his Phrygian cap which, since the French Revolution, has been called a cap of liberty, Mên was often chosen for the reverses of the bronze coins that the Romans allowed the cities of Asia Minor to mint (240). Another god found on coins acceptable to a much earlier conqueror is the seated figure on the silver minted by Mazaios, the governor of Babylon who surrendered to Alexander. Though the pose is similar to the one struck by Zeus on Alexander's own silver, he cannot be the same deity and is usually called Baal – a term that simply means a god (476–478). Mallos in Cilicia put on its early coins an enigmatic winged figure holding a solar disc. He is thought to be Ahuramazda, worshipped in one of the world's most ancient religions (479–481).

The origins of yet more monsters must lie hidden in long-forgotten cults. For example, cities many miles apart used on their coins the griffin (Panticapaion in the Crimea; Abdera in Thrace (482); Teos in Ionia) (483) and the sphinx (Chios the Ionian island (485); Lycia (484) and the Spanish Celts (344)). We may assume they are the same creatures, but the myths involving them were very different. Also similar on coins, though different in reality, were temples, altars and cult-objects. Our hypothetical collection of coins associated with religion could be as extensive as we care to make it.

The god Ammon and the silphium plant on coins of Kyrene
465 Drachm, 470–440 BC.   **466** Didrachm, 308–277 BC.   **467** Didrachm, *c.* 250 BC.

468 Lesbos. ¹/₆ stater, 450–330 BC. Ammon and eagle.   **469** Karia. Tetradrachm issued by the Persian Governor, Maussollos, 377–353 BC. Head of Apollo; Zeus carrying a double axe.   **470** Didrachm of similar design issued by Pixodaros, 340–334 BC.   **471** Tenedos. Drachm, *c.* 400 BC. Double-headed god with male and female face; double-headed axe. **472** Tetradrachm of similar design, second century BC.

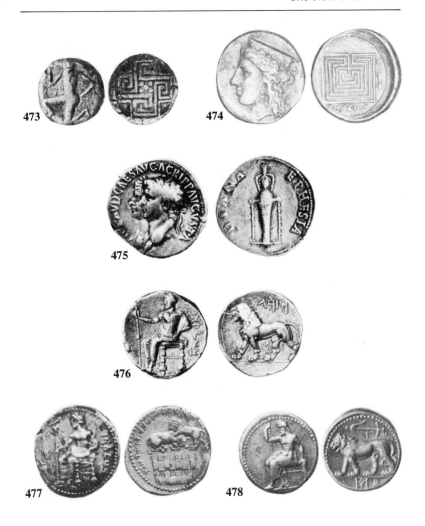

473 Knosos. Stater, 425–360 BC. The Minotaur and Labyrinth.
474 Knosos. Stater, 300–270 BC. Hera and the Labyrinth.   475 Ephesos.
Cistophoric tetradrachm, Claudius and Agrippina, AD 49–54. Statue of
Ephesian Artemis.   476 Babylon. Tetradrachm, issues of the Satrap
Mazaios, 331–328 BC. Baal and a lion.   477 Tetradrachm. Reverse shows a
lion attacking a bull above the city walls.   478 Later issue, incorporating an
anchor, badge of Seleukos I.

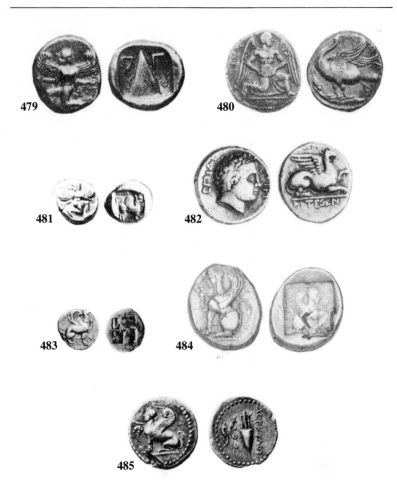

479 Mallos. Stater, *c.* 425 BC. Winged figure and conical cult object.
480 Mallos. Stater, 420–375 BC. Winged figure with solar disc; swan.
481 Mallos. Hemidrachm, *c.* 425 BC. Winged figure and a griffin.
482 Abdera. Stater, 373–360 BC. Head of Apollo and griffin.   **483** Teos.
Trihemiobol, 470–450 BC. Griffin.   **484** Lycia. Stater, *c.* 450 BC.
Sphinxes.   **485** Chios. Drachm, second century BC. Sphinx and amphora.

XXXIX. RIVER-GODS AND WATER-NYMPHS

We tend to take our water supplies for granted in this country – all we have to do is turn on the tap. Life was not so simple in the ancient world. Water had to be fetched from rivers, springs or fountains, and one of the first considerations when building a house or a village was whether good drinking water was readily available at the site. A spring or fountain (the word used when the water perceptibly gushed upwards from the ground) was a prized possession and an object of wonder. Each had its own distinctive character and taste, which lead to an established custom of visiting springs to sample the water – much as we might taste local wines when visiting unfamiliar places. Numerous legends and deities became associated with the springs and, like so much else to do with life in the ancient world, they were represented on coins.

An appropriate beginning in following this theme is the god Acheloos, the personification of the longest river in Greece. As explained in the chapters on Naples and Sicily (64–67), he was represented as a man-headed bull (486,488) and, in this guise, he wrestled with Hercules, coming off much the worse when the strong-man wrenched off one of his horns. In order to recover the horn, he had to exchange the fabulous horn of plenty, which, of course, is the cornucopia held on so many coins by various goddesses.

Other large rivers were supposed to be Acheloos' brothers, and the springs and fountains were his daughters. So, too, were the Sirens, the birds with young women's heads whose beautiful songs tempted mariners away from their courses into danger and death. Acheloos was a suitable choice for the coins of the Akarnanian League, the alliance of the cities of the district called Akarnania, which was bordered by the River Archeloos. There is a clear portrait of him on the League's staters, though it is unusual to find him depicted as a youth (487).

More commonly, he is bearded, as on the silver pieces minted in Gela, one of the wealthiest cities of Sicily. Gela stood at the mouth of the river Gelas, which is represented by the man-headed bull swimming on the obverses of its coins. Mythologically speaking, he might be a brother of the god Acheloos or Acheloos himself, who represented all fresh water. However, there is literary evidence that Gela housed a fine statue of its god in the form of a bull.

A similar bull makes his appearance on the coins of Neapolis – modern Naples. We saw in Chapter 8, the name means 'new town' and was used after the city was refounded by Italian settlers after being sacked. The original inhabitants came from Rhodes and named their city after Parthenope, one of the Sirens. She was placed on their coins, together with her father, Acheloos, in whose honour annual games were held. It would appear that he was worshipped throughout a wide area of Italy – water was precious, especially in hot climates. The cult was kept alive in Naples, which retained much of its Greek character even though it came under Roman domination at an early date.

The fountain nymph Terina had the same name as that Italian city, on the coins of which she is portrayed as a beautiful maiden. The usual reverse carries a figure of Victory in one of several poses, some of which show her seated on an amphora or drawing water from the fountain. A similar combination is found on coins from Himera in Sicily (489–492).

Victory flies above a charioteer, who is believed to be Pelops, a mythical early king who gained his bride and his kingdom by sabotaging his rival's chariot in a contest. Interest is directed to the other side of the coin which shows an elaborate scene. Himera, the city-nymph, is making a sacrifice over an altar while, in the background, the satyr, Silenos, is bathing in a fountain. The trough and lion-headed spout are clear and they give us a hint of the arrangements made for the principal water supplies in cities to be conveniently used by everyone.

Another Sicilian town the coins of which are connected with a river is Segesta. It was supposedly founded by Egostos, son of a Trojan maiden who was taken advantage of by the river-god Krimissos, who appeared to her in the form of a dog. The maiden, Segesta, is portrayed on the coins with the dog. The inhabitants of the city were not of Greek origin, being referred to as Elymi, and the myth, presumably, records folk-memories of their origins in Asia Minor and their migration to the banks of the Krimissos (80).

We have already encountered the beautiful coins of Syracuse (84–92) where generations of artists vied with each other to portray Arethusa, the nymph of the fountain on the island of Ortygia which was their stronghold. The ancient and, also, the modern city was built on this island, which dominated an excellent natural harbour and, most fortunately, had a never-failing supply of fresh water – the first essential if a city was to withstand a siege. Arethusa was given credit for Syracuse's prosperity and military successes by being placed on the majority of the city's coins. The dolphins that surround her are a symbol of sea power and the victorious chariot is an accepted prestige design, be it for a triumph on the battlefield or at the Olympic Games. Several Syracusan artists signed their dies and, if one is very affluent, one could collect a series of superb pieces that are uniquely attributable to individuals. Apart from the pleasure they would give, there can be few better investments.

Syracusan coins were admired greatly by contemporaries and copied in several cities. One of the most successful imitations is the head of Larissa, the nymph who was supposed to live in the fountain that gave the town of that name its water. It was the most important town in Thessaly, situated amid luxurious water-meadows on which fed the horses that were its best-known export (493–495).

A nymph, whose story is different from those of other young women who attracted the attention of the gods, is Sinope. Her city was on the southern coast of the Black Sea, beside the river Asopus. Her beauty attracted Zeus, whose eye for young ladies was notorious. In order to win her favour, he promised her any gift she liked – she chose virginity! The frustrated god had to grant her wish and let her spend her days in happy solitude. It is interesting to speculate on the early history behind this story and whether a reasonable explanation is found or not, one can obtain some attractive coins which show Sinope's portrait backed by a sea-eagle attacking a dolphin, doubtless, a relic of some naval conflict. A large hoard of these coins came onto the market a decade ago, so they are relatively inexpensive (496).

Another city, the nymph of which was associated on its coins with a naval success that is now a mystery, was Histiaia on the Island of Euboea. She sits on the stern of a galley on the reverses of the silver pieces and has her portrait on the obverses (497,498). Histiaia does not strictly qualify for inclusion in our fresh-water collection, for she was not a river-nymph (naiad), but a sea-nymph (maenad). However, she is included because of the way she is portrayed. The artist shows her hair floating in the water, which is very appropriate. Only the modern cynic asks how our numismatic nymphs managed to keep their beautiful coiffures when they were always getting their hair wet.

The convention that large rivers were male was continued on the coins minted by provincial cities in the Roman Empire. A bearded, mature man, swimming in the river, seems to have been the favourite image. 'Old Father Thames' may have once been thus personified. However, the cities that observed this convention were on the other side of the empire. Two had mints working for King Tigranes of Armenia. He used, on his reverses, the city-goddesses of Antioch and Damascus, at whose feet the river-god is swimming (252). The statue of this scene at Antioch was copied by other cities and, in the Roman period, the Nile and Tiber were similarly treated on coins.

486 Gela, Sicily. Didrachm, 420–415 BC. Mounted warrior; man-headed bull
(Acheloos). **487** Akarnanian League. $\frac{1}{2}$ stater, 400–350 BC. Head of
Acheloos and Apollo. **488** Hyria. Didrachm, 400–335 BC. Head of Hera;
Acheloos walking. **489** Terina. Stater, 445–425 BC. Head of nymph, Terina
(her brow obscured by a die-crack), and Nike seated on an amphora. **490** A
similar coin, 400–356 BC. Nike holds a bird. **491** Another variation. Terina
seated holding a patera; she is crowned by Nike. **492** Himera. Tetradrachm,
415–408 BC. Chariot, nymph sacrificing; a satyr looks on. **493** Larissa.
Drachm, 360–350 BC. Head of Larissa and a horse.

494 Larissa. Drachm, 350–325 BC. Head of Larissa, three-quarter face; grazing horse.   **495** A similar coin. Mare with foal.   **496** Sinope. Drachm, 365–322 BC. Nymph Sinope; sea-eagle clutching a dolphin.   **497** Histiaia. Tetrobol, third century BC. Nymph Histaia shown seated on the stern of a galley.   **498** Macedon. A similar coin believed to be an imitation produced about 165 BC.

XXXX. THE GREEKS
AND THE SEA

What would Greece be without the sea? Most of the mainland towns are built beside it or only a short distance away. The scores of islands are linked by it. Modern tourism makes the most of idyllic beaches and the shipping millionaires are reputed to dream of buying an island of their own – nothing quite compares with this as a sign of success. Much earlier seafarers traded between the Greek cities and brought the prosperity that gave rise to coinage. Anyone interested in maritime affairs might take the sea as his collecting theme and everyone concerned with Greek coins should be aware of its influence on them.

The earliest European coins were minted on the island of Aegina, within sight of Athens. At the time (sixth or early seventh century BC), Aegina was a greater commercial centre than Athens which, as we all know, eventually far surpassed her. She used, as her badge, a sea-turtle, probably alluding to her seafaring activities (103–108).

Another creature that proved popular as a symbol of mastery over the sea was the dolphin, the apparently effortless dash and agility of which still reminds skippers of small boats of their inadequacy. Taras, the founder of Tarentum, was supposed to have been one of Poseidon's sons, who was saved from drowning in a shipwreck by a dolphin sent by his father. He is shown riding it on most of the silver coins minted in his city (52–60). A few early silver pieces show another aquatic animal, the mythical sea-horse, associated with Poseidon (499). It appeared infrequently on coins, though a good example comes from Tyre, the famous Phoenician city. Its god, Melqarth, rides a sea-horse (256).

Tyre's neighbour, Sidon, provided most of the coinage needed by the Phoenicians. Its splendidly barbaric silver pieces show the king of Persia in his chariot and either the city's fortifications or a galley (253–255). Its fleet was one of Sidon's claims to fame and we, in

Britain, like to believe that the Phoenician ships reached St Michael's Mount to trade for tin, our first contact with the classical world. To the Greeks, the Phoenicians were an alien race whose customs were not admired. The same probably applied to the coins, since the Greek love of restraint required more subtle indications of maritime supremacy.

The exact reasons for the choice of a coin design often elude us. Hence, we are not sure why the crab appears on the coins of Akragas (68). It could be the attribute of Poseidon, which would appropriately balance the Eagle of Zeus on the other side. But Akragas was not a port: it stood a few miles inland, where two small Sicilian rivers met. One of them had the same name as the town, so is the fresh-water crab appropriate as a badge? It is certainly an ideal choice for putting into a circular space. One also appeared on the coins of Himera for a time. This city was occupied by Theron, ruler of Akragas, and Gelon, the Tyrant of Syracuse, in their campaign to drive the Carthaginians out of Sicily. They won a conclusive victory there and, for two generations, Akragas prospered, treating Himera as a dependency. On its coins, the crab is accompanied by a cock, instead of an eagle, to indicate that a certain amount of independence remained (72).

Another pair of cities that shared the same coin design is Sinope and Istros on the Black Sea. Though they are many miles apart – Sinope is in the middle of the south coast and Istros is in the north-west, near the mouth of the Danube (the River Ister in ancient times) – they both chose a sea-eagle sinking its talons into a dolphin. There must be a reason for the coincidence, though we do not know it. Some sort of trading agreement is possible. Both cities had large merchant fleets (496,500).

Syracuse which, as has already been said, was the most prosperous city in Sicily, had a powerful fleet. Dolphins surround the head of the nymph Arethusa on its tetradrachms, which were produced in sufficient quantities to need hundreds of dies (84–92). A rich collector might decide to specialise in these alone, but most of us would probably settle for a bronze coin that makes the dolphins the major element in its design (501). A more unusual choice was made for the litrae, very small silver pieces (502), which have an octopus on them. These creatures have been caught and eaten for many years in the countries around the Mediterranean and, probably, Syracuse was publicising its fisheries. They would have been an added bonus if the Carthaginians had succeeded in occupying Sicily. Their prolonged struggle to do so involved hiring large numbers of mercenaries and minting the money to pay them. Carthaginian tetradrachms for use in Sicily have the horse and palm symbols of Carthage backing Arethusa and the dolphins copied from Syracusan coins (268). The need for acceptability was one reason why these obverses were chosen and another may have been the desire to assert naval supremacy.

One city made the ship its badge on both sides of its coins. This was Phaselis in Lycia, an old settlement that probably chose the designs as a play on words (503,504). A phaselus was a long, narrow boat built for speed. Its prow can be seen on the obverse of staters and the stern on the reverse. A crayfish appears on coins from Apollonia Pontika, the port on the west coast of the Black Sea best known for its temple to Apollo (457,505). The anchor was its badge, giving it something in common with the Seleukid kings of Syria, who sometimes marked coins with an anchor, a dynastic badge believed to have been adopted by Seleukos I after his naval victories as Ptolemy's admiral (171,173,478).

Naturally, Poseidon, as god of the sea, was venerated in many cities and was placed on coins. Italian examples come from Poseidonia (45).

More spectacular representations of Poseidon can be found on the coins minted by Alexander's successors in the Kingdom of Macedon. Demetrios Poliorketes commemorated a decisive naval victory over the Egyptian fleet by striking distinctive tetradrachms. Nike stands on the prow of the galley blowing her trumpet and, on the reverse, Poseidon wields his trident for Demetrios (161,162).

Some years later, Demetrios built up another huge fleet and provided himself with money to pay the crews. This time, the royal portrait, complete with horns to show semi-divine status, is backed by Poseidon who stands with his foot on a rock, surveying the sea which, by implication, is also Demetrios' kingdom. Though Demetrios' plans were frustrated, his son imitated his example, after defeating the Egyptian fleet off the island of Cos. In gratitude, he founded shrines for Poseidon and Apollo, and issued tetradrachms in their honour. Neptune's unruly locks are held in place with a headband of seaweed and Apollo sits on a ship's prow which bears the king's name (164).

Historical references on coins connected with the sea can be supplemented from literature and this leads to those famous voyages carried out by the Argonauts and Odysseus, which are next covered in detail.

499 Tarentum. Stater, 500–473 BC. Taras riding a dolphin; hippocamp.
500 Istros. Stater, 400–350 BC. Two male heads (The Dioskouroi?); sea-eagle
on a dolphin.   **501** Syracuse. Bronze coin, 344–336 BC. Head of Athena;
starfish between two dolphins.   **502** Syracuse. Litra, 344–317 BC. Head of
Arethusa and octopus.   **503** Phaselis. Tetrobol, *c.* 450 BC. Prow of galley
resembling a boar; stern of a galley.   **504** Phaselis. Stater, third century BC.
Prow and stern of a galley.   **505** Apollonia Pontika. Drachm, 450–400 BC.
Gorgon, anchor and crayfish.

XXXXI. THE VOYAGE OF THE ARGO

One of the most familiar Greek myths is the story of how Jason and his companions made an expedition to retrieve the golden fleece. Apparently, it was an old, well-loved story long before Homer composed the epic of the Trojan War. Modern scholars make an informed guess that, if such a voyage ever happened, the thirteenth century BC would be the most probable period for it. Of course, all the miraculous things that occurred are myth, the additions and elaborations to the original account by generations of bards seeking to include as much entertainment material as possible and, also, to please their hosts. Robert Graves has written a fine analysis of the historical basis for myth, indicating that the story of the Argonauts was based on half-remembered wars, piracy and travellers' tales of the lands on the edge of the Greek world. He further complicates the issue by suggesting that the original expedition went in the opposite direction from that which was later believed, and visited the Adriatic, not the Black Sea. He may well be right, though, for present purposes, we shall stick to the accepted tradition.

So, to take up the story, which is supposed to have happened a generation before the Trojan War, fetching the golden fleece was a task imposed on the hero, Jason, before he was allowed to inherit the kingdom that was rightly his. This type of apparently impossible mission can be found in the folk-lore of many nations and the difficulties to be overcome tend to increase with the telling. The fleece hung in the shrine of Ares (better known to us as Mars, the god of war) where it was guarded by a dragon. It had been hung up there by Phrixus, a member of the royal family of Jason's native land, Iolchus, which was a very ancient site in Thessaly, eastern Greece. The magical ram had enabled Phrixus to escape a murder plot by fleeing to the most remote place where he would be acceptable. This was the kingdom of

Aea, generally understood to be at the extreme eastern end of the Black Sea. The later Greeks called it Colchis and we call it Georgia. Apart from being a valuable object in itself, the fleece had another attribute. Since it had been a religious offering made by Phrixus, it had the power to lay his ghost, which was haunting Iolchus because he had not been properly buried.

Neither Phrixus nor Jason appear on coins: Iolchus lost its importance by the time coinage was invented, though Colchis could be represented in our collection by a very rare fifth-century coin that shows a monster like the Minotaur – a bull-headed man. Much more easily, we could obtain a good numismatic representation of Ares (506).

Jason was set his task by the usurping king, Pelias, who had been warned to beware of a man who was wearing one sandal. Jason had lost the other one wading across a river and it reappears on the early coins of Larissa, the most important Thessalian town. Naturally, he was not expected to succeed, but he invited stalwart volunteers to join him and was soon the leader of a very distinguished group indeed. There are several lists of Argonauts. Robert Graves suggests that every city claiming trading rights in the Black Sea had to have one of its ancestral heroes in the crew. If this is so, then coins from a great many cities could be given a place in our collection. Individual discretion must decide what degree of completeness to aim at. For the moment, I should be content with Hercules, the strong-man; the Dioskouroi (500), the heavenly twins (400); and Atalanta (507), the celebrated lady athlete. All can be found without much difficulty among the Greek coins usually offered for sale.

Their ship was called the Argo. It had fifty oars, making it large for its time, but giving room for the inclusion of the heroes that tradition demanded. An unusual feature was a piece of the talking oak of Dodona, the shrine of an oracle personified on a coin issued by King Pyrrhus of Epeiros (226). Thus, the ship was able to warn of perils and even to refuse to sail unless certain ritual obligations were complied with. There is no certain representation of the Argo on coins, though there are plenty of ships to be had. An appropriate choice would be the hemidrachm of Kios in Bithynia, which shows a ship's prow and a portrait of Apollo (519). Since he was the god of embarkations, Jason sacrificed to him before setting out. His lyre often appears on coins and an example might be included to remind us of Orpheus, the poet and musician whose lyre-playing was put to good use on occasions throughout the voyage (508,509). He calmed down the drunken brawlers at the feast on the evening before they set sail and competed successfully with the Sirens, whose wonderful songs led mariners to their deaths.

The expedition might have come to an inglorious end at their first port of call, the Island of Lemnos. It was supposed to have been inhabited only by women. They had apparently quarrelled with their husbands and killed them, leaving a problem. How was the population to renew itself? The Argonauts were welcomed with open arms and had a marvellous time. Hercules, who had been left guarding the ship, grew impatient and went round banging on the doors with his club to get everyone out of bed. Though a large island, Lemnos produced only a few coins, rather insignificant bronzes, to represent it in our hypothetical collection.

Reluctantly, the Argonauts resumed their voyage and passed through the Hellespont (the narrow straits on the European side of the entrance to the Black Sea), by night, thus avoiding an attack by the Trojans, who would not allow Greek ships to go there. Here, we have a hint at the trade rivalry behind the Trojan War. When they were safely into the Sea of Marmora, the wider part of the connecting channel, the ship's company disembarked at a peninsula ruled by a king called Kyzikos. This is the name of a city on the southern Marmorean Sea coast and some confusion may have crept into the story here. It certainly gives us a reason for adding one of the splendid coins that city produced (510).

While being entertained at King Kyzikos' wedding feast, the Argonauts were informed that their ship had almost been captured by giants, but the guards had been able to drive them off. Thankfully, the ship's company dedicated their anchor to Athena, who had protected them, and acquired a new one. An anchor is the main feature of some coins from Apollonia in Thrace, while the gorgon on the reverse reminds us of other monsters to be encountered (457,505). After that incident, the Argonauts set sail again, only to be driven off course by a gale. They landed at an unrecognised spot in the pitch dark and were attacked. Once again, they drove away their adversaries, one of whom was killed. Unfortunately, daylight revealed that he was King Kyzikos, who had led his men against what they supposed were pirates. This accident proved to be the work of the local goddess who was seeking revenge against Kyzikos because he had killed her sacred lion.

After suitable apologies and funeral rites, the Argonauts sailed on. They beached the ship on the coast of Mysia, the shore of the southern Marmorean Sea. There, Hercules, who had uprooted a pine tree to make a new oar to replace one that he had broken, lost his young companion Hylas. Searches revealed only the pitcher that Hylas had taken to fill with water and it was concluded that the nymphs had lured him into a lake, as their bridegroom. Hercules was not content to leave it at that and enlisted the help of everyone he met in his search. Jason felt that he could no longer hang about waiting for Hercules, so he set sail, abandoning the strong-man who, conveniently for the myth-makers, had an opportunity to undertake some more labours.

Next, the island of Berbrycos was reached. Amycus, its king, refused the sailors food and water until they agreed to enter one of the crew in a boxing match with him. This practice was normal and those who refused were simply flung over a cliff. What political encounter or primitive religious rites this story represents is uncertain, but King Amycus had underestimated his opponents on this occasion. One of the heavenly twins, Polydeukes, or Pollux, as the Romans called him, had won the boxing at the Olympic Games. A ding-dong struggle ended with a powerful uppercut that killed Amycus. Greek boxing, it must be said, was like prize-fighting and serious injuries were common. Killings had to be atoned for, so sacrifices were made to Poseidon, from whom Amycus claimed descent.

Calling at Salmydessus in Eastern Thrace, the Argonauts encountered the blind prophet Phineus, who was plagued by the Harpies. These female flying monsters had been sent by Hera to steal his food and torment him, because he had been arrogant enough to claim the privileges of the gods and foretell the future accurately. Hera, the mother of the gods, was honoured in Elis, the state in which the Olympic Games took place. As consort of Zeus, to whom they were dedicated, she appears on coins accompanied by a thunderbolt (452).

Her Harpies were chased away and the grateful Phineus told the Argonauts how to get through the Bosphorus, the eastern straits leading to the Black Sea, which were guarded by mist-covered rocks that crashed together, destroying any ship that tried to pass. Jason was instructed to release a dove (the badge that Sikyon put on its coins) (463), which flew through the closing gap, just getting clear with the loss of a few tail feathers. As the rocks shuddered back to their place, the Argo dashed between them as fast as she could be rowed and, like the dove, escaped without damage, except to her stern ornament. The misty moving rocks were probably icebergs, transferred in the story from some more northerly situation.

When the Argonauts next went ashore, it was at a place called Mariandyne, where they were made welcome because they had killed Amycus, who had long been an enemy – a blockade of their shipping seems a likely explanation. Bad luck came in the form of a boar who savaged Idmon the Wise, with the result that he bled to death. Attack by these animals was a hazard of life in the early Greek world and several cities put wild boars on their coins (507,512). A very fierce-looking one is to be found on the issues of Lyttos, a small settlement in Crete (511). Even worse luck developed when Tiphys, the steersman, died of disease, so the Argonauts moved on to Sinope, where replacements were found to fill the rowers' benches. This city was one of the most important on the south coast and produced plenty of coins. I would choose an early one with the vigorous eagle head (513).

After their rest at Sinope, the Argonauts pushed on, avoiding the country of the Amazons and, also, the Chalybians, the iron-workers who lived by trading their wares for other necessities. The only city that featured Amazons on its coins was Soloi in Cicilia (453). They are shown attending to their bows. Possibly, at one time, this city, which is in a different part of Asia Minor from that which our heroes reached, was famous for its archers. The dies were made in such an archaic style that we cannot be certain whether the figures are intended to be male or female, but I like the idea that they are Amazons! Unfortunately, apart from the uncommon choice of Hephaestos (Vulcan) as a coin design, I would be hard-pressed to find a coin suitable to represent iron-workers and the same applies to the Stymphalian birds that were the next dangerous creatures to be encountered. They lived on an island dedicated to Ares and had a nasty habit of dropping their feathers on people. These feathers were made of bronze and came down like darts. The Argonauts defended each other with their shields and were able to row up to the island, whereupon the birds flew off.

After that, they reached Colchis and all they had to do was get the fleece. King Aeëtes refused to hand it over – it would be an anti-climax if he behaved otherwise – and Jason was again in need of divine help.

His protectors, Hera and Athena, discussed the problem and decided to enlist the aid of Aphrodite, the love goddess, who can be found on Corinthian coins (114,115). She sent her son Eros to shoot his arrow into the heart of the king's daughter, with the result that she fell head over heels in love with Jason. This princess was Medea, the witch, who appears in Greek mythology as the worker of spells and an authority-figure in her own right. Of course, she took Jason's side and her father relented sufficiently to promise that Jason could have the fleece if he performed yet another apparently impossible task. This was to harness fire-breathing bulls, plough with them, sow dragon's teeth and combat the warriors who would spring up from the furrows. Medea gave her lover some magic ointment made from the poisonous saffron crocus (still called colchicum in our gardening catalogues) which calmed the bulls. The warriors were tricked into fighting among themselves and the problem seemed to have been solved. However, Aeëtes did not keep his word and the fleece had to be stolen from under the nose of the dragon that guarded it. There are several coins which could represent the dragon. One, with a gorgon head, has already been mentioned and the Sikyonian dove is backed on staters by a chimaera (463), a creature that is part lion, part goat and part monster – dragon, let us say.

The theft was discovered as the Argonauts made their way back to the Argo and they had to fight a rearguard action to cover the launching. As we would expect, they got away, though hotly pursued. Medea was able to heal most of their wounds by means of her drugs and they returned along the route by which they had come. At least, that is what Robert Graves concludes, in spite of the fact that there are many variations to the story of the Argonauts' return. One version tells how the pursuers caught up with the Argo at Korkyra (Corfu), where attitudes to women stand out clearly in the local king's decision that, if Medea were still a virgin, she should be sent home but, if she were not, Jason could keep her. Presumably, she was not a woman to take liberties with, for she had not yet been bedded, and Jason organised a midnight wedding to cope with the problem. How the ship got to Corfu is immaterial, though there are some attractive Korkyran coins, the main features of which are a cow and calf. We could include them in our collection along with a Carthaginian stater or two that would have circulated in Libya, whither a tremendous gale blew the Argonauts when they were almost in sight of Iolchus, the end of their return voyage. A tidal wave cast the ship inland and then retreated, leaving it high and dry. The Argonauts were in danger of perishing ignominiously in the desert but, by using rollers, they managed to drag the ship as far as a lake which, unfortunately, proved to be salt. One of their number who had gone in search of food was killed by a shepherd (Ammon) (465–467) fighting to save his flock and, in turn, the shepherd was hunted down in revenge. Once again, it was necessary to atone for spilling blood so a great tripod altar that was in the ship's cargo was dedicated to the gods of the place (40,41). Thereupon, the fish-tailed Triton appeared and agreed to tow the Argo down river to the Mediterranean. Several creatures that might be Tritons appear on coins, as does Scylla, the man-eating monster who lived in the straits between Italy and Sicily. We show her on Athena's helmet, a device used by the inhabitants of the Italian city of Thourioi to show their claim to sea power (47–51). The bull on the reverse, and another from Phaistos, are appropriate reminders of what happened at the ceremonies associated with funerals. No less than twenty bulls are supposed to have been slaughtered on the death of King Amycus. Though they were stolen property, their value would have been immense and, by dedicating them to the gods, Jason was giving up great wealth.

Sailing via Crete, where the rock-throwing bronze guardian (the first steam-driven machine?) had to be overcome (514), the Argonauts returned to Iolchus and dedicated their ship to Poseidon. The last stage in the epic was for them to overcome Pelias' resistance and make Jason king. It became clear that a frontal attack on the city would result in heavy losses, so Medea resorted to a stratagem. She and her servant-girls, dressed up like sea-nymphs, came to the city and announced that the goddess Artemis had chosen to visit it. (She can be found on several different coins (515–517).) Among other things, Artemis could rejuvenate people. Medea demonstrated how this was done, first by removing her own disguise and appearing to Pelias as a young woman instead of an old crone, then putting up an old ram, boiling the pieces and substituting a lamb that had been hidden in the hollow statue of Artemis her maids had been carrying. After that, Pelias agreed to be cut up and boiled, so that he could become young again. The result will be obvious.

The last coin we should look for is one of the fifth-century silver pieces featuring a corn grain, with an incuse reverse, the only currency produced for the ancient city of Orchomenos in Boeotia, for it was there that the golden fleece found its final resting place in the temple of Zeus (518).

506 Tarsos. Stater struck by the Satrap Datames, 379–374 BC. Female head, copied from the Arethusa on Syracusan coins; head of Ares in crested helmet.　**507** Aetolian League. ¼ stater, 279–168 BC. Head of Atalanta and the Kalydonian Boar, which she killed.　**508** Kolophon. Drachm, 430–400 BC. Head of Apollo and his lyre.　**509** Chalkidian League. Tetradrachm, 379–348 BC. Apollo and his lyre.　**510** Kyzikos. Tetradrachm, 390–330 BC. Head of Persephone; lion and tunny fish.　**511** Lyttos. Stater, 320–270 BC. Eagle and boar's head.

512 Lycia. Stater, *c.* 500 BC. Boar's head.   **513** Sinope. Drachm, 480–450 BC. Eagle's head.   **514** Phaistos, Crete, Stater, 300–270 BC. Winged male, probably Talos, the rock-throwing bronze man; a bull. **515** Aetolian League. ½ stater, 279–168 BC. Head of Artemis with bow and quiver; personification of Aetolia as an Amazon ?   **516** Syracuse. 12 litrai piece, 214–212 BC. Head of Athena; Artemis with bow and hunting-dog. **517** Perge. Tetradrachm, third century BC. Head of Artemis; on the reverse, she holds a wreath and sceptre; there is a stag beside her.   **518** Orchomenos. Obol, 510–480 BC. Corn grain.   **519** Kios. Hemidrachm, 350–300 BC. Head of Apollo; prow of a galley.

XXXXII. THE ODYSSEY

This epic, attributed to Homer, tells of the adventures of the Greek hero Odysseus (or more correctly Ulysses or Ulixes – the Greek versions of his name).

He was the ruler of Ithaca, a small island roughly twelve miles by four, situated off the coast of Epeiros in western Greece. When the Trojan War began, the principal Greek leaders, Agamemnon and Menelaus, persuaded him to accompany them, though Odysseus had been warned by an oracle that he would not see his home again for twenty years. Our collection should start with coins from Ithaca though, since it had lost any commercial importance it may have had in earlier days by the time it came to produce coinage, they are only small bronzes. As one would expect, they carry a portrait of Odysseus, who is shown wearing a sailor's cap.

Troy was destroyed centuries before money was invented, though it was refounded and came to be known as Ilion (Ilium) in Troas, the north-west tip of Asia Minor. Excavations in the great mound that is the site of Troy indicate that the coin-issuing city was established in the seventh century BC on the ruins of several earlier settlements. Which one was the Troy of the Homeric epics remains uncertain. Even the date of the conflict is problematical. The thirteenth century BC is a reasonable suggestion. One would never guess from Ilion's coins that there had been a war at all. They feature a portrait of Athena and a personification of the city and, thus, are very similar to other products of the towns in Asia Minor (520).

Personally, I would represent the Trojan War by including in the collection one of the coins that show a Greek warrior in traditional fighting attire – naked except for helmet and greaves, carrying shield and sword. Good examples come from Lycia, another part of Asia Minor, though there are several to choose from (521–525). With a little imagination, he could represent a particular warrior, such as Achilles, with whom Odysseus negotiated when a dispute led to Achilles' withdrawal from the fighting.

Odysseus was useful as a diplomat and a spy because he was shrewd and cautious, as well as being renowned for courage and perseverance. These qualities appealed to Athena, who was his protectress throughout his long journey, which started after the war ended and the Greeks dispersed. Odysseus began the voyage with a large number of ships and companions, though they gradually grew fewer. The very first place he visited – Cicones, a town in Thrace – was plundered by his followers, who suffered seventy-two casualties when the people living in the neighbouring area came to the rescue of their kinsmen. Hurrying away, Odysseus encountered a fierce storm that drove him south, past Greece and on to the coast of North Africa. That area could be represented in our collection by a Carthaginian stater, since this was the currency of the most important state there. However, another possibility is a coin from Kyrene, which was a city famous for exporting the silphium plant (465–467). Rather like rhubarb, it was a drug believed to cure all kinds of complaints and, for other purposes, could be a substitute for whatever it was that kept the Lotus-eaters happy. These people were so fond of their delicious fruit that they forgot everything else and, after Odysseus' companions followed suit, he had great difficulty in persuading them to leave for home.

Navigation was simple in those days, when mariners were rarely out of sight of land, though where Odysseus went next is pure speculation. The winds drove him 'into the Western Seas' a long way from Greece, where only travellers' tales indicated what was to be found there. Since the Odyssey is the first novel (according to Robert Graves), we have every reason to distrust the geography and should not try to find coins from every place mentioned.

The little fleet reached a land that was, at first, apparently unpopulated except for large herds of goats – valuable animals sometimes put on coins like the fourth-century stater from Kelendris (35,526). However, Odysseus and his twelve close companions soon learnt that the flocks belonged to one-eyed giants who penned them up for the night. The travellers were trapped in the cave where Polyphemus lived, and he proceeded to have supper and breakfast by eating four of them. By the well-known stratagem of blinding the giant with a stake and then tying themselves to the undersides of his sheep,

Odysseus and the survivors escaped from the cave, allowing our hero to continue his adventure.

A sheep would merit inclusion in our collection and there are several numismatic rams (527,528). Perhaps the god with ram's horns, called Zeus Ammon, who appears on the Kyrenian coin already mentioned, would be suitable, too.

Unfortunately for Odysseus, Polyphemus cursed him and prayed to Poseidon to avenge him. To have the god of the sea against one was a grave misfortune in anything to do with ships. Conversely, a naval victory was ascribed to Poseidon's help, so a commemorative tetradrachm issued by the Macedonian King, Demetrius Poliorketes, would look splendid in our 'cabinet' (161,162,164). Before leaving Polyphemus, it might be as well to remember that the strong wine used to make him fall asleep had been given by Odysseus by a priest of Apollo called Maron and that a Thracian town was named after him. Its best known coins were tetradrachms with a portrait of Dionysos, the god of wine (428).

Next, the little fleet landed on the island that belonged to Aeolus, Keeper of the Winds – not likely to be found in an atlas. He was persuaded to put all the winds except the west into a bag and give it to Odysseus. Thus, a steady west wind prevailed and carried the ship towards Ithaca for nine days. It had almost arrived there when the sailors, thinking that their captain had a valuable treasure in his bag, opened it. The result was predictable – the winds escaped and rushed back to Aeolus, driving the ship with them. Poor Odysseus, full of apologies, asked again for help but was turned away on the grounds that one should not aid somebody so obviously cursed.

Odysseus was carried even further west to Telepylus – 'the Far-off Gate', one of the limits of the known world. To represent this place, may I suggest one of the outlandish bronzes from southern Spain? The strange head and even stranger creatures which these coins have on them, are the little-understood evidence of how local tribes tried to join in the commerce of the Greco-Roman world. It is extremely doubtful if they descended from the cannibals that Odysseus encountered and, even if they did, they would not have boasted of the fact. The cannibals hurled rocks from the cliffs, smashing holes in the ships, and sank eleven out of the twelve. Odysseus had been more cautious than his companions and, instead of pulling his ship on to the beach, had left it moored in a spot from which he could make a quick getaway. He was learning from experience!

Similarly, when the remaining ship reached Circe's island, Odysseus sent an advance party to spy out the land. These were the sailors who were entertained to a sumptuous meal by that sorceress and turned into pigs. Why not have a coin with a pig on it to represent them? The city of Klazomenai had as its badge a winged boar, which is suitably improbable for our story (24). When Odysseus went to look for his companions, he met the god Hermes, who gave him a flower which was a rare drug to counteract Circe's spells.

Hermes, the messenger of the gods, proved useful to Odysseus on several occasions and should have a coin to himself; one from Sybrita in Crete would be first choice (529). After Circe admitted defeat, she restored Odysseus' crew to their normal state and provided plenty of food and drink for them, so that they enjoyed a year of pleasure. Odysseus reputedly fathered several children by her – an incident that apparently caused no concern in a society that expected Penelope, his wife, to refrain from sexual relations with anyone else while she waited patiently for twenty years until he returned to Ithaca.

Eventually, the crew urged Odysseus to sail home, so he set out again. Circe advised him to consult someone who should know how to combat Poseidon's hostility and suggested a dead prophet called Tiresias. The land of the dead was supposed to be on the furthest shore of the ocean, a notion adapted by the Celts, who talked of the Isle of the Blessed. They would have had no need for coins there, though, since Britain was the remotest western island known to the Greeks, we might feel inclined to put a tribal stater into our collection (316–322). After Tiresias had been bribed with a drink of blood – an essential of life that ghosts lacked – he told Odysseus how to get home. His route was straightforward, but a temptation would be the splendid cattle of the sun god, which were kept on an island called Thrinacia, sometimes identified with Sicily. So, after spending a little time in conversation with the spirits of his dead friends and relations and, also, some interesting celebrities whom he was delighted to meet, Odysseus returned to Circe.

She gave him navigating instructions and conjured up a favourable wind which took him past the Sirens, whom readers will, by now, recognise as the winged females whose beautiful songs lured sailors to their deaths. They are not represented in this form on coins, because their appearance would bring bad luck to the issuing city (454).

However, their father, the river-god Acheloos, is. He is the man-headed bull worshipped in Italy and placed on the silver minted for Naples. Since the Romans claimed that an island near that city was the one inhabited in former times by the Sirens, a Neapolitan coin seems very appropriate (64–67). Only Odysseus heard the Sirens' song for he stopped up his companions' ears with wax, after ordering them to tie him to the mast, so he could not leap overboard and swim to the fatal island.

Their next hazard was the passage betwen the two monsters Scylla and Charybdis. One was a whirlpool, the other a many-headed monster who ate sailors. This monster was used as a badge on the helmet worn by Athena when she appeared on the coins of Thourioi in Lucania, southern Italy. At the time when they were minted, the Straits between Italy and Sicily were supposed to be Scylla's home (49–50).

Nearby, was the area where the splendid cattle sacred to Helios were kept, though his favourite island was Rhodes on the coins of which he always appeared (133–135). Odysseus made his companions promise not to harm the cattle, but he had not foreseen that adverse winds would keep them on the island for many days. The supplies given to them by Circe ran out and some hungry sailors decided to roast an ox. An enigmatic coin from the Sicilian town of Selinos shows a muscular figure, possibly Hercules, apparently about to hit a bull with his club (532). Perhaps, there was a local tradition relating to cattle-killing. The sacrifice scene on the reverse might serve to remind us that Odysseus was sometimes obliged to act similarly in order to placate the gods and the fact that he, occasionally, did not do as he should was his undoing.

As soon as he left the island where the cattle had been killed, Odysseus' ship was caught by a fierce storm. Furthermore, the angry Zeus smashed it to pieces with a thunderbolt. Both the Father of the Gods and his thunderbolt can be found on many Greek coins. All the crew perished except our hero, who clung to the wreckage for days (nine and seven are the numbers that occur frequently in mythology). At last, he was cast ashore on an island. This proved to be Ogygia, where the nymph Calypso lived. She was very hospitable and succeeded in detaining Odysseus for a further seven years. However, he was perpetually homesick and, eventually, Athena, his protectress, persuaded Zeus to allow him to go home. Hermes was sent to inform

Calypso of the decision made in the highest places and she had no option but to obey. She helped Odysseus build a raft and he set out.

After eighteen days (twice nine), Poseidon caught sight of him and smashed the raft. Fortunately, Odysseus was helped by the Cretan sea-goddess known to us as Ino Leucothea who, incidentally, was represented in art by a sea-mew or an octopus (502), for which we turn again to Sicilian coins. She lent him a veil which made him invisible as far as Poseidon was concerned and our castaway found that he had suffered his last shipwreck. Having struggled to the island of Drepane, then occupied by the Phaeacians, he was well received, treated in accordance with his royal status and taken home loaded with presents. These indicate what was the most desirable form of wealth in those days – cauldrons, tripod-altars, golden cups and purple cloaks.

All but the cloaks can be found on Greek coins and even the murex, the shell-fish that produced the precious purple dye, makes a numismatic appearance. Silver pieces from Kroton, the badge of which was the tripod (40,41), and Boeotia, which used a wine-cup, might be considered (530). Odysseus fell into a deep sleep as he neared his home, so the crew carried him ashore, stacked his presents beside him and cast off again. The king, who had given orders to ship him home, had to sacrifice a dozen bulls (like the one on our Thourioian coin) in order to placate Poseidon.

Odysseus had arrived just in time to save his household. Having kept the crowd of suitors at arm's length for years, Penelope had reluctantly agreed that her husband was probably dead and that she would remarry. Her choice of a husband was difficult, though there were plenty of young men hanging about eating Odysseus' produce, drinking his wine and seducing the maids. So, she set them a test. The future bridegroom would be the one who would string Odysseus' powerful bow and shoot an arrow through the loops on a row of twelve axes set up for the purpose. Odysseus learnt that all this was going on by paying a visit to his palace disguised as a beggar. There is a Roman Republican denarius that shows him being greeted by Argus, his aged dog, who recognised his master and then expired, thus not giving the game away (531). On the other side of the coin, is a portrait of Hermes, without whose help the encounter could not have taken place. The row of axes is a folk-memory of the double-headed axes that seem to have had a place in the early religion of the Aegean Islands. We can find them on the coins of Tenedos, a town near the site of Troy (471,472).

The rest of the story concerns Odysseus' plot to do away with the suitors. He tipped off his son, who had by this time grown from a baby to a stalwart young man, and a few faithful servants. The suitors' weapons were quietly removed from their places hanging on the walls within easy reach. Then, Odysseus entered the competition, strung the bow and shot down the suitors.

Further adventures were attributed to Odysseus as the tale was told and retold over the years. When the Roman poets got hold of it, they patriotically sited incidents in Italy. As already mentioned, some of them maintained that the Sirens' island was near Naples. Another choice was Capri. Several Sicilian cities claimed to be the original home of Circe, Calypso and even the cannibals. Their coins could be given a place in our Odyssey collection, though my own preference is to call a halt at this point.

520 Ilion. Tetradrachm, second or first century BC. Head of Athena; Athena with spear, distaff and owl.   **521** Lokris. Stater, 369–338 BC. Persephone and a warrior (Ajax?).   **522** Aspendos. Stater, 460–420 BC. Warrior and triskeles.   **523** Lycia. The Dynast, Perikles, *c*. 380–362 BC. Bearded head (Zeus or possibly Perikles); warrior and triskeles.   **524** Thebai, Hemidrachm, 302–286 BC. Head of Demeter; Protesilaos, who led the assault force, leaping ashore at Troy.   **525** Argos. Drachm, 370–330 BC. Head of Hera; Diomedes, who helped Odysseus to steal the palladium from Troy, carrying it away.

526 Ainos. Tetradrachm, 474–449 BC. Head of Hermes and a goat.
527 Delphi. Trihemiobol, 421–355 BC. Heads of a ram and a goat.
528 Kranion. Obol, *c.* 400 BC. Ram's head and hoof.　**529** Sybrita. Stater,
320–270 BC. Dionysos riding a panther; Hermes tying his sandal.
530 Boeotia. Hemidrachm, 379–371 BC. Shield and wine-cup.　**531** Roman
Republican denarius. Moneyer: Caius Mamilius Limetanus, *c.* 82 BC. Head of
Mercury (Hermes); the returning Odysseus welcomed by his dog.
532 Selinos. Didrachm, 466–415 BC. Hercules jumping on to the Cretan bull,
which he is about to strike with his club; river-god Hypsas sacrificing.

FURTHER READING

VIRTUALLY ESSENTIAL
Sear, D. R. (1978 & 1979) *Greek Coins and their Values*, 2 vols. Seaby, London

VERY USEFUL GENERAL WORKS
Davis, N. (1967) *Greek Coins and Cities*. Spink, London
Davis, N., Kraay, C. M. (1973) *The Hellenistic Kingdoms*. Thames and Hudson, London
Head, B. V. (1963) *Historia Numorum*, reprinted. Spink, London. First published in 1911, this is the only one-volume standard work on Greek coins.
Jenkins, G. K. (1972) *Ancient Greek Coins*. Barrie and Jenkins, London
Plant, R. (1979) *Greek Coin Types and their Identification*. Seaby, London

VERY USEFUL SPECIALISED WORKS
(suited to the not very experienced collector)
Gobl, R. (1971) *Sasanian Numismatics*. Klinkhardt and Biermann, Braunschweig, Germany
Meshorer, Y. (1967) *Jewish Coins of the Second Temple Period*. Tel Aviv, Israel
Mitchiner, M. (1977) *Oriental Coins and their Values, Vol II: The Ancient and Classical World*. Seaby, London
Sellwood, D. (1980) *An Introduction to the Coinage of Parthia*, Spink, London
*Youroukova, Y. (1976) *Coins of the Ancient Thracians*
*Zograph, A. N. (1977) *Ancient Coinage*

*Both translated and published by British Archaeological Reports, 122 Banbury Road, Oxford.

These and a great many other numismatic books are obtainable from: B. A. Seaby Ltd, Audley House, 11 Margaret Street, London, W1N 8AT, and Spink & Sons Ltd, 5, 6 and 7 King Street, St James's, London, SW1Y 6QR. Both firms supply a free list of available books.

INDEX

Abdera, 191, 261
Achaean League, 76
Achaeans, 30
Acheloos, 40, 41, 44, 265, 266, 288
Actium, 130, 195
Aegina (Aigina), 19, 63–8, 80, 271
Aesillas, 79
Aetna, 46, 49
Aetolians, 98
Agrippa, 95
Ahuramazda, 261
Akarnania, 72, 257
Akarnanian Confederacy, 73
Ake, 164
Akragas (Agrigentum), 44, 45, 48, 272
Alexander I, King of Macedon, 89
Alexander Balas, 110
Alexander the Great, 14, 59, 75, 76, 81, 89–95, 99, 103, 120, 148, 164, 193, 200, 228, 261
Alexander Jannaeus, 177
Alexander, King of Epiros, 34
Alexandria, 109, 121, 122, 123, 126, 129, 130, 144
Allen, D., 201
Alyzia, 72
Amalthea, 40, 41
Amazons, 252, 279
Ambrakia, 74
Ammon, 91, 193, 259, 281, 286
Amphipolis, 92, 193
Amphitrite, 187
Anaitis (Anat, Anahit), 107–9, 151, 220

Anaktorion, 72
Anaxilas, 45
Antigonos Gonatos, 97
Antigonos Monopthalmos, 96, 103, 104, 105, 121
Antimachos, King of Bactria, 229
Antioch, 105, 124, 158, 177, 261
Antiochos I, Soter, 106
Antiochos II, Theos, 107, 124, 228
Antiochos III, the Great, 107–8, 125, 126, 165, 229
Antiochos IV, Epiphanes, 82, 83, 108, 126, 175
Antiochos VII, Sidetes, 110, 175
Antiochos VIII, Grypos, 111
Antiochos IX, Kyzikenos, 111
Antiochos XIII, Asiatikos, 111
Antiochos Hierax, 107
Antipater, 96, 121
Aphrodite, 69, 72, 130, 138, 280
Apollo, 25, 46, 89, 97, 105, 186, 200, 229, 273, 276
Apollodotos, King of Bactria, 229
Apollonia, 73, 255, 273, 277
Arados, 164
Archaic coins, 16–22, 46, 71, 79
Archelaus, 156
Archidamnos, 34
Ardaser, Sasanian King, 220–1
Ares (Mars), 148, 186, 275
Arethusa, 47–9, 170, 267, 272
Argonauts, 40, 275–83
Argos, 65, 73, 79

Argos Amphilochikon, 73
Ariarathes I, King of Cappadocia, 155
Ariarathes IV, King of Cappadocia, 155
Ariarathes VI, King of Cappadocia, 155
Ariarathes IX, King of Cappadocia, 155
Ariobarzanes, 156
Aristotle, 25, 74, 90
Armenia, 111, 158–9, 212
Armorica, 200
Arsakes, 211
Arsinoe II, 123, 124, 194
Arsinoe III, 125
Artabanus, King of Parthia, 214, 221
Artavasdes, King of Parthia, 214
Artemis (Diana), 16, 79, 99, 148, 281
Askalon, 123
Asklepios, 145
Astakos, 72
Atalanta, 276
Athena, 55, 59, 60, 69, 90, 122, 143, 156, 193, 200, 229, 231, 241–4, 251, 255, 277, 284, 288
Athens, Athenians, 13, 31, 48, 55–62, 63, 65, 71, 72, 74, 80, 89, 90, 96, 223, 228, 229, 241, 247
Attalid Dynasty, 143
Attalos III, King of Pergamum, 144
Ausculum, 140

Babylon, 92, 103, 104, 120, 124, 213
Bactria, 108, 228–36
bankers' marks, 6
Bar-Kochba, Simon, 180
Bellerophon, 69, 242, 257
Beneventum, 141
Berenike, 124, 129
Berytos, 163
Bithynia, 148–50
Boeotia, 289
Britain, 90, 169, 198, 287
Bruttium, 74, 184–90
Byblos, 163, 164

Byzantium, 195, 223

Caesar, Julius, 76, 83, 129, 130, 149, 195, 198
Caligula, 195
Cappadocia, 149, 155–7, 158
Carrhae, 213
Carthage, Carthaginians, 43, 46, 49, 75, 98, 107, 140, 164, 169–74, 188, 272, 285
Cassius, 83, 156
Celts, 97, 106, 194, 198–207
Ceres, 259
Chandragupta, 104
Characene, 214
Chares of Lindos, 81
Chimaera, 257, 280
Chios, 261
Cicero, 144
Cilicia, 144
Cistophoric Tetradrachms, 144
City-State, 13–15
Claudius, 84
Cleopatra I, 126
Cleopatra II, The Wife, 126
Cleopatra III, The Sister, 127
Cleopatra VII, 125, 129
Cleopatra Thea, 110, 111, 126, 127
Colchis, 276, 279
Colonies, 13
Commius, 201
condition of coins, 2
Corinth, 65, 69–78, 97, 242, 257
Crassus, 213
Crete, 19, 79
Ctesiphon, 213
Cumaeans, 39
Cybele, 246, 260
Cyprus, 96, 126, 127, 129

Damascus, 92, 121, 123, 158, 223, 268
Danube, 106, 137, 200
Darius I, 64
Darius III, 90, 91
dates on Greek coins, 7, 143
dealers, 1

defects in coins, 2–3
Delos, 83
Delphi, 33, 138
Demarete, 47
Demeter, 65, 188
Demetrios Poliorketes, 81, 96, 97, 104, 105, 121, 143, 273, 286
Demetrios I, Soter, 109
Demetrios II, Nikator, 110
Demetrios I, King of Bactria, 230
denominations, 6–7
die-sequence, 4–5
Diodotos I, King of Bactria, 228
Diogenes, 76
Dione, 138
Dionysos, god, 126, 144, 152, 192, 194, 245–9, 286
Dionysos, Tyrant of Syracuse, 49, 170
Dioskouroi, 276
Dodona, 138, 276
Domitian, 243
Dyrrhachium, 74

Ecbatana, 107, 212
Echinos, 73
Edessa, 222
Egypt, 91, 103, 110, 120–34, 223
Elis, 278
Elymais, 108, 109, 214
Emporion, 200
Epeiros, 73, 137–42
Ephesos, 16, 152, 260
Epidamnos, 74
Etruscans, 29, 184–90
Euainetos, 48, 170
Eukleidas, 48
Eulaios, 126
Eukratides I, King of Bactria, 229
Eumenes I, King of Pergamum, 143
Eumenes II, 143
Eumenes, Syracusan die-engraver, 48
Euthydemos I, King of Bactria, 229
Euthydemos II, King of Bactria, 229

forgeries, 3

Gades, 163
Gauls, 97, 99, 138, 148, 198
Gaza, 123, 223
Gela, 44, 48, 266
Gelon, 44, 46, 48, 170
Gobl, Robert, 220
Gorgons, 149, 185, 255–8
Gotarzes I, King of Parthia, 212
Gotarzes II, King of Parthia, 213
Graves, Robert, 239, 275, 276, 285

Hadrian, 180
Hannibal, 31, 36, 108, 148, 171, 188
Heliokles, Bactrian-King, 230
Helios, 80, 81, 82, 288
Hellenic League, 90
Hephaestos, 279
Hera, 25, 138, 245, 250, 278
Herakleia, 139, 251
Hercules, 40, 49, 81, 90–2, 98, 165, 186, 194, 229, 230, 250–4, 276, 278, 288
Hermes, 287, 289
Herod Antipas, 178
Herod the Great, 177, 178
Herod Agrippa I, 178
Herod Agrippa II, 178
Herodotos, 17, 58, 63, 148, 163, 241
Himera, 44, 46, 48, 170, 266, 272
Histiaia, 98, 267
Homer, 90, 250, 275
Horace, 184

Ialysos, 79
Iliad, 90
Ilion, 284
Illyrians, 74
Incuses, 18, 44, 63, 71, 192
India, 104, 105, 108, 228–36
Indus, 92
Ipsus, 96, 105
Isis, 122, 125
Ithaca, 284, 286

Jason, 275–83
Jericho, 153
Jerusalem, 108, 178–80, 223

Jews, 109, 175–83
Joppa, 123

Kalymna, 26
Kamiros, 79, 80
Karia, 82, 260
Kassander, King of Macedon, 81, 96
Katane, 46
Kaulonia, 23, 24
Kelendris, 19, 255, 285
Kimon, 48
Kios, 276
Klazomenai, 287
Kleomenes, 120
Knosos, 260
Korkyra, 73, 74, 280
Koronta, 72
Kotys, 194
Kroisos (Croesus), King of Lydia, 17, 18
Kroton, 23, 25, 30, 289
Kushans, 231
Kyrenaika, 126
Kyrene, 259, 285
Kyzikos, 277

Laodike, Wife of Antiochos II, 107
Laodike, Queen of Pontos, 151
Laodike, Wife of Ariarathes VI, 155
Laodikeia, 246
Larissa, 267, 276
Lemnos, 277
Leontini, 46, 75
Lesbos, 152
Leukas, 73
Liberalia, 247
Lindos, 79
Livia, 145
Locroi Epizephyrioi, 74
Locris, 141
Lucania, Lucanians, 34, 139
Lycia, 19, 261
Lydia, Kingdom of, 17–19, 260
Lysimachos, King of Thrace, 81, 97, 105, 143, 191–4, 200, 242
Lyttos, 279

Ma, 151, 156, 260
Maccabees, 175
Macedon, 81, 89, 96–102, 105, 106, 137, 152, 193, 194, 245

Magna Graecia, 23–8, 138, 185, 187, 188
Mallos, 19, 261
Marathon, 58, 82, 247
Marius Aquillius, 152
Mark Antony, 129, 130, 156, 177, 195, 213
Maroneia, 191, 192, 245, 286
Marsyas, 256
Masada, 179
Massilia, 200
Mazaios, 260
Medea, 280
Medes, 107
Megalopolis, 247
Melkart, 164, 165, 259
Memphis, 127
Mên, 151, 260
Menander, Indo-Greek King, 231
Mende, 246
Mesma, 75
Messenians, Messana, 33
Metapontum, 23, 25, 30
Metropolis, 72, 92
Mithradates II, King of Parthia, 212
Mithradates VI, King of Pontos, 60, 128, 151, 152, 158, 194
Mithras, 151
Moloch, 169
Mostis, 194
Mytilene, 152

Naples, 39–42, 266, 290
Naxos, 246
Nike (Victory), 41, 47, 59, 83, 90, 97, 106, 143, 170, 187, 200, 266, 273
Nikomedes I, King of Bithynia, 148
Nikomedes II, King of Bithynia, 149
Nikomedes III, King of Bithynia, 149, 155
Nikomedes IV, King of Bithynia, 149, 153

Nikomedia, 148
Nysa, Queen of Cappadocia, 155

Octavia, 130
Octavian (Augustus), 130, 145, 156, 195, 213
Odrysae Kingdom, 192, 193
Odysseus, 39, 284–92
Olympia, 252
Olympic Games, 14, 25, 45, 64, 89, 278
Olynthos, 192
Orchomenos, 282
Orescii, 192
Orodes II, King of Parthia, 213
Orpheus, 40, 276
Osroes, King of Parthia, 213

Palladium, 143, 242
Pan, 45, 97, 247
Pantikapaion, 247, 261
Parasemon, 18
Parion, 255
Partheniae, 33
Parthenon, 58, 59
Parthenope, 39, 40, 266
Parthia, Parthians, 108, 110, 130, 156, 158, 211–19
patina on coins, 3
Pegasos, 69, 152, 156, 242, 255
Pella, 193
Peloponnesian War, 58, 60, 72
Perdiccas, 103, 104, 121
Pergamum, 107, 108, 110, 143–7, 152
Persephone, 141, 171
Perseus, 90, 98, 149, 255
Perseus, King of Macedon, 83, 99, 194
Persian Empire, 18, 58, 64, 65, 90–2, 148, 164
Persis, Kingdom of, 214
Petelia, 188
Phaistos, 252, 281
Phalanthos, 25, 33
Pharnakes, 153
Pharsalus, 195

Phaselis, 273
Philetairos, 143
Philip II, King of Macedon, 75, 89, 90, 193, 199
Philip III, King of Macedon, 92
Philip V, King of Macedon, 82, 98, 148
Philip VI, King of Macedon, 98
Phoenicia, Phoenicians, 163–8
Phraates IV, King of Parthia, 213
Phrygia, 246, 260
Phrygillos, 48
Plato, Bactrian King, 230
polis (city state), 13–15
Polybius, 107, 109, 229
Pompey, 83, 111, 153, 156, 159, 165, 194
Pontos, 149, 151–4
Pontius Pilate, 179
Populonia, 185
Poseidon, 25, 33, 47, 97, 187, 255, 256, 273, 278, 286
Poseidonia (Paestum), 23, 25, 29, 31, 273
Prusias I, King of Bithynia, 148
Prusias II, 148, 149
Ptolemaic Empire, 120–34, 165, 194
Ptolemaic Era, 7, 122, 124
Ptolemais, 111, 123
Ptolemais, 111, 123
Ptolemy I, 81, 96, 120–3, 137
Ptolemy II, Philadelphos, 123
Ptolemy III, Euergetes, 124
Ptolemy IV, Philopater, 124, 125
Ptolemy V, Epiphanes, 125
Ptolemy VI, Philometer, 126
Ptolemy VII, Neos Philopater, 127
Ptolemy VIII, Euergetes (Physkon), 126, 127
Ptolemy IX, Soter II, 128
Ptolemy X, Alexander, 128
Ptolemy XI, Alexander II, 128
Ptolemy XII, Neos Dionysos (Auletes), 128, 129
Ptolemy XIII, 129
Ptolemy XIV, 130
Ptolemy Keraunos, 106, 148
Puranas, 230

Pydna, 99
Pythagoras, 25, 26, 30
Pyrrhus, King of Epeiros, 35, 74, 97
    137–42, 187

Rhegion, 23, 25, 74
Rhoda, 200
Rhodes, 79–85, 96, 121, 152, 288
Rhoemetalces, 195
Roman coins, 35, 41, 186
Rome, Romans, 27, 29, 34–6, 60,
    82–4, 98–9, 107, 108, 109, 111,
    125, 126, 128, 130, 137–41,
    143–5, 149, 151–3, 155–6,
    169–72, 177–80, 184–8, 194, 195,
    198–202, 211–14, 220, 247

Sadalas, 194
Salamis, 58, 66, 123
Samnites, 139
Samos, 19
Sapur, Sasanian King, 222
Sarapis, 122, 125, 259
Sasan, 220
Scipio, 108, 188
Scylla, 251, 281, 288
Scythians, 212, 213
Segesta, 45, 266
Seleukia-in-Piera, 105
Seleukia-on-the-Tigris, 104, 124,
    212, 213
Seleukid Empire, 103–19, 158, 165,
    175, 194, 228
Seleukid Era, 7, 104, 165
Seleukos I, 97, 103–6, 143, 273
Seleukos II, Kallinikos, 107
Seleukos III, Keraunos, 107
Seleukos IV, Philopater, 108
Selge, 255
Selinos, 44, 45, 48, 288
Seltman, Charles, 26
Seuthes II, King of Thrace, 192
shekel, 165, 179, 180
Sicily, 43–52, 141, 169–72
Sidon, 92, 108, 123, 163, 164, 165,
    271
Sikyonia, 257

Silenos, 245, 266
Sinope, 267, 279
Sirens, 39, 266, 277, 288
Sirinian Pyxos, 23, 25
Soloi, 252, 279
Soison, 48
Sosibios, 125
Spain, 169, 201, 286
Sparta, Spartans, 33, 34, 48, 59, 65,
    67
storage of coins, 3
Strabo, 169
striking process, the, 4–6, 23
Sulla, 83, 128, 152
Susa, 213
Sybaris, 23, 25, 26, 29–32, 241
Syracuse, 44, 46–9, 75, 140, 170,
    267, 272
Syria, 97, 105, 109, 111, 159

Tabaristan, 223
Tanit, 169, 171, 259
Taras, 33, 34
Tarentum, 23, 25, 33–8, 138, 141,
    187, 200, 271
Tasciovanus, 201
Tenedos, 260, 289
Teos, 19, 261
Terina, 266
Thasos, 194, 200, 256
Thebes, Thebans, 250
Theopompus, 184
Thermae, 48
Thermopylae, 65
Thessalian Confederacy, 242
Thourioi, 31, 281, 288
Thrace, 19, 99, 152, 191–7, 245
Thucydides, 58, 73
Tiberius, Roman Emperor, 145, 156,
    172, 178
Tiberius Gracchus, 144
Tigranes, King of Armenia, 111, 153,
    156, 158–9, 212, 268
Tigranocerta, 159
Timoleon, 75
Tiridates I, King of Parthia, 211
Tiryns, 251

Titus, 180
Trajan, 213
Tripolis, 163, 164
Troy, Trojans, 46, 275, 277, 284
Tryphon, 110
Tyre, 108, 123, 163, 164, 165, 271
Tyrrheion, 72

Valerianus, 222
Vespasian, 179, 180
Vologases I, King of Parthia, 213

Wappenmünzen, 55
weight standards, 6, 16, 18, 71, 79
widow's mite, 177

Xenophon, 192
Xerxes, 65
Xusro I, Sasanian King, 223
Xusro II, Sasanian King, 220, 223

Youroukova, Y., 191

Zankle-Messana 23, 25, 44
Zeus, 35, 91, 106, 138, 145, 148,
    187, 188, 200, 241, 245, 250, 252,
    260, 267, 278, 288
Zipoetes, King of Bithynia, 148
Zoilos, 98